HOW A BASE JUMPER SAVED ME

A GUIDE TO OVERCOMING ANXIETY, FEAR AND PANIC DISORDER.

CHRIS BREEN

Copyright © 2024 by Chris Breen

All rights reserved. No part of this publication may be reproduced, distributed or transmitted in any form or by any means, without prior written permission by the author or publisher.
Email: chrisbreenauthor@gmail.com

Cover design, illustrations and internal typeset by Tanya Breen.
Special thanks to Amy Doak and Kirsten Macdonald for their invaluable expertise and countless hours of editing and encouragement.

Chris Breen. Melbourne, Victoria 3000.
1st ed. Paperback ISBN: 978-0-6459933-0-1

The information provided in this book is intended for informational and educational purposes only. The content provided within these pages is not a substitute for professional medical advice, diagnosis, or treatment. Always seek the advice of your doctor or other qualified health providers with any questions you may have regarding a medical condition.

This book is not intended to provide specific mental health advice, and its contents should not be used to replace the guidance of a qualified mental health professional. The author has made every attempt to provide information that is accurate and complete. The author, editors, and publisher are not responsible for any consequences or damages arising directly or indirectly from the use of information in this book.

If you are in crisis or believe you are experiencing a medical emergency, contact your doctor or call 000 (if located in Australia) or contact Lifeline on 13 11 14.

For the young man at 26 who desperately searched
for a book like this to guide him.

CONTENTS

Introduction		1
01	My Story	5
02	Anxiety & How it Rolls	27
03	Evolution of Fear	47
04	The Power & Weakness of Your Fear Centre	67
05	The Body & How It Works	77
06	Just a Thought	95
07	What's Happening in Your Head	121
08	Promoting Panic	133
09	Putting it into Perspective	165
10	Retrain Your Brain	191
11	Drivers of Anxiety	209
12	The Mainstream Buddhist	227
13	A Gut Feeling	247
14	L.E.T.'s Get Physical	259
15	Simple, Practical Fixes	285
16	Different Types of Treatments	295
17	Snakes & Ladders	303
18	Cheat Sheets	313
Acknowledgements		337
References		338

HOW A BASE JUMPER SAVED ME

"ONE DAY YOU WILL TELL YOUR STORY OF HOW YOU'VE OVERCOME WHAT YOU'RE GOING THROUGH NOW, AND IT WILL BECOME PART OF SOMEONE ELSE'S SURVIVAL GUIDE."

AUTHOR UNKNOWN

INTRODUCTION

If you are reading this book, fair chance you or someone you love or care about has been hit fair and square between the eyes with this nasty little bastard called Anxiety. If you're really unlucky, you may have gone on to develop an Anxiety disorder.

I've worked in the health care industry for over 25 years: as a nurse, then as a paramedic. During that time, I have worked with many people suffering from Anxiety and Anxiety Disorders.

The most challenging patient I have encountered through these years was ME.

Despite my experience and qualifications, I still struggled for many years to manage this debilitating disease. As a father of young men, I want to share my knowledge to try and make things a little easier for those of you out there who are ready to tackle their Anxiety.

The book is aimed at a **Drug Free** approach giving you a resource and information about Anxiety, paired with a toolbox of strategies and tips. These tools have been researched and based on my path to recovery and hopefully, they can be implemented into your life to restructure old unhelpful habits, beliefs, thought patterns and behaviours.

There is no real easy way out of your Anxiety aside from putting in a significant amount of hard work and elbow grease to nail this beast.

Different resources and treatments will work for some people at various times and not so much others, but you are most welcome to give my tools a crack to help your recovery and reclaim your life along with any other options you have available to you.

This information didn't just come to me in a dream or on a little platter (I wish it were that easy!!). It is the result of years of personal trial and error, triumph and, of course, heartache from experiences of Anxiety and Panic Disorder. An apprenticeship spanning 25 years and still going, we are always learning.

I have read numerous books and literature on topics that range from philosophy, spirituality, psychology and pathophysiology (stuff about the body and how it works) along with anything else remotely connected to Anxiety and Fear.

My personal and professional life along with the help of therapy and deep academic diving, real-life practises and case studies have gifted a platform of knowledge.

Over the decades, the combination of experience and knowledge had allowed me to gain insight into a condition that I had little or no knowledge about when I first began to suffer from it. You can't beat an opponent you have no experience, skill or understanding about.

There was also a life changing moment when I was in Switzerland watching some Base Jumpers jumping off a massive mountain that shaped my perception and idea about Anxiety forever which I will discuss more so during the book that will hopefully change you too!

I have always felt, my Anxiety has always given me a sense of being held back, and I felt I was not able to move forward in my life with relationships, sport and career until my recovery.

It seemed there was always some roadblock in the way, stopping me from achieving my goals. This was not only scary but also frustrating. Regardless of your levels of Anxiety and how it affects you, this book can help you progress forward towards your dreams and passions, just like I have.

INTRODUCTION

If you only get 1% or 50% out of this book or maybe a few little Ah-Ha moments, then I will feel that my work has been for something and I have helped achieve my goal to help you.

I have complete empathy and compassion for everyone who has experienced this condition at any level and wish peoples knowledge of its power was more understood.

Hence, my desire to write a book. Along with my personal experience, as a paramedic, I also witness and treat numerous patients that are distressed and in genuine Fear as they have little or no understanding of what's happening to them and why.

I can see how Fearful they are, and it upsets me enormously that they are suffering and are also not afforded the understanding and treatment they so much deserve.

The pandemic really shone a light on the amount of people either developing or suffering from Anxiety and it's detrimental effects. It was becoming so obvious that this mental health condition has an impact on not just a few, but a significant portion of population and it seemed like it's EVERYWHERE.

This only motivates me more to help.

I believe that too many people are suffering unnecessarily because they have not been shown the RIGHT way to win this battle.

This topic, and this book, is my passion. My motivation is to help and give you something I never had at the start of my suffering: Hope and Knowledge.

Happy reading, good luck and take care.

Cheers, Chriso

"I STARTED TO FEAR AIR (EVEN THOUGH I RATIONALLY KNEW THAT BREATHING AIR IS WHAT I NEEDED TO LIVE), HEAT, SMOKE, WATER, FOOD, NOISE AND EVEN THE THOUGHT OF BEING OUTSIDE. THE SKY SURROUNDING ME WAS TOO CLAUSTROPHOBIC."

CHRIS BREEN

CHAPTER 01

MY STORY

As mentioned in the introduction, I am writing this story to help others who are dealing with the unfortunate "curse" of suffering from Anxiety and Anxiety disorders and to give some inspiration and hope that there is a way of getting your life back and living it fulfilled.

One of my main issues, in the beginning, was not having a guide or any answers as to how to combat my Anxiety and Panic. It seemed that no one had any answers for me which I desperately needed except for a "pill" such as an antidepressant or benzodiazepine (sedative) which I was a little dubious about because I was anxious, not depressed. It was a categoric NO for me with any drugs but probably could have had a few sedatives to help me sleep from time to time in hindsight.

Recovery is not a quick fix as Anxiety is a multi-faceted condition that needs to be addressed in several different ways and strategies. It affects people in different ways too. Everyone has their own story and life experiences that have created their Anxiety in the first place.

Overcoming this mental illness was the most challenging, most constant, severe and taxing thing I have ever encountered.

It was relentless and refused to let me rest or take a break like some type of demonic figure in my head. It was a constant companion that I couldn't shake 24/7. And I mean 24/7 believe me.

There were many times that I wanted to tell others about my suffering. I also wanted to share my bravery as well about how I was continually striving to overcome my Fears and anxieties. Instead I chose to live my life with a bullshit mask on to hide the truth of my suffering. That was due to the shame I felt about having a mental illness.

Not being able to share my suffering did create a degree of sadness.

Well, here I am, not ashamed anymore and I'm going to let it all out and tell the world...

You can get back the life you had, and I hope you enjoy my story.

WHERE IT ALL BEGAN

I grew up the youngest of eight children in a little country town in Victoria, Australia, with a population of around 5,000 people. I was raised amazingly by my beautiful mother. She was a single parent that created a loving environment for us and did an amazing job caring for all 8 children (5 sisters and 2 brothers) nurturing and educating us as best as she could.

However, despite her best efforts of creating a safe and comfortable home, I reckon my Anxiety started from an early age — around five-years-old from memory. It was largely centred around my parents' divorce and the Fear of losing my mother and potentially having to relocate to another city. My father had moved to Melbourne, which was three hours drive from my home town.

Before the divorce and until my father moved away, the home environment was full of anger, domestic violence and alcohol abuse. Unfortunately there was physical and verbal abuse in the home, scenes of smashed chairs, tables and holes in walls was a common occurrence and he destroyed the very fabric of our family unit. I remember the silence in a house full of 10 people the morning after an 'outburst'. It was almost deafening as everyone tried to come to grips with the results of the night before. How my poor mother and older siblings kept it together still inspires me to this day. It also made me aware of how one man can cause so much destruction.

After he left, it seemed my Anxiety was only present when I was away from home (especially at sleepovers or school trips) or when Mum went out socialising. My lack of control and not knowing her whereabouts ramped up my Fear of her potentially leaving or dying. My Fear of having to live with Dad sadly was off the charts.

My Anxiety increased severely when she found a new partner. It wasn't the partner that was the problem. It was me! Each time they went out for a meal or a social event, my Anxiety was heightened as I worried about her not making it home or the possibility she'd be killed in a car accident (sadly, the kids who lived two doors down from us lost their mother in a car accident which made this a genuine Fear). I was always thinking about the worst-case scenario, the one that ended with me having to leave home and live with my Dad.

If she wasn't home by a certain time I felt was appropriate, I would fret, not sleep and lay awake for hours praying and begging God to bring her home safely to me and us.

I would sit at the front window or sit out the front of the house looking down the street hoping to see her car coming down the road constantly wishing she would be home safe. My siblings had no idea I was doing this and to be honest, even back then I knew it was silly but couldn't help myself.

It was a fucking nightmare often based on unfounded Fears and of no fault of Mum.

I often remember saying to myself that if I can just get to the age of 16 or so, I hopefully could look after myself and not need to move away from my home. I just needed someone to be there for me if she dies until I was old enough to care for myself.

My Dad passed away in 2020 and there was a lot of things as a child, adolescent and adult I needed to unpack about the past. There was huge amounts of anger and disdain towards him. Fortunately, I was able to move forward with the past and understand the world he lived in with his own emotional torment and addiction which provided a sense of peace and forgiveness.

GROWING UP WITH ANXIETY

This background Anxiety about Mum started to take its toll over the years and at around the age of 15, I started developing physical symptoms that also created more Anxiety. It started with heart palpitations and episodes of shortness of breath. This progressed to digestion problems like bloating, reflux and nausea with a general sense of feeling unwell more often than not. In turn, this created extra stress and Anxiety. To be fair, I had never put 2 and 2 together and assumed that my physical symptoms were some undiagnosed condition that hadn't been found yet.

I was always looking for the physical source of my symptoms and after visiting the local GP; it seemed there were no answers. The doctors were unable to find the cause of my symptoms.

I suppose as I got older, it became part of me and I just accepted that I had these underlying physical symptoms and stressors and I had to get on with it. Life simply had to be lived.

At the age of 18, (a week before moving away for University) whilst watching a movie and from seemingly nowhere I started to get these really crazy heart palpitations. I mean the ones where your heart is fully racing and beating erratically trying to jump out of your chest. I absolutely shit myself because not only were they quite violent in nature, they also kept taking my breath away which was really frightening. They would come and go sporadically and for varying lengths of time often lasting up to 20 minutes. Living in the country, we didn't routinely call for an ambulance.

I made an appointment with my GP, and he couldn't find anything or pick anything up on his E.C.G. (heart machine). I asked him if I was OK to continuing playing sport, and he quickly replied: "No, as you might have an arrhythmia that could kill you and may need to be defibrillated"! Yep, those paddles they put on your chest in the movies to try a revive you! My immediate thought was WTF (although, this was the 90s, so I would have said it outright!). What horrible and frightening thoughts to have right when you are moving away from home for the first time and living in a strange environment.

My Fear was compounded by the fact that I couldn't exercise "in case" I needed specialised treatment or it ended in cardiac arrest. I decided to not listen to the Doctor and exercise anyway (although I continued to worry). I worried about walking up a hill, riding a bike or any form of exertion really that increased my heart rate. It was just another underlying Fear I had to deal with. It just seemed that my world was full of stress and Fear all the time. Gee, it was tiring but I had also developed an ability to almost live a double life, one with Fear and the other with Fear but a quashed version. (I found out a few years later that my palpitations were episodes of 'ectopics' that are skipped beats and are primarily benign.) It did, however leave mental scars. The other part to this story is the fact that I loved playing football and being part of a club/team. This was taken from me due to potential of this arrhythmia (or supposed) being detrimental to my health.

My new life at University helped provide a distraction that limited the intensity of my Anxiety. It was still there, just not at the same levels I had become accustomed to.

After many years of partying and distracting myself with alcohol and any other form of excitement, I eventually graduated with a Bachelor of Health Sciences Nursing degree (it took me five years to obtain a three-year degree, but I had a bloody great time in the process, trust me). I then moved to another city to start work as a nurse. I met a gorgeous girl at the age of 23 (who eventually became my wife), and things seemed to be looking up. I felt relatively free from all of those old symptoms, and life was pretty good. I often reflect on this little window in my life with gratitude and relief as I had a chop out from my usual Fearful challenges.

A TRAGEDY

Unfortunately, this happiness and reprieve was short-lived. When I was 25, I made a shocking discovery — my beautiful, amazing, intelligent and loving sister had died aged 32 and I was the one who found her dead and decomposing in her bed. Yep, that fateful day at around 7pm on a Sunday on a cool April night when my world turned upside down.

It was not like any Sunday as it was better than that. My girlfriend and I had had a lovely day heading out for lunch and watching a new release movie at home (The Sixth Sense). I had been given the day off from my nursing shift randomly because of a rostering mistake and I was making the most of it – how lucky was I.

Having many siblings in the family generally means that birthdays are regular and this particular day happened to be one of my other sisters birthdays. Because I was supposed to work, I didn't make the trip up to the country to help celebrate her birthday.

This was how I became the person to discover my sister dead in her home. My family was enjoying the day all together and had realised that no one had heard from my big sister (who also lived in Melbourne) which was very odd. They contacted me to ask if I had been in contact with her at all and that answer was obviously NO.

As we lived in close proximity to each other, I jumped in the car and headed around to her place. The warning signs should have been there from the start as her mailbox was full, her car was in the driveway and her neighbour telling me that she hasn't seen her in a week or so which was abnormal. Unfortunately, I couldn't gain entry to her home.

I brushed it off as perhaps a business trip she failed to tell anyone and left it like that!!

This was mid afternoon and concerns and worry from the whole family started to snow ball. Something wasn't right and we needed answers. I couldn't access her home until another neighbour came home from work (he had a spare key) – so I waited for a few hours.

Eventually, I got the call he was home and drove back around. Killer Queen from the band Queen was on the radio as I pulled up and all I had to do was gain access to her house, walk in and prove that she was not at home and away somewhere else.

Well, fuck me, how wrong was I. As soon as I walked in, the smell and stench of that flat was absolutely horrendous and almost debilitating. I walked into every room except her bedroom knowing what I was just about to find and discover - Heartbreaking to say the least but also traumatising. This was the moment my life flipped on its head, nothing I had ever experienced had come close to this and the amount of insurmountable grief I was about to start feeling. The brutality of such an experience is something I often witness in some of my patients family members when they have the same experience and I feel so sorry for them and what they have just copped - it is just devastating!

How can any human with normal emotions live and move on with this scene or scenario? What was life going to be like after this and what had I lost?

Well, She was the most incredible sister any brother could ask for, and suddenly she's gone, just like that.

She was a sister that always made me smile and be so proud to be her brother, was incredibly generous and always super "cool" because she was the city girl with the great job and fashion sense. She seemed to have it all with her wisdom and knowledge of life. She would always be a there when I needed her for advice and love.

It was like she could do no wrong in my eyes, and I had complete admiration for her in everything she was and did. Why, Why, Why????

The mental picture and the impact of that situation would prove to become the most significant experience of my life. (Or one of many)

A person you love so much is gone so quickly and the physical pain and heartache post her death was so palpable I could feel the grief manifest into physical pain throughout my body driven purely by emotion. It was so FUCKED!!!!

Emotional pain and numbness were so extreme, I hope and wish I never feel like that again—total devastation.

Although it may seem hard to imagine, this was the start of much worse things to come. Her death was so unexpected, and the cause of death was never determined, so my belief systems (the ones that had me treading water in life at best) were starting to crumble, and fast.

The grief was insurmountable. I had little to no coping strategies for such a traumatic event. It was such a difficult time, trying to not only cope with her loss (and I still miss her deeply) but also trying to understand and comprehend how we can just die. And how the next person in that random firing line may well be me

This made my ability to be optimistic seem impossible, and it triggered all those old health Fears. After all, no one could ever find a physical cause for my symptoms. Maybe I'm next? It became apparent to me that I may have something undiagnosed and heaven is closer than I thought. Of course, I now know that it was Anxiety driving these thoughts.

THE STORM IS BREWING

I staggered through the next 12 months trying to make sense of what has just happened to me and what life and death are all about. A young man trying to find his place in this world which was not overly promising to be in to be honest, I was just shattered.

So just to be different and completely desperate to live again, I found myself heading on a two year trip to London. Maybe an opportunity to break away from the heartache and grief in my life and try a new beginning. Anything would have to feel better than my current emotional state. What could go wrong I thought??

On my first ever overseas trip from Australia to Singapore, I copped my first Panic Attack when I got off the plane. The humidity was so high, I had never experienced anything like it before, and I felt that I couldn't breathe. The air was so thick. WTF!!!! Talk about suffocating, scary and overwhelming from out of the blue. I was fresh off the plane on my new adventure and suddenly scared shitless and really not sure what to do. So in true Chris fashion, had a very scary and shaky cigarette and silently prayed this thing that happened would go away. The Fear did actually subside after a couple of hours and I quickly brushed it off as some weird breathing problem caused by too many cigarettes... and for the record, I am an ex-smoker now.

I remember feeling as though I had dodged a bullet that day Gee whiz, I had no idea what was in store in the very near future.

Fast forward 6 months into the trip and having had the fortune of experiencing travel through Turkey and Scotland and finding some work, we were settling into London life and part of me was feeling a sense of relief and happiness for the first time since my sisters passing. Maybe the storm had passed and a positive turning point of happiness was just around the corner.

Well, fuck me, I had another Panic Attack on the Tube (London underground rail system) that nailed me. It was BIG and scary to say the least. This one was different to the first one in Singapore and so random. So out of the blue and it lasted a lot longer as well.

I was absolutely distraught about what had just happened and will try a paint a picture for you of what it felt like and am sure others can relate.

What does a BIG Panic attack feel like? Well, let me tell you what it was like for me.

It started like this: Gee, I am feeling a super anxious at the moment. That's weird, I'm just on a train cruising into the city to go shopping, and I have no reason to feel like this.

Then I noticed a combination of a few things. Firstly my palms, forehead and underarms were becoming sweaty and trembly. Additionally, I could only describe my thoughts as starting to race but in a terrifying way. My chest was beginning to feel warm, then hot, and surges of adrenaline were starting to coarse around my body. I also started to feel hotter and hotter all over, which prompted me to take off my jacket. The air became thick, and my breathing began to feel shallow, fast and suffocating all in one. All I knew was that I needed to get off the train but couldn't because I was stuck underground and trapped. Before I know it, all systems were firing. My mind, brain and body were fully ignited with Fear and absolute stress – the overwhelming desire to run and die all at the same time. I was sure this was the end of my life, and I was going to suffocate right in front of everyone on the train just like that. BANG, BANG, BANG. The explosion of my overzealous nervous system fired off, leaving me in a state of pure and utter Panic.

God fucking help me, please. What the hell has just happened? Oh my God, oh my God. Please help me. Anyone. I'm so scared, and I don't understand why this is happening. Get me out of here.

What happened next was just as Fearful. I got off the train, out onto the platform and into the fresh air and then BANG. It happened again. *Oh no, this can't be right, I am off the train, and now it's happening again.* This went on to happen four more times that day, and that's when I knew my life was in trouble (if it wasn't already).

I hadn't had any issues with claustrophobia before getting on the train that day, but it was brewing. I also think what compounded the issue was that my London experience coincided with September 11, 2001, terrorist attacks in New York. The propaganda surrounding that focused on the next terrorist bombing site — the Tube.

Every time the Tube got delayed underground, my mind would often wonder if we were going to be blown up next and what possible chance would I have of surviving.

Within the space of 24 hours, I felt as if my world was turned upside down. This was the start of my Nervous Breakdown – something that took years to come back from. In such a short period, I lived in a world of being petrified, had regular Panic attacks with extreme levels of Anxiety and yet I still had no comprehension of my condition. Even now whilst writing this, I feel the total destruction I endured and the endless fight for freedom of my Fears.

HIDING THE TRUTH

I was so amazed at the speed of my mental health decline that I thought I must have contracted a virus or something equally unusual that affected my mind or brain. This obviously wasn't the case, but the idea resulted in 'naming' this mystery condition. I started referring to it as 'Cyrus the Virus'.

It became a sort of code between my girlfriend and I. If I needed a break when we were out socially, or I wanted her to know that I was struggling to cope, all I needed to say was: "Cyrus is back" (actually never left – just got more severe) and she knew what was happening. It was all part of the cover-up to stop people from finding out about this terrible secret that I was struggling to deal with.

Every single fucking waking moment of every second of every day started with the same thing. Fear!!!! I Feared everything from trains to buses; from shops to confined areas; from being alone to being in a crowd. My mind would play tricks on me with thoughts of losing control of my mind and ending up in a psychiatric unit. Being tied up in one of those white jackets with the arms tied together and being drugged up so much I was incoherent.

There was often urges of wanting to lash out — to hurt people or destroy things whilst in shops for no reason what so ever. It was relentless and devastating to be me every moment of the day. I couldn't get a break from my mind which was so ignited with Fear, reality was non existent. Regardless of what was happening in my life — good or bad — it seemed like this screaming was coming from inside me. I was terrified continuously and struggling to cope. In fact, for a while, I wasn't coping at all. I was better off dead.

My mind broke down completely, just two months after that day on the Tube. I started to Fear air (even though I rationally knew that breathing air is what I needed to live), heat, smoke, water, food, noise and even the thought of being outside. The sky surrounding me was too claustrophobic. If I mustered up the courage to go outside, I had to deal with the claustrophobia of the sky coming down on me, the million and one other Fears and triggers that I had somehow developed and the constant threat of another Panic attack which seemed to be on speed dial as they were so frequent.

I had lost 12 kilograms in 3 months, looked so pale and unwell with a gaunt withdrawn look to me. I felt like sleeping was not an option as I would struggle to sleep more than a few hours per night.

I felt so exhausted, that I used to hide and pray in local churches often laying between the pews for respite and trying to regain some energy.

Churches were often open but vacant so it was a place of solace both with hiding my Fear and also asking God for any reprieve from this "thing" in my head that wouldn't give me a break with shear rumination of anything and everything I was Fearful of. The amount of bargaining I did in those pews with God was out of control as I would have given anything to set myself free.

I would often say that "if I had a million dollars" I would give it away to have some peace and freedom from my head and if that could happen, the transaction was easy I promise you!!!

You can probably see the demoralising situation I was in and lack of hope I was facing also. It was literally a second by second life I was living with any given second being a petrifying one.

Most people with Anxiety can at least avoid certain situations or places that trigger their stress. I was annihilated and unable to AVOID anything. Air, water and food are all a bit tricky to avoid. I felt like I could never rest.

It was hell on earth, to say the least, and to make matters worse I was 20,000kms from home. The only shining light was my beautiful and supportive girlfriend. She tried her hardest to help and support me without judgment even though she had no idea how to help me and couldn't comprehend what I was going through.

This was the most challenging point in my life, and to be frank, I was struggling to want to live. I felt I couldn't ever self-harm, or commit suicide though because we had just lost my sister, and my poor family had already been through enough.

I was trapped, desperate and ashamed of myself for being weak. I was a loser with mental health issues. This was my constant internal dialogue that I had developed. I wanted to tell someone, but the shame was too great. I hated myself, and I didn't want anyone to have to deal with the 'freak'. Interesting self-talk right?

I had become the person who is scared of anything and everything. By now, I'd also built up a bit of a shield. I was that cool, bulletproof country boy who wanted to keep that persona going. The exterior was up, and the interior was a debacle.

In late January 2002, my girlfriend and I travelled to Egypt to escape the London winter. At that time, not many tourists were really travelling in general as a result of the recent 9/11 attacks. Especially to a country like Egypt. However we decided to go anyway. We did not want to live in Fear that a terrorist attack would happen to us, and stop us continuing to travel as we had planned and worked so hard for. How ironic hey?

As it turned out it was possibly the safest time to travel, even though it was extremely quiet for the peak tourist season, we met and toured with some fantastic fellow Aussie travellers. On the surface it was a great trip. However Internally for me, and for the majority of it I continued to suffer from Panic attacks. I became so great at hiding it from everyone, no one had any idea. I was still my larrikin self, enjoying a laugh and a beer, all the while constantly suffering.

On a quiet clear evening, camping on the banks of the Nile, our group was sitting around a campfire, listening to stories and looking above at the stars. In this moment I felt the most overwhelming sense of claustrophobia, I was terrified, of everything. I felt suffocated from THE SKY, the feeling it was enclosing on me — yet we were literally surrounded by endless space and air. We were in the MIDDLE OF NOWHERE, and it was here I realised there was NOWHERE I could go to ESCAPE this – I prayed that night, please end my existence, it's too much now. God didn't come to the party on that request!

After, Egypt we somehow made a quick trip back to Australia for a wedding, and I remember feeling so relieved. I had put all my Anxiety egg causes into the fact that I was overseas and thought for sure that being home would save me, that things would go back to normal. On the contrary, it magnified my Fears even more. It wasn't the environment or location that was the problem; it was my head. (I still had little concept of my condition.)

MY STORY

We delayed our return trip for various reasons, and I hoped my girlfriend would see how sick I was. Perhaps we could stay home for good. The reality was, she had no idea how sick I was. Anxiety and Panic can't be measured, and it is impossible to observe.

She kept telling me: "if you let this stop you, it will kill you". She knew how proud of a person I was, and not going back to England would eat me up. She was right, but now I was even more petrified. I had to return to the place where it all started.

I was now scared of everything ever invented or experienced in life, sicker than I had ever been and now contemplating going back! Brave or stupid I thought?

The day we flew back to London, it took me 20 minutes to walk 150 metres from the family home to the shops because of the intense agoraphobic condition I was in. My jelly legs were struggling to allow me to walk, plus the massive Panic and suffocation I felt. I had no power in them at all, and they often gave way, making me look liked I was drunk. My legs were either too stiff and unable to bend or completely floppy and weak.

I was a mess, but despite that, less than seven hours later, I was at the airport and ready to board my flight to London. I hit an all-time Panic Attack record on that plane – I experienced one every 20 minutes or so, and it's safe to say I didn't exactly feel a million bucks when we landed.

The truth is, I became an expert at hiding my petrified mind. I travelled the world, meeting new people, partying, making new friends and looking as though I was having the time of my life. I was suffering internally and in so much pain. It was my little secret and, weirdly, I felt I had to protect it.

Despite my daily world of complete Fear being present, I somehow continued with our trip around Europe whilst hanging on by a finger nail. I didn't want to let my girlfriend down. This was her dream, and all I could think was to not ruin it for her. Why fuck up two people's lives, right?

The Europe trip in mid 2002 lasted for almost 4 months and I actually made it through with a smile for the rest of the world but clearly not for myself.

THE BASE JUMPER

There are life defining periods in your life that you look back on and realise they were the moments that change your path.

Towards the end of our travels backpacking around Europe, in August 2002, we were staying with other backpackers at a camping ground in the small town of Lauterbrunnen in Switzerland.

Each day we would explore and walk the surrounding mountains, watching others mountain bike riding and seeing the base jumpers, jump off the side of the cliffs above our camp making their way down the valley below.

The surrounding views, were unlike anything we had ever experienced. It was magic. But don't worry (no pun intended) my mind was still suffering with continuous Anxiety and Panic.

At the end of a big day hiking we were cooking our dinner in the camp Kitchen. It was here that I witnessed a group of base jumpers jump off the side of the cliff, near the camp where they would eventually open their parachute and float down in the valley below. I watched in amazement, at the excitement of this group, at the cheers and the pure LOVE of the adrenaline rush they were getting from leaping off the side of a massive mountain! I started to question, how can one persons Fear be terrifying and another's Fear be pure joy and excitement?????

It was in this moment I realised that my perception of Fear could be changed. The way I see it and think about it. The reality that perception is something we have the power to alter. It was then,

I realised that a **Base Jumper** has saved me!

It was this trip that I found hope in the form of a **Base Jumper** and the turning point of my ability to tackle my Panic and Fear head on — it was fate working it's magic and if I never got back on that plane, who knows where I would be now!

The time frame for my suffering was close to a year day in day out of pure dread, Panic and Fear before a shift was made after a **Base Jumper** epiphany.

We will delve into this epiphany throughout the book and explain what happened to help me out of this massive hole.

ACCEPTING REALITY

The only thing I was proud of myself during this time was that I never gave up. I refused to let this beat me. Everything I researched or studied about this condition always ran the same theme.

Forums and comments online often stated things like "I am nearly better, except for being on buses" or "when I am in the car" would be typical. It was a condition that was scary and pretty much, not curable. What hope did I have?

My best mate's brother also had Agoraphobia, and he was the only point of reference for me. Unfortunately, this only escalated my Fear as he had a difficult time and still has with this condition as far as I am aware.

In a way, though, this made me more determined to beat it — to prove it can be done. I was once told to just learn to live with it and do the best you can. My immediate internal response was always: Get Fucked! There has to be a way, and I will keep searching until I get better.

I kept asking myself "why me?" (of course, I suppose I could have easily have asked "why not me?") although now I believe the reason is apparent: to help others in the same boat.

I want to give hope and a sense of relief because that was what I always wanted. Someone to say 'it's going to be OK' and 'we can help'.

FROM MENTAL BREAKDOWN TO A CAREER AS A PARAMEDIC? NOT THE OTHER WAY ROUND

I always knew that I wanted to be a paramedic after spending a week on clinical placements with the Bendigo Ambulance Service way back in 1998 during my nursing studies. That week on placement ignited my sense of purpose in life and it was from there, I knew exactly what job I wanted to do. My enthusiasm and excitement for my career exploded exponentially and it certainly was a different feeling that a nursing career had (which was not a lot to be honest).

The plan from that moment was to finally graduate, earn some cash and look at studying paramedicine down the track after a few years nursing. Part of my life's journey didn't factor in the death of my sister, an overseas trip and of course a nervous breakdown in the form an Anxiety disorder.

My dream of becoming a paramedic did raise the question with me and those close to me of "would doing such a highly stressful job" be the best thing for you considering your recent and current situation and mental health?

Absolutely, it did?

I had been through hell and back and the last thing I wanted to do was head back into this hole I spent a long time digging out of. The prevalence and risk of developing a mental health condition in the emergency services is very high compared to the general population. It is obvious why this is the case given the significant trauma and stressful cases paramedics see and do on a daily basis.

The advice or concern my family and even I had was generally geared around the fact it's often the job that creates the mental health problems, (paramedic) not the other way around. It was a fair point.

MY STORY

By the time I had applied to become a paramedic, I was confident that I had put in the time and effort along with the tools and strategies to deal with such a complex, stressful and challenging role. I realised that I probably had a better chance coping with the job after my breakdown and recovery (than the years prior to my breakdown), as I now had a massive war chest or arsenal to help deal with the role.

It was time to put it into practise and after joining the Ambulance Service in South Australia in 2004, I soon found many times where stress and Anxiety were very much a natural part of my job. Anything from car accidents, to shootings, hangings and complex sick patients were subjected to me on a daily basis.

I was being tested professionally, mentally and also academically. It was amazing, scary and exciting all in one. I was living my dream and yep, coping quite well with my Anxiety and all it tried to throw at me. My years of hard work and strategies were paying off and I was feeling very much in control of my mental health.

There has been one particular job that does stick out at me which happened on December 17, 2017. It was a magnificent sunny, warm day full of good vibes and feelings here in Melbourne.

I was working with a great friend of mine and we had just transported a little boy to hospital who had fallen out of a tree from around 4 metres high with potential for significant injuries. We felt like we did a great job caring and managing his injuries and after finishing that job, we were ready for a coffee and lunch.

Driving back through the city of Melbourne, we got dispatched to a case in the CBD which we thought was a 15 year old vs car.

The job was only 200 metres from our dispatch coordinates so off we went. Upon arriving, I looked at my partner as we pulled up and some expletives were said as we both looked out the window of the ambulance just witnessing a scene of something much more than 1 patient.

We had just driven into something looking like a war zone!

There were people scattered all over the road, a car half stuck on a bollard that looked as though it had rammed into very hard.

Police everywhere along with thousands of onlookers out doing their Christmas shopping. The noise and vibe was deafening.

What had just happened was a person had driven high speed into 18 people crossing the street taking them out like a ten pin bowling ball would do in the alley. The screams and cry for help seemed to stretch far and wide.

This is the job, most paramedics don't ever want to be first to as it can really test your capacity to do a good job and deal with the most extreme pressure.

Nevertheless, we were it and it was game on to try and help these people.

To make matters worst, some of the equipment we needed to help document and identify the patients wasn't available to us, so we needed to think on our feet and do the best we can.

It was the most stressed and intense 30 minutes of my working life. Trying to help and care for 18 patients scattered around an area the size of approximately 50 metres had its challenges. We needed to identify who was the sickest, prioritise them and get the relevant resources available to come and help manage and transport to hospital.

It was a shit show to say the least and very scary. I had never seen anything like it in ambulance before and had no time to compute what we were facing or had just transpired. It was so hard to manage due to the shear volume of patients and acuity of their trauma which was significant.

We were able to get plenty of resources to the scene within a short period of time and the extra support and hands on the ground proved beneficial for us and also the patients.

Unfortunately, one patient died 8 days later in hospital whilst the other 17 survived.

MY STORY

The job felt so chaotic and intense, I felt my head spinning whilst on the scene and for several hours and even days after it. It really pushed my mental health as I felt that I didn't perform as well as I had liked and maybe I could have done better (even though all 18 patients got to hospital within 30 minutes).

It was in the days post the case that I wondered how I would cope and deal with the stress of such an event. I wondered if this would reignite my Anxiety and cause me to spiral out of control and back into the dark hole I once lived in.

Fortunately, those legitimate Fears I questioned did not appear or become reality. I had a sound system of dealing with stress, Fear and Anxiety and along with sharing my experience with other colleagues, family and friends I managed to stay in control and deal with the stress in a normal, rational manner that any well rounded mentally sound person would. This gave me great confidence in my strategies and tools and hope that one day I can share these with others.

I am now in my 40's, and since my recovery, I have continued my career as a paramedic. My wife is still by my side. I'm a father of two amazing young men. I look back and often wonder how I ever survived or dealt with such a problematic consuming mental health condition.

Of course, it has also taken this long to admit to my friends and peers that I have or have had mental health problems. The sad thing is that I should be proud of what I have achieved. I think a person's character often shines when they endure adversity, and I can safely say that I passed this particular test with flying colours and a bloody distinction.

I am going to show you my way of recovery in the hope that it lets your heart smile again. I want you to become the person you are have always wanted to be, without this debilitating condition taking control.

There are so many of us suffering in silence and feeling the stigma of mental health. Let's try and stop the suffering from now on. Read on and let's tackle this together.

> "THE BRAVE MAN IS NOT HE WHO DOES NOT FEEL AFRAID, BUT HE WHO CONQUERS THAT FEAR."
>
> NELSON MANDELA

CHAPTER 02

ANXIETY & HOW IT ROLLS

WHAT IS ANXIETY?
(AKA: THE THING IN MY HEAD THAT WON'T PISS OFF)

Wouldn't we love to just 'get over it' and 'forget about it'? Unfortunately, it's not that easy to do. Our brains and minds have gone off track a little, and we are overwhelmed by Fear.

Anxiety and Anxiety Disorders are a mental health condition. They are debilitating and create a world of pain and suffering that often reduces quality of life.

People with Anxiety Disorders will do anything to alleviate the symptoms and will use all sorts of behaviours to escape them. Often though, that can mean it follows them around everywhere like a little puppy dog causing long-term effects on their emotional and physical health.

Suffering from Anxiety causes us to become trapped in a spiral of Fear that is almost impossible to get out of. It's changing this spiral that is the key to recovery and improved quality of life.

Anxiety is and can be a normal part of life. Your body responds to Anxiety when required and it is necessary for survival. It can have a positive effect by promoting heightened arousal for situations like job interviews, school exams or other types of performance associated with work, sport or our academics.

'Normal' Anxiety is temporary and resolves once the situation stops and the result or outcome is realised. This is the skill non-sufferers can do better than sufferers – completing the loop. It's a skill I've failed with more times than I can count before my recovery.

Anxiety Disorders, however, can become more than just temporary worry or Fear as they often continue past any stimulus or situation. This compounds the problem and extends the suffering for much longer.

There is a common thread for those of us that suffer from Anxiety. It involves several persistent, excessive worries, Fears or concerns to everyday life that has no end in sight. We tend to become super **fixated** or **focused** on our Fears; we jump to **conclusions** (especially ones of the Worst Case Scenario variety). We think the **threat** is inevitable, meaning we refuse to take on any other evidence that the threat may be false.

This condition can get you in a variety of different ways with different scenarios affecting us for various reasons with different triggers. Fun, hey?

ANXIETY & HOW IT ROLLS

There are several subgroups of Anxiety Disorders that are all under the same umbrella.

These subgroups are called:
- Generalised Anxiety Disorder (GAD)
- Post Traumatic Stress Disorder (PTSD)
- Social Anxiety Disorder or Social Phobia (SAD)
- Obsessive-Compulsive Disorder (OCD)
- Panic Disorder (Agoraphobia)
- Specific Phobias
- Depersonalisation and Derealisation

Genetics, learned behaviour, chemical changes in the brain and unhelpful/negative thinking all play a role in increasing the chance of us potentially developing these disorders.

Additionally, research into the gut and gut health has a significant impact on our Anxiety as well. The science is still relatively new but gaining momentum, and I think that sooner, rather than later, we might find treating Anxiety is assisted with managing both the gut and the head in mainstream medicine.

With all of my research, I have found that we need to address our body and mind in a multitude of ways, this is what I want to teach you.

We will learn how to address our genetics aimed at our DNA; see how our behaviour has been learned; understand how our body, mind and brain work; and also look at our diets and what we can change to improve our Anxiety and, ultimately, our life.

Our primary approach is from a Cognitive Behavioural Therapy (CBT) model. This aims at addressing our unrealistic or misguided thoughts – the ones that set up our Anxiety in the first place. We will also understand our bodies reaction to Fear in a lot more detail. This will be addressed later in the book.

FIGURING OUT HOW YOU'RE WIRED

We are naturally wired for a certain level of Anxiety through a danger bias (tendency to sense Fear) that allows our brains and bodies to continually look for threat or danger to help keep us alive. Fair enough, right? Very helpful.

We can detect danger or negative situations faster than the good stuff. It's a bloody great design, I will admit. This wiring has kept us alive throughout the ages. If you think about it, if we were never on guard and watching out for danger, then we'd probably be extinct from predators that caught us off guard a long time ago. The fact the human race is alive and well proves the theory that our ability to detect danger has been genetically passed down. Therefore, it's impossible to avoid our genetic makeup and anatomy that produces Anxiety and Fear. Once upon a time when a tiger or bear would threaten and potentially kill us, evolution allowed us to develop a survival detection system. However, these threats have virtually gone or are at least not a reality in civilised society.

Unfortunately, stress at work; technology; overloaded, fast-paced lifestyles; and social pressures are the new tiger and bear.

Great, I hear you say. I now feel equal parts reassured and stuffed!

Well, all is not lost. Just because we've been wired for Fear doesn't mean we can't live a happy and harmonious life. I promise.

OK, SO WHAT DO I DO ABOUT IT?

Before I can help you, YOU need to work out if Anxiety is your problem.

You have probably been feeling like crap for such a long time, and you may not even be aware that Anxiety is the cause.

To get the ball rolling, below is a list of stuff that may be familiar to you. You might have felt, or experienced, some or most of the symptoms depending on your situation.

Don't be alarmed by the extent of the symptom lists (especially if you're ticking heaps of boxes). This is a general overview, and there are potentially plenty more. You may have others you have also identified and can add to the list yourself.

It seems that Anxiety can create a variety of symptoms: both physically and mentally.

Remember, we are just trying to get an idea if this is you, or not.

Please note: This information is not a diagnostic tool but rather a guide to see where you're at.

Naturally, if this does resonate, seeking professional help is always recommended. Self-diagnosis isn't helpful (especially when you assume the worst!) so starting with a professional or even online survey/checklist is a useful start.

Let's check out what this beast can produce:

PHYSICAL SYMPTOMS

- Gasping for air even though you're not moving or exercising (I can't breathe).
- Suffocating or feeling a sense of hot, stuffy air.
- Fast or pounding heart.
- Getting choked out or tightness in your throat.
- Chest tightness or pain.
- Sweating like a pig all over the body, flushed in the face, feeling hot or chilly, getting the shakes.
- Dizziness and feeling faint (sometimes like passing out).
- The urgency to wee or poo.
- Trembling or shaky (jelly legs).
- Dry in the chompers (mouth or throat).
- Tight or sore muscles (feeling stiff).
- Pins and needles in arms, fingers, legs, toes or mouth.
- Feeling crook in the guts (sick or nauseous).
- Hyperventilation (breathing too fast for no reason).
- Nervous sounding voice (wobbly sound).
- Tunnel vision (losing vision from the outside).

ANXIETY & HOW IT ROLLS

EMOTIONAL SYMPTOMS

- Feeling edgy, jumpy or jittery (like a cat on a hot tin roof).
- Feeling pissed off, frustrated and impatient over bugger all.
- Freaking out (scared, terrified or Fearful) when should be feeling safe.
- Feeling nervous, tense and wound up (buzzing around like a blowfly).

BEHAVIORAL SYMPTOMS

- Wanting to get the hell out of there (run or escape the situation).
- Staying clear of situations where there are threat and danger (avoid).
- Wearing out the carpet (agitation and pacing).
- Freezing or inability to move (like you're wearing concrete boots).
- Constant wanting someone tell me it's going to be OK.

COGNITIVE (THINKING) SYMPTOMS

- Unable to cope with anything and everything.
- Fear of losing my shit (going crazy or mad).
- Fear of losing control (doing something without being able to control it).
- Fear of getting sick and being 6ft under (serious illness, injury of death).
- Worried about getting judged by everyone as a freak.
- Unable to remember bugger all (decreased memory or poor memory).
- Can't think correctly or without reason.
- Freaky images, thoughts or memories in your head.
- Being easily distracted.
- Perceptions of detachment or unreality.

BLOODY HELL!!

You may feel like some of these symptoms might ring true for you and, if so, it might be an idea to keep reading!

Let's take some time to narrow down some of the subgroups of Anxiety, and one might resonate with you. Remember, It's OK if you identify yourself in more than one though. It's in understanding and acknowledging that we can get back on track.

Below is only a guide with the different types of Anxiety and if you require more information, seek professional help and assistance.

LET'S BREAK IT DOWN:

GENERALISED ANXIETY DISORDER (GAD)

What is it?

There's no doubt about it, Generalised Anxiety Disorder (GAD) is a real energy sucker! People with GAD find it difficult to overcome or rationalise their concerns even though they are aware of the situation.

As the Anxiety is constant, their levels of fatigue, energy and sleep are affected. They cop heaps of muscle tension, aches, sweating, agitation and trembling and they often have more crap days than good. If the signs and symptoms hang around longer than six months, you may be in this category.

Signs & Symptoms

The main symptom is full on the worry that won't stop. It causes havoc on your ability to carry out tasks like work, study, relationships or daily activities.

Common Thoughts

"I feel worried all the time and can't seem to stop worrying."

"Little or big things worry me, even basic jobs, school stuff or simple tasks."

"I always feel as though something bad or terrible is going to happen to me."

"The future is always terrifying, and I often think the worst happening all the time."

Who is at risk?

- It tends to lean towards women more than men.
- Can occur at any age group, young or old.
- People with GAD may often describe themselves as 'worriers' and have been like this for as long as they can remember, not knowing what causes it.

THE SUFFERERING DOESN'T
HAVE A FINISH TIME
AT THE END OF EACH DAY.

POST TRAUMATIC STRESS DISORDER (PTSD)

What is it?

This one particularly likes to affect emergency services and armed forces servants and is an absolute prick. It can affect anyone, though.

Post Traumatic Stress Disorder or PTSD is a particular set of reactions that can develop in people that have been through a traumatic event. That is, they have experienced or witnessed an event that threatened their life or safety, or others around them, and this leads to feelings of intense Fear, helplessness or horror. This can be a car accident or another serious accident; physical or sexual assault; war or torture; disasters such as bushfires or floods.

People with PTSD often re-live the experience: feeling Panic or extreme Fear similar to the Fear they felt during the traumatic event. Apart from the traumatic event itself, other risk factors for developing PTSD include the history of trauma or previous mental health problems, ongoing stress and lack of support.

Signs & Symptoms

As mentioned above, extreme levels of intense Fear, helplessness and worry. Elevated levels of Panic and extreme Fear.

Common Thoughts

"I see terrible images of the scary event all the time that causes me horrendous Fear."

"I have horrible nightmares all the time and can't sleep."

"I feel scared all the time."

"I stopped going to the shopping centre because it brings back memories of the little boy being run over in the carpark."

"I used to be happy and fun but know I just feel nothing or numb."

"My friends and family are different now; nothing feels the same."

Who is at risk?
Affects both women and men equally

SOCIAL ANXIETY DISORDER OR SOCIAL PHOBIA (SAD)

What is it?
Social Anxiety Disorder (SAD) can also be known as Social Phobia.

People who are shy or inhibited socially in their nature, as well as children who are clingy or shy, are at particular risk.

Having a history of being poorly treated, embarrassed or humiliated in a situation in the past can attribute to create this phobia.

There is an increased risk if it runs in families with a history of Anxiety Disorders. A learned attitude or behaviour from other family members can also bring forth SAD. For example, a parent demonstrating exaggerated distress about seeing new people.

Signs & Symptoms
This one is especially tough given we are such social animals by nature. People suffering from social disorder become concerned when they think everyone has an opinion or judgement of them, which can lead to intense Anxiety.

Additionally, they think they are being criticised and humiliated by others which can also make them feel embarrassed. They are super concerned about how people will view and judge them.

Common Thoughts
"I feel embarrassed in front of other people all the time."

"I often get worried people are judging me for any reason."

"I will worry for days or weeks before an event where other people will be and can judge me."

"I like to stay away from places where there are other people as I find it difficult making friends or keeping friends."

"I always feel like blushing, sweating, trembling or get a nervous voice around other people."

"I often feel sick or nauseous with other people around."

"When I show signs of being nervous around others, it makes things worse for me."

"Because I get nervous around other people, I act different than normal, and it often makes my relationships even harder to keep."

Who is at risk?

- More women than men appear to develop the disorder.
- Generally begins in adolescence.

Although it's perfectly normal to feel nervous in situations where you might come under the scrutiny of others. Whether they'll be strangers or people we know, (for example, giving a speech at a wedding or presenting at a conference), it becomes a concern when the problem is disabling or distressing, and when avoidance is preferred. The behaviour affects the person's ability to function or contribute.

OBSESSIVE COMPULSIVE BEHAVIOUR (OCD)

What is it?

OCD sufferers often perform acts from their compulsions or obsessions to alleviate the distress or neutralise the thoughts created by their levels of Anxiety.

Signs & Symptoms

It seems OCD can develop from the combination of genetic and environmental factors as well as family history, social and psychological factors.

There are also environmental or learned behaviours, like developing a handwashing compulsion after getting sick from contact from another person, animal or plant.

Observing similar behaviours by family or friends can influence you and build momentum.

Common Thoughts

"I need to do certain things or actions in a way to make me feel better like washing my hand's lots or keeping things clean."

"If I don't do it right, I get anxious and stressed."

"I feel embarrassed and don't want to tell anyone.'

"I often hide my actions from others."

"Sometimes, my thoughts are terrifying like I want to hurt people."

"I often need to count items or objects such as my clothes or footpath blocks when I am walking to feel better."

"I need to hoard items such as junk mail and old newspapers."

"I often get urges that are unwanted and worry me a lot."

"I feel dirty all the time and feel contaminated with germs."

"I get apprehensive if I haven't checked to see if the doors locked or stove's off."

Who is at risk?

- Children as young as 6 or 7 can show signs or symptoms.
- Mainly develops around adolescence.

PANIC DISORDER (PANIC ATTACKS)

What is it?

Otherwise known as Panic Attacks, these are nasty, nasty buggers and you wouldn't wish them on your worst enemy. It's the ultimate destroyer. An Attack involves a period when you are full of intense Fear (freaking out). It can build up from nowhere and combines intense body sensations with super scary thoughts. Depending on your understanding, they can last from 30 seconds to 20 minutes and are s#*t and terrifying.

Signs & Symptoms

Panic Attacks can flare up quite often for some. When it hits regularly, it becomes very disabling it reduces your ability to perform some or all daily activities due to intense Fear of having more (in other words have bad/scary days and life's crap).

After a Panic attack, most people are fatigued – exhausted and mentally drained. Often feels like you've have been hit by a truck.!

Some people can have Panic attacks several times a day, every couple of months or years, and some will even have them waking up from their sleep.

Common Thoughts

"I am so petrified, freaking out and Fearful that it's bloody unbearable."

"I think I may die with this."

"I can't breathe properly and suffocate."

"I'm having a heart attack." (heart is beating flat out)

"I am having a stroke; my fingers and toes are going numb."

"I think I'm going crazy about losing my mind."

"Something is choking me."

"I feel out of my body, and nothing is real."

"I'm really dizzy and faint."

"I'm sweating everywhere."

"I am always stressed about having another Panic attack and what's going to happen next time when I have one."

"I don't want to go to some places or situations in case it causes another Panic attack."

"What if I have something medically wrong with me and the doctor got it wrong, and my Panic attack ends bad."

Who is at risk?

- Panic Attacks can be quite common and can affect up to 40% of the population at some stage in their life.
- Women are affected more than men.
- It seems to develop in early to mid-twenties or mid-life. It can affect people of any age but is significantly less in children or older people.
- There is no specific cause noted for Panic disorder. Still, several physical factors can contribute to its development like people with lung problems, thyroid issues and irregular heartbeats.
- Also having a history of really sad or bad life experience/s can increase the probability (for example, death of a loved one, sexual or physical abuse or ongoing high levels of stress).

AGORAPHOBIA (A-GOR-A-FO-BIA) - (ASSOCIATED WITH PANIC ATTACKS)

What is it?

Agoraphobia is a type of Anxiety Disorder in which you Fear or avoid either places or situations because you believe if you have extra or more Panic attacks. You may not have the ability to escape, and you feel embarrassed or helpless.

The cause is primarily the Fear of suffering a Panic Attack and not being able to help, resolve or control the situation without further suffering or any assistance.

This can happen anywhere from being in public or crowded places, confined spaces, public transport or open spaces.

They often suffer one or more Panic attacks in a particular place and start to avoid that person, place, situation or thing eventually narrowing their ability and environment to the point of being housebound. In extreme cases (absolutely terrible place to be in, believe me. I've been there, and it's awful).

SPECIFIC PHOBIAS

What is it?

They are getting freaked out by one particular thing, or things, in any given situation, activity, animal or object. It can be quite a normal response if the reason is legitimate or dangerous with stuff like snakes, spiders, certain insects or heights and aeroplanes all being 'usual' things to have a Fear of. Additionally, something like the sight of blood or vomit also fit into this category. When the reaction is extreme, though, there is an issue.

There is an increased risk if it runs in families with a history of Anxiety Disorders. A learned attitude or behaviour from other family members may be detrimental (for example, a parent demonstrating exaggerated distress about dogs or spiders).

Research has shown that children of people with moderate to severe depression are three times more likely to have an Anxiety Disorder or a Specific Phobia than with non-depressed parents.

A Specific Phobia can also be brought about if someone has witnessed or experienced a traumatic event (for example, bitten by a spider and becoming unwell may then create a Fear of spiders).

Signs & Symptoms

Some people can react by imagining an exaggerated or irrational response to danger with feelings of Panic, Fear or terror that are out of whack to the actual threat.

These types of excessive reactions may indicate a Specific Phobia.

Common Thoughts

"I get Fearful of certain things like heights, snakes or bees."

"I know my Fears are irrational, but I can't stop them."

"The last time I saw a spider, I had a Panic Attack."

"I want to take the kids to the zoo, but I am too scared of even seeing a snake even though it's in the cage."

"I feel petrified that I may come into contact with a large dog so I would rather stay at home because it's safe."

"It's tough for me to keep down a job because I'm petrified about coming into contact with a bee on the way to work."

Who is at risk?

- The first symptoms usually arising in childhood or early adolescence.
- Any age group if the experience is severe and not able to be rectified or rationalised.

DEPERSONALISATION AND DEREALISATION

What is it?

These two conditions can be a part of Anxiety and exposure to long-term stress or trauma. They can also have devastating effects on the individual who experiences them. It can also affect individuals who suffer from Depression, Bipolar Disorder, Schizophrenia and Borderline Personality Disorder, to name a few.

They are closely connected and often overlap each other. It can be a challenge to see the issue when you're not attached to yourself or your outside views or perceptions.

Depersonalisation (more physical) can give the person a sense of being detached from themselves and that they don't belong to their feelings, emotions and sensations. It's a total lack of sense of self – almost as though they are not themselves.

Often their experiences seem blurred or hazy, giving them a sense they're not real and that only ramps up their Anxiety.

It's often described as a feeling like you're present, but you're not inside yourself. That other people exist and are close to you, but you're not connected to them like you used to be.

There's also no connection to your body and your movements.

Derealisation (more thought, or cerebral) relates more to the way a person sees the outside world and their perceptions. A sense of their surroundings not having the same meaning and understanding, giving them a more surreal or shallow view.

This can affect their sense of taste, smell and sound, making things seem not as real as they should be.

Sufferers often describe their feelings or derealisation as being similar to watching their lives through a TV screen; that they are 'observers' of their experiences and lives.

It is common for them to have experiences of Deja vu at regular intervals also (for example, places they know quite well can seem foreign, or feelings towards loved ones may be limited).

It is believed that constant worry and intrusive thoughts fuel this symptom of derealisation and heightens one's Anxiety even to Panic.

This, of course, creates a cycle of Fear and worry and often reduces the person's ability to deal with the condition because they tend to avoid situations or circumstances that fuel their Anxiety.

Because they are somewhat detached from their reality, their ability to process information is difficult because their experiences are not seen as their own.

Both of these conditions seem to come from the mind trying to protect itself and creating a defence mechanism.

Due to the high levels of stress and Anxiety, the mind defaults to 'checking out' of reality, as it's too tense and stressful. It will default to an imaginary entity to help out and take the load off the pressure for some time. Unfortunately, this can just make matters worse.

These conditions are challenging to deal with and overcome. Given the fact that high stress and Anxiety are triggers for the conditions, then it would be advisable to try and reduce these levels to decrease recurrence.

Additionally, understanding the fact that it's not real, and only a default symptom of Anxiety may help alleviate extra Anxiety and stop the cycle.

Well, that was fun, wasn't it? If you're feeling like some (or even many) of those things are looking all too familiar, you've probably got that jittery feeling in your belly. You may like to put the book down at this point and walk away. What if I told you that recognising the problem was one of the hardest parts though? If you've made it this far, you should be proud. How about reading on and learning how to understand this bastard a little more? After all, knowledge is power, right? [1-9]

CHAPTER 03

EVOLUTION OF FEAR

HOW OUR BODY MAKES THIS HAPPEN

You're probably asking yourself: why does it have to be me with this condition, and why can't someone else have it?

I don't want to play this game of Fear and didn't sign up in the first place. Yep, I can hear you from here.

I know because I used to say this all the time. The fact of the matter is, once the nasty little bugger (Anxiety) decides to play ball, there is no way out (until you read this book, of course!)

There may be several reasons for WHY ME?

As mentioned earlier, many are not your fault. Genetics, physical or mental trauma or learned behaviour as a child or adult are things that are out of your control. However, some factors are things you have control over like diet, understanding your physical symptoms, and the way you think.

First, we need to go back to the beginning of how our brains and bodies work and how they developed through time to work out this jigsaw puzzle.

Did you know everyone plays this game of mental wellbeing daily, whether they realise it or not? The only difference is that some are engulfed with Fear, and others have it under control. Most people are not even aware they are participating in the game in the first place.

The road back to taking charge of our minds is long and often lonely, but it's very achievable. First of all, you need to understand how it all works.

FEAR THROUGH EVOLUTION

Apparently, we all have a brain.

Some people who know me well would argue if this is true!!!!!

OK, when we started as humans (a bloody long time ago), we could keep ourselves alive but did it naturally and without a lot of thinking. We were good at getting the basics right: eating, breathing and reproducing.

Over time and thanks to evolution, it became apparent that we needed extra brain power for survival or the edible old human species would end up extinct. We were getting eaten and killed too easily by anything that found humans tasty!

Luckily, we were able to develop a new survival system through time that was very efficient and enabled us to flourish as a species. Fast forward and look at the capacity we have today.

Alrighty, did you know we have developed three brains (yep three) over our history? It doesn't always feel like it (some days I wonder if I've even got one running), but a lot is going on up there without us realising.

The first brain developed was the **Reptilian** Brain.

THE EVOLUTION OF FEAR - THE 3 BRAINS

REPTILIAN: 1ST
Automatic (Subconsious)
Survival/Reproduction

MAMMALIAN: 2ND
(Limbic)
Automatic (Subconsious)
Emotions/Fear & memory

NEOCORTEX: 3RD
Rational or
thinking brain

Reptilian Brain:

- It developed long before I was born.
- Does the basics well (keeping us alive by helping us breathe, eat and drink, reproduce, etc.).
- Not much of a thinker (wouldn't win a Rubik's Cube comp).
- Pretty much automatic (all the action goes on in our subconscious).

As we kept evolving, it became apparent that although the Reptilian brain kept us alive, we needed a bit more brainpower and things like emotions to get the job done.

After all, if we are going to reproduce, it would be nice to feel some emotion like love for our partner/s. So, sure enough, along came to the Second brain called ***Mammalian***. It has been around forever too.

Mammalian Brain:

- Sits on top of the Reptilian brain.
- Brought some great new tools with it (it's home of the 'Fear centre' that is called the Limbic System).
- It also houses emotions, feelings and memories.
- Remembers good and bad stuff (like danger) well.
- Has the ability to get the body 'pumped up' for action (a unique little trigger, the Amygdala).
- Not much of a thinker either.
- Also automatic (in our subconscious).

Now, what do we have happening?

There are now two brains that are great at keeping us alive, providing us with feelings and memories, but neither of them is the sharpest tools in the shed.

So, evolution created a third brain called the **Neocortex**. Yippee! This one can think (therefore referred to as the 'Thinking Brain').

Neocortex Brain:

- The three brains work together and compare emotions and memories (that's what helps Keep us alive – especially if some bad stuff has gone on).
- It can tell us that there is danger (and then choose running or fighting).

The **Reptilian** and **Mammalian** brain don't like thinking too much and basically, respond to what the Neocortex (thinking brain) tells them.

The Neocortex can act like an ON/OFF switch by working out the problem, seeing if it's going to be an issue and then making a decision.

It can tell the other two brains to cool their jets and that 'it's OK, there is no danger here, thanks very much.'

In other words, we can turn off our Fear and Anxiety once it has started to fire, but we can't always stop it initially. This is OK, as long as we understand that Fear is something that is created unconsciously AND consciously.

Let's keep reading to find out more:

PULLING APART THOSE THREE BRAINS

When it comes to the feelings of Fear and Anxiety, the combination of those three brains has some fantastic little parts. These are the important ones: Check out the diagram!

Below is some information about the brain and some anatomy and it's role.

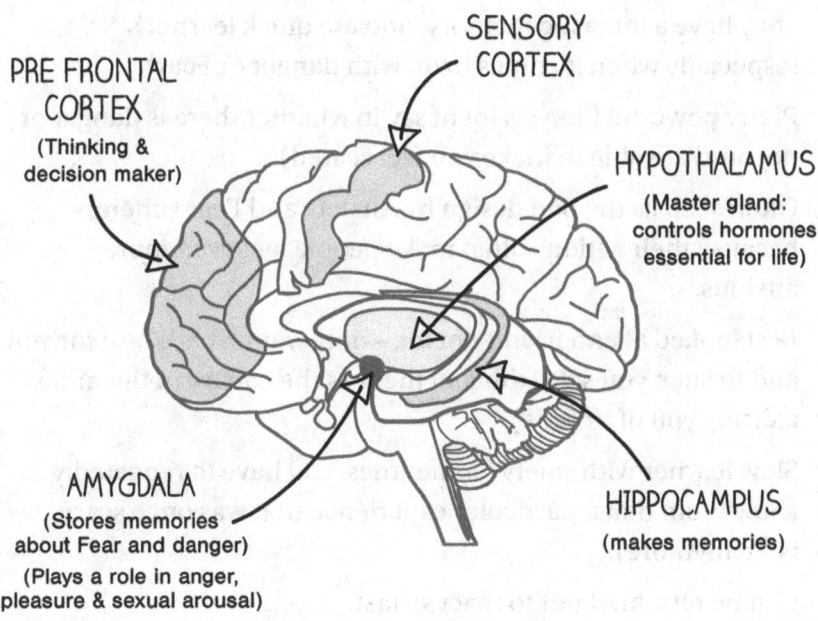

Amygdala (A-Mig-Dah-Lar) – *The Canary In The Mine!*

For those who are unfamiliar with this saying, let me fill you in. You see, back in the day before all the fancy technology we have now, miners had no way of detecting danger in the mines (especially gases like methane and carbon monoxide that could prove to be fatal). So, some smart dude (who may have also been a little lonely) took his canary down the mine for the company and perhaps a little conversation. Unfortunately, the canary died, and so did he. The other miners got wind of this and realised that canaries could be used to detect danger whilst they were underground. They all went and got one for themselves, and so more miners survived as they waited to see the fate of their canary before either continuing work or leaving the mine. The canary, my friends, is a little like the Amygdala. It detects danger and alerts us to any threat (whether it's imagined or real or unseen).[11]

- There are two of them (yep, twins!).
- They live in the Limbic system (that's the Fear centre).
- They have a fantastic memory, and are quick learner's (especially when it comes to do with danger or Fear).
- Pretty powerful (have a lot of say in whether there is danger or not, and are able to make you feel scared).
- Often seen as the bad design by Anxiety and Fear sufferers because their actions often make people feel even more anxious.
- Best looked at as a friend not foe - only want what's best for you and to keep you safe (think of them as the canary in the mine, alerting you of trouble).
- Slow learner with safety (sometimes, you have to repeatedly show them that a particular experience that was once scary isn't anymore).
- Can be retrained not to react so fast.

- Other emotions like happiness, sexual arousal, pleasure and anger are also part of their job.
- Amygdala motto is *"protect first, think later"*.[10]

Helpful info alert!

Did you know that when you are born, the Amygdala is fully developed? That means it can act like an adult and detect danger or Fear easier – no need to learn it first.

The downside of them being fully developed at birth is it's effect on children. Their ability to process Fear is minimal. They have to rely on adults around them to help understand Fear. Children watch their parents or carers, looking at body language, facial expression and voice tones. If they are looking and sounding scared, it can activate them. This can help explain how Fear can be learned at a young age.

There are two little Amygdala that are almond-shaped in structure. They work tirelessly to recall memories of past events. They get a reputation for dealing with Fear, but they have an association with pleasure responses such as reward also. They can influence the release of hormones that make us feel scared or rewarded.

When we experience something positive or rewarding, there is a release of a hormone called dopamine. It creates feelings of being satisfied, fulfilled and contented. This can lead to us thinking clearer, which, in turn, help us make good, sound decisions that are entirely rational.

On the other hand, if Fear or threat is experienced, hormones like Adrenaline and cortisol create feelings of anger, worry, stress and agitation. This leads to poor, irrational and reduced thinking that makes poor decisions. We become fixated and focused on the threat and find it challenging to think through the issue.

Research has demonstrated that the Limbic System (Amygdala's home) has a stronger effect or power over our prefrontal cortex (thinking brain). This is important to understand as the emotion of Fear (or pleasure) will grab hold of you first with a strong reaction. This is why it is vitally important to breathe deeply before reacting (I will talk about this in more detail soon) so your brain can catch up and rationalise thought before you do anything. (12)

Hypothalamus *(Hi-Po-Thel-A-Mus)*

- Controller of the brain and help's process information.
- Produce lots of hormones that control body functions (sleep, body temp, hunger and thirst).
- The gland that gets the message from Amygdala to activate the hormones that go off like a firecracker.

Hippocampus *(Hip-O-Camp-Us)*

- Controller of the brain and help's process information.
- Produce lots of hormones that control body functions (sleep, body temp, hunger and thirst).

Thalamus *(Thel-A-Mus)*

- Get's information from the five senses and send that to rest of the brain for processing.

Sensory Cortex *(Sen-Sore-E Core-Tex)*

- Get's information from your sight and hearing, make sense of it and pass it on to the rest of the brain.

And Finally:

Prefrontal Cortex *(Pre-Front-Al- Core-Tex)*

- Lots of thinking and make lots of decisions with the information it has.
- Help's us behave in the right way *(mine is a little stuffed!)*.
- Can shut off the Fear centre's cause for concern (can tell the Amygdala to stop).

- Thinking/thought power can change how we make decisions regarding Fear and Anxiety (I just need to be influenced the right way).

SENDING INFORMATION THROUGH THE BODY

The three brains wouldn't be any good unless they could get some information sent to them to make some decisions in the first place.

They are assisted in getting information through the Central Nervous System (CNS), Peripheral Nervous System (PNS), Somatic Nervous System (SNS) and Enteric Nervous System (ENS).

I don't want to bore you or get too clinical here, so I'll try and simplify the roles these nervous systems have to increase your understanding. Remember, **knowledge is power.**

All sensory information is detected within the body and sent to the brain for processing. All nervous systems help do this, and below is a quick look at their roles.

Central Nervous System *(CNS)*

- The brain and spinal cord.
- Has nerves that work super fast, called myelinated nerves.
- Main job is to deliver messages like a rocket.

Peripheral Nervous System *(PNS)*

- Made of nerves outside the CNS that collect information from everywhere.
- It's messages aren't as fast as CNS but still really quick as they run on unmyelinated nerves (which work a little slower).
- Neurotransmitters (chemical messengers that help pass on information from one nerve to another) help it to deliver messages.

- The main neurotransmitters it uses are Noradrenaline and Acetylcholine. A bit like using the post and a logistics company to get your mail. *Lol!*

Somatic Nervous System *(SNS)*

- Great at sending messages to the brain for processing through all five senses which are smell, sight, touch, taste and sound.

Enteric Nervous System *(ENS)*

- Does it's handy work from the gut (intestines).
- Sends messengers via neurotransmitters called serotonin, dopamine and norepinephrine.
- Uses the Vague (Vegas) nerve to shoot through messages.
- Can work alone and can have a strong influence on your mental health.

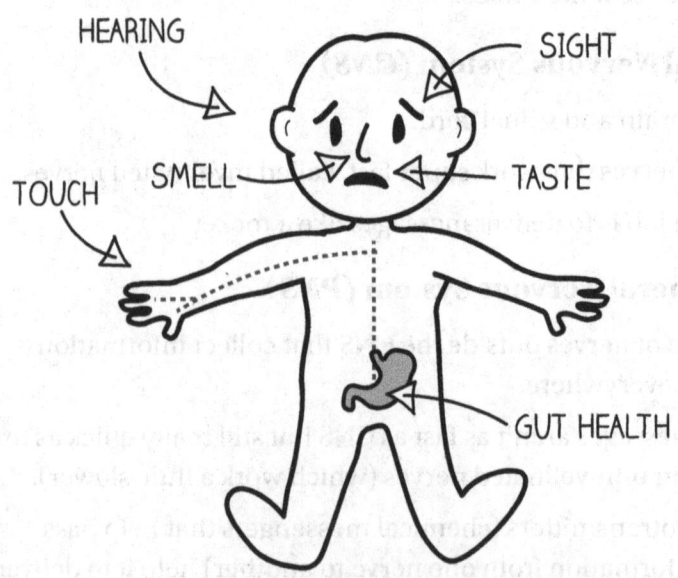

WE ARE ALWAYS SCANNING FOR DANGER
(AUTOMATICALLY).

The ENS is quite essential when it comes to our mental health, especially Anxiety and we will discuss this in more depth later in the book.

When the four nervous systems combine all their sensory information, it is shot off to the brain for assessment. This is important for you to know, because it is all of those elements combined that decide if danger is imminent or not (and therefore trigger Anxiety or Fear).

Why is it so important to know how all this sensory information is transported?

Well, guess what? In our brain, there's a section called the Limbic System (I mentioned it earlier: it's where our canary, the Amygdala, lives). Without us even realising it, all those sensory information passes by the Limbic System, automatically scanning for danger.

The issue with this is: information can be acted upon before it's even been processed by the brain. This is the reason you can get an anxious or Fearful feeling without also understanding why. I used to get stumped on this all the time – feeling scared and Anxious and never knowing what brought it on. This, of course, created more Fear, and the spiral continues. Before you know it, you've gone from zero to 100. This is why it is so essential to understand how your body works.

For example, the smell of smoke from burning wood when your next-door neighbours burn off old rubbish may cause your body to react and feel anxious without much thinking. Maybe you were involved in a fire and got burnt (either slightly or severely previously), and it generated a traumatic experience as a child or adult. The Fear centre recalls the smell of smoke and assumes the same traumatic event is happening all over again. The Fear centre can't tell it's not dangerous smoke, that it's just a burn-off or not. All it can detect is similar circumstances, and it reacts accordingly. It can't tell the difference between an old memory and the burning wood.

OK, I KNOW THE SENSORY STUFF... NOW WHAT?

Well, I am so glad you asked that exact question?

The brain (all three parts) collect all the information given to them to help work out if it's a real danger or not. As mentioned earlier, it can work with the Pre Frontal Cortex (the thinking part of the brain) to act as the ON/OFF switch to your Fear (thank God for that). That thought (or thoughts) helps determine if we fully activate our defence system or not (run, fight or freeze).

When there is a real threat of danger, or our Anxiety has been activated, there is another system enabled that prepares the body for action (I told you evolution had given us an excellent survival system). However, the problem for those of us with Anxiety is the effects of this system. The physical symptoms it produces are often misunderstood and, in turn, drive our Anxiety even higher.

Autonomic Nervous System (ANS)

Let me introduce you to the ***Nervous System***:

- Get's the message from the 'thinking brain' to either let loose and produce a lot of energy and Fear or to chill out and relax the body.
- Is made up of two parts: Parasympathetic (the handbrake – rest and digest, feel calm and relaxed) and Sympathetic (the accelerator – feel strong, energised, alert and (sorry) Anxious).
- When the Parasympathetic response is activated, then calmness and clarity prevail.
- When the Sympathetic response is activated then Fear kicks in, and the result is fight/flight/freeze.

If the S*ympathetic Nervous System* is given the green light to act, then it releases hormones that create our symptoms, and they are not always well received.

They are ***Adrenaline, Noradrenaline*** and ***Cortisol.***

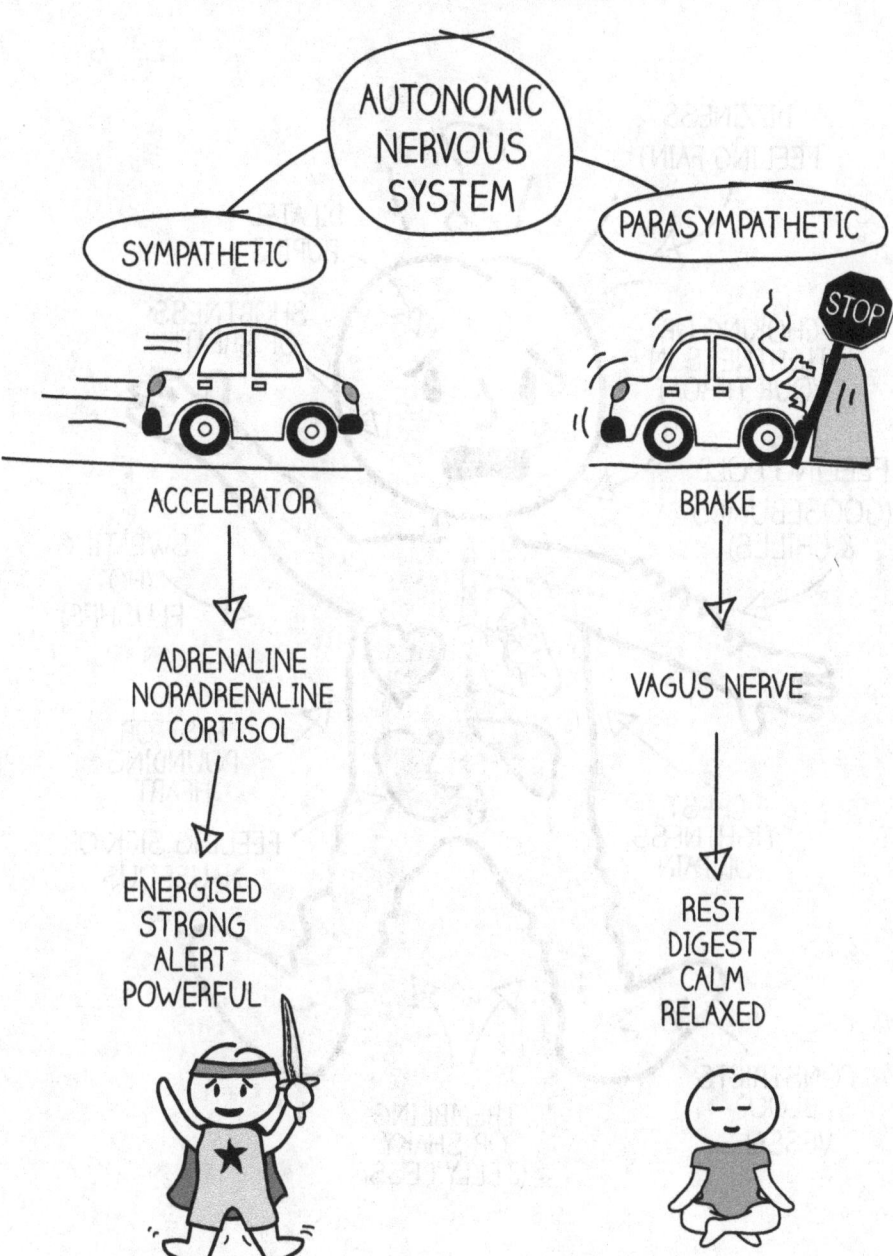

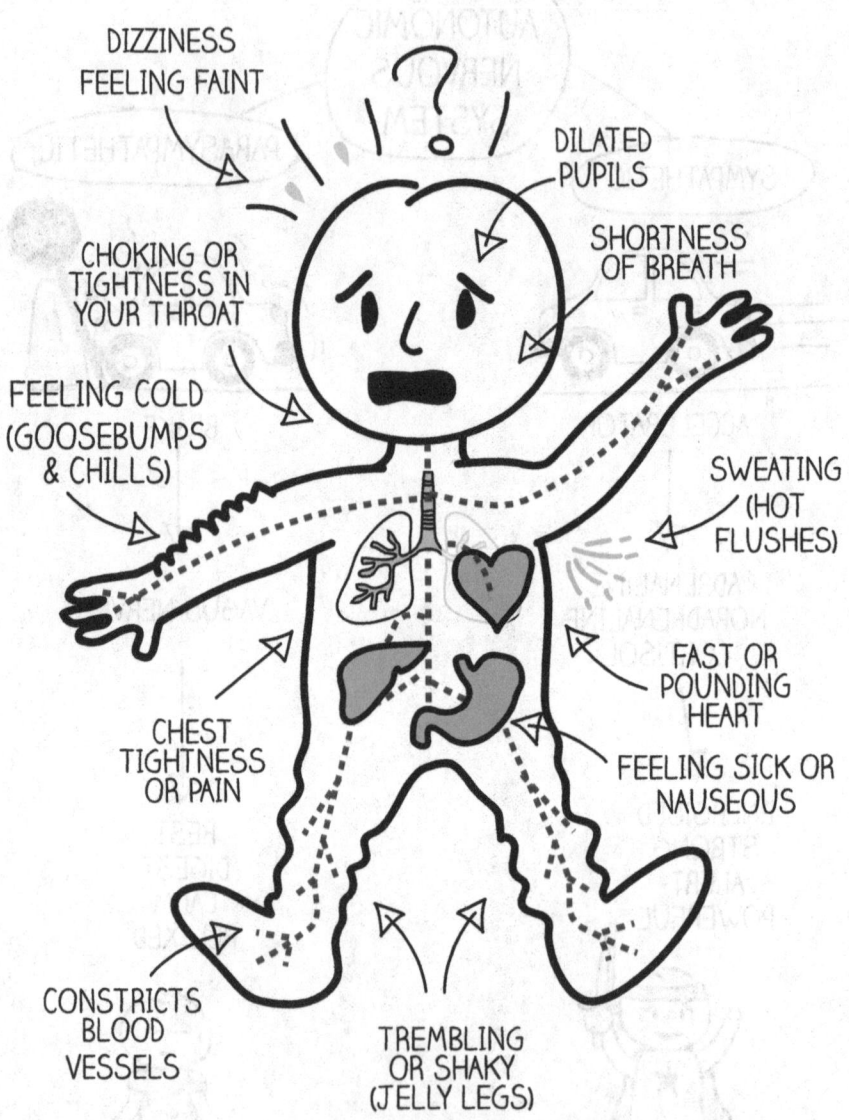

Adrenaline *(Ad-Ren-A Lyn)*

- The hormone that packs a punch.
- That response called the fight/flight/freeze is it's handy work.
- Found in the adrenal glands.
- Makes you feel energised, powerful and scared by giving you more blood, oxygen and sugar.
- Make body parts either go faster or get tighter.
- Works on RECEPTORS named ALPHA and BETA.
- ALPHA and BETA live in the heart, lungs, skin, eyes, blood vessels... *just about everywhere.*
- Actions are short lived within the body.

Noradrenaline *(Nor-Ad-Ren-A-Lyn)*

- Cousins with Adrenaline and do similar things (like a backup to help out).
- Pretty much create the same result (refer to the picture of Adrenaline's handy work below).

Cortisol *(Core-Te-Sol)*

- Live in the adrenal glands.
- Known as the master stress hormone.
- Bit slower off the blocks compared with Adrenaline and Noradrenaline but aren't far behind.
- Good at keeping your body going after they have acted.
- Will keep your body fuelled with extra sugars for energy, regulate fluid around the body keep your blood pressure down and maintain adrenaline levels.
- Not much help to your immune system as it can weaken it a little.

- Responsible for you not being able to think clearly when stressed as it affect's your brain (SORRY!).
- Can be released often, and over a long period, It can slow down the production of serotonin (which helps make you happy) which means you can become more depressed because of it.

Our understanding of these actions is pivotal to gaining freedom from Anxiety and Fear. Once you appreciate that they are simply chemicals acting on receptors that either make things go faster, slower or tighter, you can see they won't last forever. They can also be shut down by thinking helpfully about what the chemical actions are doing and how that's a good thing.

If the Parasympathetic system is given the green light, we can counteract all the actions of the Sympathetic nervous system – making us feel calmer and relaxed.

Dopamine *(Do-Pa-Mean)*

- Motivates you to seek out pleasure and also regulates how you perceive pleasure (for example, finding joy in eating certain foods like cake or lollies).
- Good at helping you work out how to survive by keeping you focussed.
- Helps you feel euphoric, happiness and bliss.
- Helps you move and learn to get away from danger and keep you motivated.
- Affect your ability to think correctly (rationally) when scared.

Oxytocin *(Ox-E-Tow-Sin)*

- Good at helping you socialise and feel love towards other people.
- Sometimes referred to as the love hormone.
- Produced in the hypothalamus in the brain and can tame the Amygdala.

- Released when a making love, giving birth and when Mum is breastfeeding.
- Helps relieve your stress and Anxiety.
- Helps people who struggle with social Anxiety the most as I promote trust, openness and a stronger, positive connection to others.

Endorphin *(En-Door-Fin)*
- Like your own personal narcotic and help block pain and help you feel good.
- Works on opioid receptors in the brain creating a little party of happiness.
- Gets released when you exercise.

Serotonin *(Ser-O-Tone-In)*
- Neurotransmitter mainly produced in the gut but also in the brain. It can affect just about all of the brains 40+ million brain cells.
- Helps you feel relaxed, calm, happy and more emotionally stable (in other words, it evens out those moods).
- Low levels of it are believed to increase the probability of feeling depressed and anxious. [12, 13]

Let's look below at the Vagus nerve and what it does and can do for us.

Vagus Nerve *(Vey-Gus)*
- The tenth cranial nerve and the longest in the body. It help's out the parasympathetic system by helping control the heart, lungs and gut responses slowing them down.
- Start's at the head and work down past the neck, chest and then to the gut region.

- Great at relaying sensory information on how the bodies organs are going and also working on motor responses as well.
- When activated, can slow down the heartbeat and reduce blood pressure, breathing rate and digestion and generally make us feel calmer.
- Stress and Anxiety can inflame it.
- Can communicate with the brain from the gut. It's called the gut-brain axis, and up to 90% of it's signals come from the gut along the nerve to the brain (that means, if the gut is unhappy, then it can upset your emotional wellbeing).

Activating the Vagus Nerve *(the calmer)*

If you want to activate the old nerve to help feel more relaxed and calmer, here are some ideas.

1) Cold shower, swimming in cold water and putting your face into cold water or even cold drinks get me going (although I appreciate that some people don't love the idea of these).

2) Gargling water and tongue depressors stimulate the muscles in the throat near the nerve. If you produce no tears, keep gargling until you do every day.

3) Singing, chanting or humming also helps stimulate muscles in the throat attached to this nerve. (Think the mantra when meditating).

4) Laughing full stop helps.

5) Deep breathing, and breathing slowly, is one of the easiest most powerful actions you can do as it activates it through the chest and gut region.

6) Meditation, Yoga and Tai Chi allow deep breathing and relaxation, thus activating the nerve.

7) Probiotics and eating healthy help keep the gut healthy, which in turn reduces inflammation of the nerve and it's signalling.

8) Tensing your gut muscles and bearing down as if you're going to have a bowel motion helps get me activated *(you can't be serious, Chris?? Yes, yes I am).*

Worth a try and effective. [85, 86]

"I LEARNED THAT COURAGE WAS NOT THE ABSENCE OF FEAR, BUT THE TRIUMPH OVER IT."

NELSON MANDELA

CHAPTER 04

THE POWER (& WEAKNESS) OF YOUR FEAR CENTRE

TAKING THE SMART ROAD

You know how the three brains have evolved and that your Fear Centre is not going to change the way it rolls (firing off like a firecracker at a New Year's Eve celebration). You see how Fear is sensed, interpreted and activated in our brain and bodies.

Now I will show you how it all comes together – how Fear tricks you, but also how you can beat it. First, we will address the physical effects, and then we will unpack how to attack our thoughts (source of Fear). This is **First Aid** for Anxiety and Fear.

Physical Fearful symptoms are produced in two different way. There is a very speedy way of creating Fear and another, slightly slower way (which is still super fast but takes a little longer to kick in). Stay with me here; it will all make sense in a moment.

The second, slower, version is the one we are going to focus on.

The first quick and messy route has us on toast because it's so fast and has no thought inclusion, all action and no thought (a bit like me in an argument according to my lovely wife!)

It's quick and messy and is what you feel when you're startled. It reacts to anything (random noises and images out of the blue are good examples). For example, when someone hides behind a door and jumps out scaring you, or your bushwalking and almost stand on a snake but jump out of the way just in time. It almost feels like you jumped before you saw the snake.

Often you react before even thinking, and sometimes you'll give a little yelp. This is a smart route as we can defend ourselves or move out of harm's way.

We have no chance of stopping this reaction and have to understand it is going to happen without any control due to its speed and nature.

The second route also utilises the same process as the first (activating a response) but adds in some thought to determine if the threat is real or not. (Imagine waking up next to me, the first response would be to jolt out of bed, but then it would be like, 'yep no danger with this spunk!' Ha!)

This second route allows a bit of thought into our scared brains and bodies and is what Anxiety sufferers feel most. The horse has bolted, and we are desperately trying to rein it back in.

THE POWER & WEAKNESS OF YOUR FEAR CENTRE

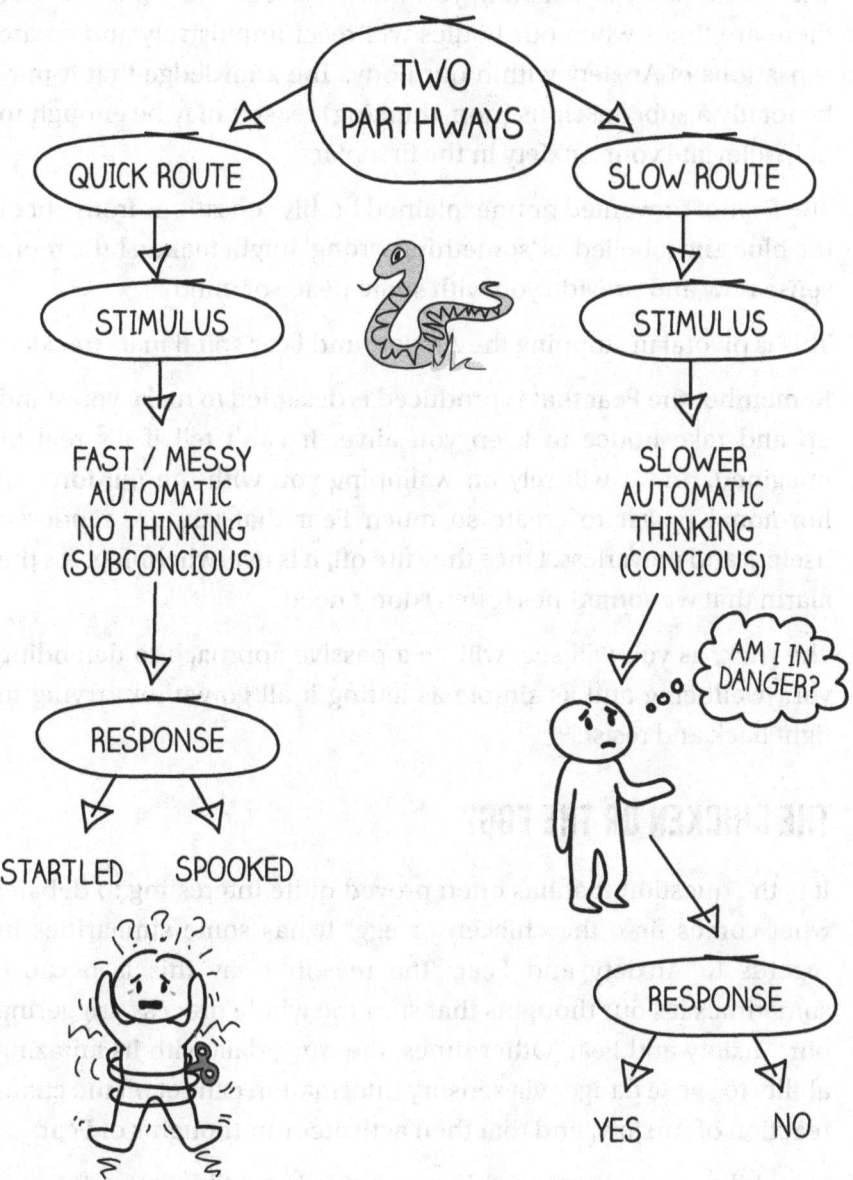

MOTTO: **Protect first, think later**   NB: **Both routes happen at the same time.**

WHATS YOUR POINT?

The whole point of teaching you this is because you will see that there are times when our bodies will react impulsively and create sensations of Anxiety within our body. The knowledge that it may be totally a subconscious (non-thinking) reason may be enough to help alleviate your Anxiety in the first place.

The Fear of unwanted or unexplained bodily sensations from out of the blue and labelled as 'something wrong' might make a little more sense now and provide you with some peace of mind.

This is pivotal in stopping the Anxiety and Fear spiral in its tracks.

Remember the Fear that is produced is designed to make you stand up and take notice to keep you alive. It can't tell if it's real or imagined, and it will rely on walloping you with the full force of hormonal power to create so much Fear that you are rendered useless and powerless. Once they fire off, it is overwhelming. It's the alarm that we sometimes (often) don't need.

The trick, as you will see, will be a passive approach to defending your wellbeing and as simple as letting it all go without trying to fight back and resist. [12,13]

THE CHICKEN OR THE EGG?

It is the question that has often proved quite interesting to debate: what comes first, the chicken or egg. It has some similarities in regards to Anxiety and Fear. The reason I say this is because sometimes it's our thoughts that start the whole process, triggering our Anxiety and Fear. Other times, the Amygdala with its amazing ability to sense danger via sensory information can set off the chain reaction of Anxiety, and that then activates our thoughts of Fear.

The ability to understand this concept is incredibly powerful as it allows you to know why you are feeling this particular way.

One great example is that you are feeling Anxious, and you weren't even thinking about anything that would scare you. This then creates more Anxiety and stress because you don't understand where the feeling came from in the first place.

However, once you understand that the Amygdala was simply doing its job in the background. It subconsciously picks up on all sensory and auditory stimuli around you and therefore setting your Anxiety into action, it allows you to see why you have become anxious initially but not dwell on it. The 'worry about where the worry came from' used to get me all the time before I was able to work this out.

Here's an example. Let's say you had a stressful/Fearful/scary episode causing you to feel Anxious and claustrophobic three months ago while you were in a supermarket getting the groceries. You felt uneasy and were happy to leave asap with your groceries.

You have been able to continue about your regular daily business since then and have little recollection of the event. The conscious brain has filed it away in the back of the brain.

However, the Amygdala still recalls the event and, one day, when you're out grabbing a few things, it sends a message to the brain setting your Anxiety off. This explains why you feel Anxious when it seems your thoughts weren't focused on anything that would cause Anxiety in the first place. It's the Amygdala marrying up the situation and recalling a level of Fear in similar surroundings, with similar smells and noises. i.e the supermarket.

If we can look at the Amygdala as our friend, a positive action that is merely trying to help and alert us, then it goes a long way in helping us understand our condition. The beauty of understanding this means that the next step would be: "OK, I appreciate you're alerting me that I have been Anxious or scared in this situation before, but I'm alright now, and there is nothing to concern me here." You can shut off your Anxiety by allowing the conscious brain to get things back on track.

SOMETHING TO TRY!

Whether your conscious or unconscious thoughts are driving your Anxiety, merely recognising that it is one, or the other, is sometimes enough to let your conscious mind take over. It doesn't matter which particular order the process takes, because we adjust the understanding of our brain function to deal with the situation at hand.

Let me explain a little more.

Say you were suddenly feeling Fearful, but there was no particular conscious thought noted. When you feel the Fear, check in with your mate Amygdala and ask if there has been an event similar, or the same, in your past. The answer will most likely be yes. Even if the situation is different, the feeling that is generated is the same. Once you have that awareness, you can apply your conscious brain and helpful thinking to turn off your Anxiety. It's like a little voice in your head acknowledging: "Yep. I remember an incident like this before. It's OK now. I am safe."

Alternatively, let's assume it was your conscious worries that were driving the Fear feeling. Acknowledge those thoughts ("yep, I see that") and apply your helpful thinking to switch the Off button.

For me, this process took time and practise. I needed to be continually doing this in my head. The reality was, I had experienced lots of incidences in different places, and situations and I needed to let my Amygdala know that I was safe frequently. It gets easier and eventually resolves if done regularly, passively and consistently.

Revisiting the supermarket example from earlier, let's look at how the Amygdala works its magic both unconsciously and consciously.

Feelings First

I walk into the supermarket to get some milk. I'm having a lovely day and not thinking about anything in particular. Maybe how much money I have in cash to pay for the milk. Suddenly, I start to notice I am feeling Anxious!

I ask myself why? I recall thinking about money, rather than the Anxiety attack I had three months ago, so I know it's not my thoughts that drove the Anxiety I am experiencing now.

Therefore, I ask Amygdala if any events would trigger this Anxiety. Guess what? There was an event. Three months ago. I'd just pushed it from my conscious mind. Amygdala picked up on a variety of sensory stimuli and coincidental events and just wanted me to be aware that Fear has been here before so I'd best be on the lookout. The little fella is merely trying to help.

Once I'm armed with this knowledge, I can respond. "It's OK. I'm fine, but thanks for alerting me." Allow your conscious brain to work through shutting off the Fear. I know it sounds trivial and almost too simple, but the power of this process is enormous, I promise. So many times, I would become wired – spiralling thoughts and Anxiety – as I couldn't understand how or why I was feeling so Anxious about something in the first place.

Understanding this basically helps reduce the spiral of Anxiety and empowers you to regain your composure.

Thoughts First

I walk into the supermarket to get some milk. I am noticing that I am thinking about that time three months ago when I had an Anxiety attack in the supermarket. I can feel that thought triggering my Anxiety. I am aware that I am Anxious, and I permit myself to acknowledge the thought and the reason. I can also remind myself that today is a different day and a different set of circumstances. I can stop the spiral by applying my conscious brain and using that strategy to regain my composure.

I am here to show you that no matter what type of Anxiety you are suffering, there are specific strategies you can apply to each one of if they escalate. I want you to use them with a sense of understanding and a feeling of empowerment.

Fear is often not knowing the result or simply just the unknown. In Anxiety and Panic, it is often the case of not knowing where it will end or how severe the attack will be that generates even more Fear.

With the strategies listed later in the book, it doesn't matter what stage of the Anxiety/Panic cycle you're at as you will have the tools to combat each one. As you move through each step, no problem, there is a different strategy to employ and with that, a feeling of confidence that you will be able to deal with it.

This helps immensely in giving you the feeling that you know the unknown and can understand the result – something that reduces the Fear.

FEAR CONDITIONING - THE ENDLESS CYCLE

As we delve into this next section, I am aiming to explain along the way how our little minds work. Our bodies and minds are amazing machines with many facets involved as to why we, as a species, are still alive and thriving.

Fear Conditioning is essentially when we get a Fear response by teaming up a non-scary object or thing with something that creates discomfort or a level of unease/stress. For example, when someone is shown a picture of a brown cow (non-scary) followed by a loud, high pitched noise (creator of unease/stress).

If this is done often enough, the person starts to create a Fearful/stressful response to the brown cow and an association with high pitched noises that create unease or stress. When your discomfort or stress is based on Fear or Anxiety, then it becomes *Fear Conditioned*.

That high pitched noise is distressing and driving the person crazy, so the last thing they want to hear is another bloody high-pitched noise or see a brown cow.

The brain joins the two things together – remembers that the brown cow and horrendous noise will create unease and discomfort. This then becomes a Fearful response and gets stored away for any future events that involve high pitched sounds or brown cows.

The other interesting thing to note is that if this noise-and-brown-cow scenario was performed in a white room with rainbows on the walls, then the brain of the person can also start to associate white rooms and rainbows with the Fearful/stressful response. That can also kick start your Fear (aren't our brains fun!)

The brain is always seeking out patterns and trying to put things in boxes. How likely an event would occur if A (brown cow) and B (loud noise) happen. It then tries to predict the outcome. If you have the same result a few times, the brains predictor centre gets on the front foot and creates a Fearful response. Additionally, if it has C (white room) and D (rainbows) as well, then the equation of A + B + C + D equals Fear, then lookout.

Let's look at a famous experiment by Russian scientist Ivan Pavlov in the late 1890s who was studying classical conditioning and noticed dogs salivated when they saw food which he labelled an unconditioned response (A). He then got a bell (neutral stimulus) with no food, and yep you guessed it, bloody nothing happened. In other words, no salivation (B). So he then started conditioning the Dog by ringing the bell next to the food and noticed salivation (C). Interesting hey and here is the clincher! He started ringing the bell without the food and Bingo; the Dog started a response by salivating. (D)[14]

Fear conditioning works in the same way, except there is an added Fearful stimulus. In regards to the dogs, maybe adding in an electric shock with food present instead of the bell would produce salivation even after the food was removed.

This helps to explain why our Anxiety seems to creep into our everyday lives and begins to affect almost everything that we touch, see, experience or even smell. It throws all the ingredients into the pot to predict if there is a potential for danger or not.

HOW A BASE JUMPER SAVED ME

It associates all Fearful responses and surroundings with the event, even though they are not dangerous and are deemed safe. This information helps explain why you are getting Anxious in places or at events when you never used to.

It's still OK, though, as we can use our strategies to stop the circuitry of Fear and association. We can retrain the brain to see that everything is safe.

That's why it's so important not to create an attachment to the *Amygdala* and *Hippocampus* (the place that stores Fearful memories) with a Fearful thought or response. There are ways to bypass or nullify that Fear Conditioning, and I will run through these in the upcoming chapters.

I know what you're thinking: hurry up and give me all the information I need... I'm desperate here! Read on; it's all coming.

CHAPTER 05

THE BODY & HOW IT WORKS

FACING THE INEVITABLE

The renowned Swiss Psychiatrist, Carl Jung, said: "What you resist, persists."

Just like you can't walk on a broken leg and expect it to heal itself, dealing with Fear and Anxiety magically requires some awareness (don't Panic, we'll tackle this slowly).

Remember all the bodily sensations that were listed in Chapter 3, along with the diagram of the Sympathetic Nervous System and his effects? Well, they are the sensations we're going to address, to begin with. What I want to provide you with, is a First Aid approach... a bit of a checklist for you to have a crack at.

Like it or not, we have to deal with the body and the sensations produced in the state of Anxiety and Fear. All those feelings you hate and would much prefer to hide from. They feel like our enemy and are scary. However, the first thing I want to say is this: "They will never hurt or kill you." I promise. They are, after all, Fear working its (sometimes unhelpful) magic. I hope to adjust your thinking about your sensations from being an enemy to a **FRIEND** with extra understanding and time.

Excellent. How do we stop that?

Great question!

The first part in helping with your Anxiety and Fear is knowledge and understanding of how Fear works: what causes it and the result it has in your body. Fair to say that we have ticked these boxes.

Soooo...how do we stop it?

Well, I'm glad you asked. There are two strategies for dealing with these unwanted or unexplained bodily sensations that i use. **P.A.C.E** and **BREATH**.

You can use one, or both, depending on the sensation and it won't cause any additional Anxiety if both are used. If we can resolve or settle the sensations, then it has a knock-on effect, allowing us to feel a lot more relaxed.

Whilst you can't stop the sensations initially, you can minimise their effects. With some practise, this will get quicker, easier and more effective.

P.A.C.E

The first strategy is called **P.A.C.E.** It works on changing your point of view towards your sensations. We are trying to be a little clever and bypass any Fearful attachment in our Amygdala.

The reason we are trying to achieve this is that in not attaching a sensation with a Fearful memory, the triggers are stopped being produced.

Remember, our thoughts can switch off the *sympathetic* response.

They can stop the feedback loop of Fear being produced in the future, and also at the moment, you are Anxious. The *Amygdala* and *Hippocampus* are always trying to marry up Fearful memories and thoughts with situations, and this is the feedback loop we want to bypass.

BETTER OUT THAN IN

In my work as a paramedic, I deal with patients in cardiac arrest. When resuscitating a person, a requirement is to defibrillate any arrhythmia's with electricity, and this is measured in Joules. What we are trying to achieve is to permanently knock out the electrical charge in the cardiac cells that are making the heart muscle fibrillate or 'quiver'. In theory, this tries to get the heart's pacemaker to take over and start beating in a regular rhythm.

There are times when we charge the defibrillator and the underlying rhythm is Asystole (no electrical activity at all) which means defibrillation is not required. With the defibrillator fully charged and ready to deliver 200 Joules, that energy needs to be discharged or dumped, which is done by pushing a button to release it. If we don't do this, us poor Paramedics may get a massive discharge of energy delivered to us.

This got me thinking about when our bodies are fully charged with adrenaline and stress hormones. What happens if we don't discharge that energy? It stays inside of us, creating a whole lot of physical stress and trauma to our body. If this is allowed to happen, time and time again, then disease and physical symptoms can develop.

So, why do we tend to hang onto this extra energy that is produced through Fear? If we were being attacked or in danger, fight or flight allows us to use this energy, and it is dissipated. Fantastic, right? We get fuelled up, and it's released as a tool to fight back or run.

However, this is not the case with Anxiety in our world's. Therefore, we need to discharge this energy from our bodies to decrease the trauma and damage that builds up over time.

This is where *P.A.C.E.* comes in. Primarily, it would help if you remembered that *Fear fuels Fear, and consent stops it*.

That means if you fight Fear sensations with Fear, it will grow and grow and grow into the ugly monster you have probably been experiencing.

However, Fear will go missing and lose its power when you *CONSENT* to it, become *PASSIVE* and *OBSERVE* it, get *ANGRY* with it or *EMBRACE* it.

P.A.C.E.

P. *PASSIVENESS AND OBSERVATION* of bodily sensations without judgement helps stop the feedback loop and turns off our Fear because there are no thoughts of Fear fuelling it.

A. *ANGER* towards your sensations reduces Fear by sending the message that enough is enough. Once again, this interrupts the feedback loop and helps reduce our Fear.

C. *CONSENT OR PERMITTING* these bodily sensations helps stop the feedback loop of Fear because the message coming through is that it's all OK. We are going to roll with it. There is no fuel to add to the Fear fire.

E. *EMBRACING* the Fear and challenging the symptoms to increase in severity. This might sound terrifying, but it's my favourite tactic and has always been the most effective for me. You might think I'm a giant weirdo, but I also tackle this step with a smile promoting feelings of happiness. Don't judge it 'til you've tried it!

P.A.C.E. is the first strategy I use to stop and reduce the effects of my physical symptoms when they are in full swing. Their power and strength are impossible to ignore.

THE BODY & HOW IT WORKS

Think of it like letting everything go through to the wicketkeeper without touching it with the bat.

Some of you out there will be very unimpressed with this. I can hear you now: "Is that your strategy, mate? You're kidding yourself. I'm not doing that. It's far too dangerous and scary to feel these sensations. They'll run rampant forever."

My response to that perfectly understandable reaction is: "Why not give it a try?"

By tackling the feelings head-on, you will be able to see that your body is working fine. The shitty sensations are not physically doing anything terrible at that moment. Working through the steps can give you confidence in overcoming those feelings, and allows you to really understand what you're thinking and how you can alter those thoughts to more helpful ones.

The more you practise, the easier it becomes, and the more power you have.

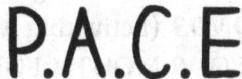

FEAR FUELS FEAR - CONSENT STOPS IT!

BREATH

The second strategy to dealing with those unwanted bodily sensations is through **BREATH** or controlled breathing. Correct breathing can calm our mind, thoughts and overactive body sensations by activating the Vagus nerve (head back to Chapter 3 if you've forgotten about this one). This can be activated via deep breathing into our belly. Doing this properly really helps calm you down.

Correct breathing also acts to restore two different levels of gases in our bodies: oxygen (O_2) and carbon dioxide (CO_2). They are super important to keep maintained because when they're out of whack, they create constriction in vessels and increased breathing (I'll go into this more when I talk about Hyperventilation shortly).

Here are some breathing techniques to use as a strategy against your Anxiety.

RULE OF 4'S is BREATHING IN THROUGH YOUR NOSE FOR *4 SECONDS*, then into your BELLY region and HOLDING YOUR BREATH FOR *4 SECONDS* (activating vagus nerve), and then BREATHING OUT OF YOUR MOUTH FOR *4 SECONDS*. This is a total of 12 seconds per cycle.

If it's tough for you to do 4 seconds, try starting with *2 SECONDS* or *3 SECONDS*, then building up to *4 SECONDS* over time. (If you are hyperventilating, you'll find strong resistance to holding your breath, but it will settle – I promise).

N.B This works excellently for severe Anxiety and Panic!

Another technique is:

BREATH HOLDING for *5-10 SECONDS* at a time, then try and breathe slowly, especially whilst breathing out. Do this until symptoms settle, and when you feel you can control your breathing rate again or just to reset your breathing rate in general, which can increase sneakily when you are stressed.

THE BODY & HOW IT WORKS

This is a little ripper as well:

PURSED LIP BREATHING is BREATHING IN THROUGH YOU NOSE FOR *4 SECONDS* into your BELLY and then BREATHING OUT FOR *5-10 SECONDS* through pursed lips. This is a little slower in effect but well tolerated until your breathing rate slows down. It's a great tool to help you relax and become calm.

Great little chiller outerer!!

Remember that several pretty scary physical symptoms can appear when we're in a state of Anxiety and Fear. Some of these can be tamed with BREATH, other with P.A.C.E. Both strategies will help in nullifying the effects of your Anxiety.

It's important to note that these strategies do take time to work. They won't resolve any unwanted sensations straight away. A general rule of thumb is that the longer you have been Hyperventilating or Anxious, the longer it will take to settle, sometimes up to five or ten minutes longer, or even more. Give it time and practise, and I promise you will see the results for yourself.

REMEMBER FEAR FUELS FEAR — CONSENT STOPS IT

Let's look at some examples of symptoms that are produced when Anxiety and Fear rear its ugly head (and what you can do when that happens).

N.B I always recommend you seek medical clearance first before trying these exercises for your safety.

Racing heart/Palpitations - As you can see in the diagram, adrenaline activates the B1 receptors in the heart, causing it to beat harder and faster. We also know that this is a normal response - it's just doing its job. Good employee, hey!

Imagine if the heart didn't beat faster when in danger? It would be hard to run or fight if blood wasn't getting to the body.

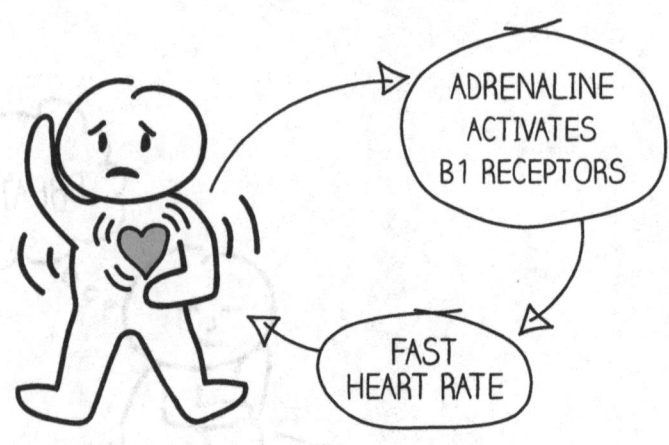
RACING HEART

THE BODY & HOW IT WORKS

USE: ANY OF THE P.A.C.E STRATEGY

Hyperventilation/Shortness of breath/Suffocation/Air hunger -

Hyperventilation (puffing like a steam train) is a fancy word used to describe an increase in breathing rate and depth. This can be caused both psychologically (in the head) or physiologically (in the body).

In our case, it is obviously in our head because we're Anxious and Scared (and freaking out!)

The symptoms associated with Hyperventilation are: shortness of breath, increased breathing rate, feeling suffocated, feeling of not getting enough air, uncontrollable breathing, dry mouth, pins and needles in fingers, toes and lips, chest tightness, general muscle tightness, hand cramps or possible tetany (muscle contraction)... *Gee, doesn't that sound like fun.*

It seems crazy to get all these symptoms from breathing too quick, right? It's super handy if we are running away from something, but it has devastating effects on how we feel if we're sitting in the lounge room or on a bus. I will try and explain how the tactic works so you can appreciate why my strategy is so effective.

Our breathing centre in the brain (medulla oblongata) requires both oxygen (O2) and carbon dioxide (CO2) to regulate our breathing rate and depth. The levels act like little signals telling us to either breathe faster or slower.

Most of us think that it's ***a lack of*** oxygen that makes us need to breathe more when hyperventilating. However, it's the level of carbon dioxide that drives the breathing centre more.

By understanding this, you can appreciate why less breathing is more helpful. In this state, you don't need more oxygen.

As Anxious humans, we have this unlucky ability to throw the old O2/CO2 system out of whack. When we are breathing normally, these two gases work great as a team, and the result is helpful, quiet breathing that meets the body's needs. When we hyperventilate, a few things happen to throw a spanner in the works.

Firstly, we breathe out too much CO2 by breathing too fast. Technically, if that's done long enough, it can stop us from breathing. Remember, it's the CO2 level that drives the breathing centre. This is what happens when people hyperventilate before trying to swim underwater for as long as possible. They pass out, as they essentially stop breathing and become unconscious and drown. Don't worry; this won't happen to you. The worst you will be feeling is faint or dizzy (and also, you're not in a pool trying to hold your breath).

The brain realises there's a mismatch in the two gases and activates the breathing centre to breathe even more ...causing complete confusion making it a whole big bloody issue, creating feelings of shortness of breath, suffocation and air hunger.

In turn, this adds to your initial problem with your breathing making you feel out of control.

What is needed to restore law and order, and start breathing normally, is more CO2 in your body and less O2. You might have heard of treating people who are hyperventilating with a paper bag around their mouth – having them breathe in and out of it?

If you breathe out CO2 into a bag and breathing in extra CO2 it will increase the CO2 levels in the body, thus settling the respiratory centre and breathing becomes back to normal range. Clever really.

To give you a little more background, O2 needs CO2 to help release O2 into the bloodstream and to the organs and tissues. If there's not enough CO2 in the body, the body runs at a low level of O2 and, in turn, the respiratory centre needs to breathe faster. Can you see the spiral and chaos created when these two gases aren't at their normal levels?

All this shortness of breath activates the Sympathetic system and triggers all those hormones that increase heart rate, sweatiness, shakiness and increased shortness of breath from the increased heart rate.

That's why it's so important to understand this science to gain power over your breathing. The good news is that it's easy to fix! Regulate your breathing by merely using one of the **BREATH** strategies listed earlier.

The other by-product of hyperventilating can be pins and needles in fingers, toes and lips; chest tightness; general muscle tightness; hand cramps or possible tetany (muscle contraction). This is because of the lack of CO_2 acts to ionise calcium in our blood vessels.

Guess what a decrease in calcium does in your body? It helps constrict blood vessels, and this causes contracted muscles. Therefore, fingers and toes have a reduced supply of blood (which is carrying the O_2). O_2 is needed for nerves to work correctly, and without it, you will get pins and needles.

So, the muscles are contracted thanks to decreased calcium, the O_2 and blood supply is limited due to constricted blood vessels, not enough O_2 is getting to the cells and producing lactic acid, and this all generates pain. Phew! [15]

HYPERVENTILATION

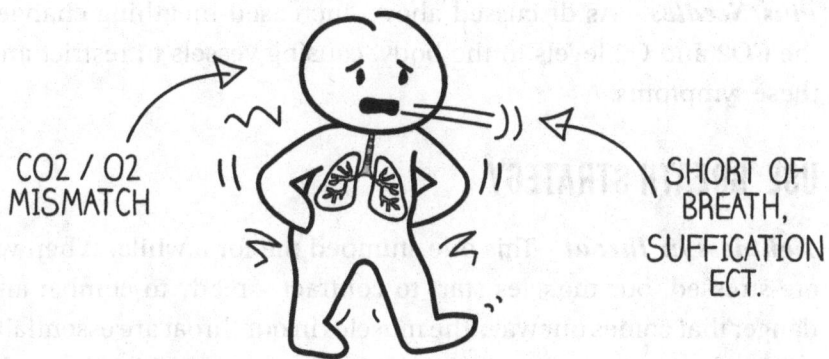

YOU GUESSED IT, USE: BREATH STRATEGY.

A WORD ABOUT EXERCISE

In case you're wondering about being breathless or breathing too much when you're exercising (mimicking Hyperventilation), it's completely safe. Any form of exercise is excellent and will not result in what the Hyperventilation mentioned above does.

The reason for this is that CO_2 is a by-product or waste from cells metabolising when energy is required. Now, because exercise or increased bodily function requires energy, extra CO_2 is produced in the body and needs to be removed, and that is done by INCREASED breathing. This is one of the reasons why we breathe faster and deeper when exercising. This will normalise the CO_2 levels in conjunction with O_2, keeping the breathing centre happy and relaxed. So, get out there and start exercising!

Dizziness – When we breathe too much, or faster than our bodies require, there is a decrease in CO_2 in the systems as discussed above. This causes blood vessels in our bodies to constrict (whether it's in your arms, legs or head). This creates constriction in our brain vessels, that restrict blood flow, that in turn make you feel dizzy. We need to regulate our CO_2 and O_2.

USE: BREATH STRATEGY TO SORT THIS OUT.

Pins/Needles – As discussed above, increased breathing changes the CO_2 and O_2 levels in the body, causing vessels to restrict and these symptoms.

USE: BREATH STRATEGY

Tightness In Throat - This one stumped me for a while. When we are stressed, our muscles start to contract – ready to combat any danger that comes our way. The muscles in our throat are essentially made of up smooth muscle that is also found in the blood vessels.

That creates the tightness feeling but don't worry: you won't choke, and it won't close over. This will also cause some action in the ENS (the gut) that can activate nerves, and that may play a role in the tightness when Anxious.

USE: P.A.C.E OR BREATH

Tightness In Chest – Again, muscles are contracted by the Fear response feeling tightness in the chest wall, making it feel constricted and also difficult to breathe freely. When Anxious, there is also a tendency to breathe shallow as well.

Please note though; chest pain can be serious. Don't ignore it, and always get it checked out by your doctor to determine that it is Anxiety-related.

USE: P.A.C.E OR BREATH

Muscle Tightness (General) – Basically, the body is primed and ready to activate all its energy with maximum blood supply and glucose at its disposal. Not actually using this energy causes tension and tightness.

USE: BOTH P.A.C.E OR BREATH

Sweating Or Sweaty Palms/Soles – The body starts to heat up when stressed and sweat is when it's trying to cool itself – it's the body's air conditioner. If you think about it, when the system is in overdrive through stress, the internal physical mechanics are not dissimilar to exercise, and we sweat then as well.

USE: P.A.C.E

Facial Flushing/Feeling Hot – The body is heating up, and the metabolism is working hard along with increased blood pressure causing flushing. The perfect way to deal with this is to try once again and increase the facial flushing with your imagination) which in turn stops it in its tracks paradoxically.

Stomach Nerves/Butterflies – Blood is primarily diverted from the gut as it's required in the extremities (your leg and arm muscles, and heart and lungs are all getting geared for action). Digestion is therefore significantly slowed down, causing a fluttering/butterfly feeling. I try and create an abundance of butterflies and pretend they have babies. It sounds counter-intuitive but making them fly around my stomach essentially stops the sensation.

Sometimes, it can be persistent, and another little trick is to pretend I'm a belly dancer – getting my stomach and muscles to suck in and out and that tricks the body into resetting.

USE: P.A.C.E

Goosebumps – The erector pili muscles on the surface of the skin are activated, causing them to stand up, giving the presentation of goosebumps and hairs on end.

USE: P.A.C.E

Inability To Think Clearly – Whilst in the grip of a Panic Attack or Fear, high levels of cortisol and adrenaline deliberately create the inability to think clearly so you have the chance to run or fight without thinking. Breathing deep, slow breaths gives you time to regain perspective and rational thinking before reacting slowly.

THE BODY & HOW IT WORKS

IRRATIONAL THOUGHTS

USE: BREATH

Irrational Thoughts/Fear/Going Crazy - Have you ever thought about why your thoughts are so ridiculous, and you Fear going crazy?

Well, apart from a bunch of hormones creating the inability to think clearly, there is also another explanation. As you are aware, your Fear centre is so much better at delivering messages than your thinking brain. It's powerful enough to push a variety of alerts or signals to your brain if it believes there is danger.

Because it has this superpower, it will start detecting all sorts of different forms of danger and alerting us if the message isn't heard clearly. As alerts are coming from everywhere, it starts to affect what you're thinking and causes you to have irrational thoughts (revisit the Fear conditioning section in Chapter 4). The brain wants to predict outcomes and associates all types of events and experiences with one another when Fear has occurred. This, in turn, creates chaotic, irrational thoughts.

Let's say you have an Anxiety Attack in a shop, on a hot day. As you start to delve into the causes of the Anxiety in the shop, other thoughts appear like. Was it the narrow aisles? Or was it the stuffiness in the shop because it was hot? Or is it just shops in general?

USE: BREATH OR P.A.C.E

Feeling Of Wanting To Run Or Get Away – Another Fear classic here. The flight part of fight/flight comes into play as we have a massive urge to run or leave the environment. It's another survival mechanism built-in, but you will find that there is no need to go anywhere. Just sit with the urge, and it will pass.

USE: BREATH OR P.A.C.E

Needing To Urinate – When our bodies are stressed, lots of things happen internally. Our body is ready for action and needs to fight or run. The urinary bladder wall relaxes, giving a feeling of wanting to pee. Also, it's a form of blood pressure regulation as our blood pressure increases during stress.

USE: P.A.C.E

Needing To Defecate – Ever heard the expression, 'nearly shit myself!' when someone is frightened? Similar to urination, our body doesn't need that king brown sitting in your bowel and could do with the lighter load! Once again, bowel control is always maintained as long as you're aware the urge is caused by the stress response. The rectum and colon are activated, creating this sensation.

USE: P.A.C.E

Dry Chompers (Mouth) – That feeling when you're dry in the mouth is caused by adrenaline decreasing salivation production and lacrimation (tears).

USE: P.A.C.E

Shaking – As our whole system is primed for either running or fighting, the adrenaline in our system is flowing through our body, creating an adverse effect of shaking/trembling. I find it useful to encourage these sensations and let them pass through.[13,15,16]

USE: P.A.C.E

I haven't covered every physical sensation related to Fear and Anxiety here. Sometimes, we get our own little special thing/sensation. I would encourage you to look back at the section on the effects adrenaline, noradrenaline and cortisol on different parts of the body and various organs. These guys are all part of the Fearful Response Team and create so many more sensations not mentioned.

N.B As mentioned previously; it's always great to get the barrage of diagnostic tests and examinations for physical symptoms first. Once you've been given a medical clearance from doctors, you can safely assume that Anxiety might be a more severe issue than perhaps you realised. Always rule out a physical cause first. It's best to be safe than sorry.

HOW A BASE JUMPER SAVED ME

"YOU ONLY HAVE CONTROL
OF 3 THINGS IN YOUR LIFE:
THE THOUGHTS YOU THINK,
THE IMAGES YOU VISUALISE,
AND THE ACTIONS YOU TAKE."

JACK CANFIELD

CHAPTER 06

JUST A THOUGHT

Anxiety and Fear need to be addressed on multiple levels. It's a multifaceted condition. We have learnt strategies to deal with the physical sensations in our body with **BREATH** and **P.A.C.E.**, so now we have to address strategies to deal with our thoughts. After all, they're the ON/OFF SWITCH to our Fear. Before we tackle the strategies that manage our thoughts, I want to talk a bit about perception.

Robert Kiyosakim, a successful businessman and author, said: "It's not what you say out of your mouth that determines your life, it's what you whisper to yourself that has the most power."

Another way of looking at this is: what we perceive becomes our reality.

PERCEPTION, PERCEPTION, PERCEPTION.

The way you view something can alter how it can affect you.

We have looked at what happens in the body and brain to understand the process of Fear and the effect the Fear has on us. We change how we see the sensations and change our Fear about them.

We have also noted that we are stuck with our Fear Centre and current operating system. It's here to stay, and nothing can change how it rolls. I hate to be the bearer of bad news, but Fear is here to stay. Accept that fact, but please remember we can also reduce it!

The good news is that we can do a couple of things to make our Anxiety a little more tolerable. One being able to turn down its intensity and ability to react (more of this later in Amygdala training) and the other is changing our perceptions (point of view) about Anxiety and its symptoms.

This can result in us beginning to live a happier, more fulfilling life without this bloody crap going on in our head. Sound good?

This chapter will cover our Thoughts, the way we think and the realisation that our current thoughts can be depressing like some cranky, old bugger.

With my Anxiety, I had the body sensations stuff covered with my medical background, and I had complete acceptance of that. My big downfall was flawed, thinking and not understanding that my thoughts were so unhelpful and destructive.

Our thoughts have the power to control how we feel and act. If we're not feeling great, often this is the reason why.

This realisation or education can be another significant step in smashing our Anxiety out of the park. It can give us freedom from relentless Fear, stress, sleeplessness and unhappiness.

So, where to start?

It almost seems too simple. Recognise our Thoughts determine how we feel, and how we act, so we just need to change our Thoughts...

THOUGHTS DETERMINE FEELINGS
Yep, it's that simple. And it's that hard.

UNHELPFUL NEGATIVE THOUGHTS - PRODUCE NEGATIVE FEELINGS

HELPFUL POSITIVE THOUGHTS - PRODUCE GOOD FEELINGS

Most of us are on autopilot with our thoughts. We don't even realise what we are thinking most of the time. The weird thing is, these thoughts determine how we act and feel. It's the basis of our personalities. Our thoughts shape who we are. (Deep, huh! Deeper than euphemism)

We smash out around 70,000 thoughts a day, so obviously, it's hard to keep on track of them all. However, if we can try to bring a bit more awareness to them, then we can begin the process of recovery. People with helpful thoughts don't tend to suffer from

HOW A BASE JUMPER SAVED ME

Anxiety. Anxiety has a hard time hanging out with helpful thoughts and generally pisses off!

Our subconscious mind plays a huge part in automatic thinking. It's incredibly powerful and is essentially programmed by our conscious thoughts (that's the thinking brain).

The subconscious stores and listens to what we tell it, so if it's always negative and Fearful, then the result is that it responds in the same negative way. The good news is we can reprogram it to start responding in a more helpful, rational way.

There are a few things that need to happen to get us back on track.

So are you ready to dig deep, put in some hard work and make real change in your life?

Remember that you have been thinking a certain way for a very long time now. You've created certain habits and patterns of behaviour, but if you put in the effort, it can make a massive difference to you, and I promise you this: *magic can happen and it will - if you practise, practise, practise.*

OK, so did you want to know what sets up our Anxiety and Fear in the first place?

Drum roll, please!!!!!

Well, it is thoughts and images of the WORST CASE SCENARIO happening in that situation/event you are currently in!

Yep, we Anxiety fuckers go straight to the top and conjure up pure bloody Fear. Worst case scenario is the **ROOT** of our Fear.

Identify this, and then we can understand how our thoughts can get out of control and create the spiral of Fear we get ourselves into.

I will use the analogy of me working as a paramedic, trying to help a patient.

We turn up, assess the patient with collecting a history verbally and physically, obtain vital signs and any other information needed. Once we have assessed the patient, we can treat him or her appropriately.

If we just rolled in and tried to guess what's wrong at a glance without any proper assessment, we would not do an excellent job at all would we?

Soooooo, for us to help our Anxiety, we need to work out what the cause of our suffering is in the first place, and that is by identifying the Worst case scenario!!

Awesome Chriso, a great start!

Now here is the clincher. These bloody Worst case scenario thoughts and images are a little sneaky and become automatic, so we often don't realise they are even said or visualised. The first thought leads to the second (both shit and scary), and we still haven't yet worked out Anxiety is firing up the mind and body in an instant.

Fuck me, just like that!!!!!!

OUR GAME PLAN AT A GLANCE

The way you view something can alter how it can affect you.

We have looked at what happens in the body and brain to understand the process of Fear and the effect the Fear has on us. We change how we see the sensations and change our Fear about them.

STEP 1) Recognise our WORST CASE SCENARIO thoughts or images when anxious (become aware).

STEP 2) Recognise the first and second thoughts as they set up our Anxiety/Fear spiral.

STEP 3) Determine what we are thinking and ask yourself if it's helpful or unhelpful.

STEP 4) Get some backup and evidence to refute or change our thinking to a more helpful/realistic way. Rebut the fuck out of it.

STEP 5) Put the new you and your thoughts into action from above (you will feel like a brand-new dude).

STEP 6) **Practise, practise, practise** (steps 1 through 5 on repeat).

It looks quite simple and, to be honest, it is. The problem is sticking with the Game Plan. Our Fear has intruded our thoughts for so long; it's hard to imagine thinking another way regularly.

A simple tool is by asking yourself ***W.H.A.T.*** when anxious. This is on the run FIRST AID for our Anxiety.

- **W.** What am I thinking when anxious? (Worst case scenario image/ thought- Root cause Fear).
- **H.** How did I come up with this thought?
- **A.** Am I using evidence to back this thought up?
- **T.** Try being more realistic or helpful in my thinking and improve it.

STEP 1) **RECOGNISE WORST CASE SCENARIO**

Now we've established that the root of all Fear is the *Worst Case Scenario* or the most dreaded. This, combined with your First Automatic Thought are massive in nailing your Fears and slamming the Fear back in its place.

Most people who suffer from Anxiety tend to think Worst Case Scenario as often as possible and, as a bonus, they exaggerate the probability and severity of the result. It's a very distinct symptom that's found quite commonly in Anxiety.

If you have an unhelpful thought, this is a quick little exercise that helps, and it can be done on the spot, in your head. ***FIRST AID STUFF!***

This is what i do in the heat of the battle.

1) Identify the *Worst Case Scenario*.

2) Identify the *Best Case Scenario*.

3) Now settle for the middle ground between the two. The option that will best help alleviate Fear and Anxiety. Be aware that your condition propels you towards the most dreaded/worst case. Be aware that it needs adjustment so as not to become fixated on it.

4) This can be helpful, but it is a quick fix and requires more work when you get the chance. It has to be investigated further to put it into perspective. The Fear comes from the thought of not being able to live or cope with the *Worst Case Scenario* and the idea our world will become a nightmare.

This may be true (if it happens), but we also need to accept that even the worst type of emotional pain and suffering eventually resides and life becomes liveable again. It may take time, but things do improve (trust me on this one. I have been there).

Most people who are not overly Anxious may tend to think *Worst Case Scenario* initially but can pull it back into a more realistic perspective and often await the outcome of what is happening before responding to the actual event or situation.

For example, a non-anxious kid may fall off his bike and hit his leg hard on the road. He may initially think, I have broken my leg. But on further assessment realises that, although painful, his leg is straight, there are no wobbly bits and the force of the hit was only moderate and not enough to break a bone. Therefore, he has reduced the *Worst Case Scenario* to a more helpful one.

If you can accept, rebut, cope and expose yourself to the *Worst Case Scenario*, then your Fear and Anxiety dramatically diminishes. This, along with other thoughts, need to be altered.

So let's tackle the *Worst Case Scenario* thought.

There are two parts to this exercise. The first is identifying and writing down YOUR Worst Case Scenario, and the second is writing down YOUR *Coping Strategy or Game Plan and then Visualise you coping with it being a reality.*

FIRST PART - IDENTIFY WORST CASE SCENARIO

So, let's start by working out what our **Worst Case Scenario** is and writing it down.

To put it into perspective, we now need to ask ourselves how probable the *Worst Case Scenario* is?

Some questions you can ask yourself are:

1) What is the *Worst Case Scenario*? What image comes into my head?

2) What is the probability, or percentage, of the *Worst-Case Scenario* happening?

3. Can I accept the fact of it happening?

4) How would I cope with the *Worst Case Scenario* happening?

5) How can I make the *Worst Case Scenario* more realistic?

I won't lie; this can be challenging, so be gentle on yourself as strong emotions may be induced. However, always remind yourself that it is imagined. If you feel it's too challenging, leave it for a bit and try to revisit it at another time when you have, more strength and energy.

SECOND PART - COPING GAME PLAN

> ***Warning:*** This is a super powerful tool I use, and it can create feelings of high stress and Anxiety. I want you to remember that it is imaginary and not real. You are stronger than you think, and you are a warrior. This is also optional as an exercise but truly has terrific benefits if you persist. GOOD LUCK!

This is a visualisation exercise imagining the Worst case scenario you have written down earlier.

When answering these questions, put as much detail in as possible. Things like how you felt both physically and mentally; how you look and reacted to the event; how your family and friends are feeling; and how you are coping with the actual event happening. You are trying to make it as real as possible with smells, sounds and tastes included as well. The more information, the better.

Now, if you have done it correctly and have written down your own relevant Worst Case Scenario, the next step is trying to imagine living with the reality of it happening. How you are feeling and life after the event. Spend 20-30 minutes daily visualising.

I know this sounds scary and hard, but over time, you will notice your Anxiety with both feelings and images starting to reduce towards the Worst Case Scenario and how you feel about it (and that's exactly what we are after). We are aiming to reduce it by half, or even more.

1) Write down how you would cope with this happening. Things like how you would live your life at work, school or socially? How can you get some quality of life and be somewhat optimistic? How can you reduce its effects? And what have others done to cope? Try and write done as much as you can that will help you cope if the Worst Case Scenario happened.

2) Now this time, try and visualise yourself living in a world successfully coping with the Worst Case Scenario being part of your life. Do this until you can start to feel and imagine yourself being more comfortable and tolerable of the event. You are living your life with reduced Anxiety and stress, like previously, imagine your interactions with friends, family and own life feeling improved with the beautiful smells, tastes and sounds being present also.[8]

BUT WAIT, THERE'S MORE

1) Make sure you keep visualisation going once you feel anxious and don't stop then.

2) Keep the imagination work going until there is a reduction in your Anxiety.

3) Make sure the Worst Case Scenario is real and significant for best results.

4) Make sure the Coping Game Plan is realistic and something you can imagine for real.

Wow, that's pretty full-on and remember that the option is there to start with the first task before taking on the second visualising the COPING PLAN.

Below is something that I use to help reduce my worst-case scenario in a statistical sense called Micro Mort of Risk.

MICRO MORT OF RISK

When we are dealing with Anxiety and Fear, sometimes trying to calm ourselves and thoughts are difficult to do.

As you have seen, some of the questions for you to ask are regarding probability and percentages of things happening.

These form statistics and facts to help bring our Anxiety back to a more realistic perspective.

For example, what is the probability of me dying watching T.V.? I would say very small, if any, so we are OK with that risk. It is a simple example as we all know the answer. Bugger all!!!

When things get a little more complicated, or the task has more risk, than our Fear can go up.

Thankfully, especially if you're a numbers person, there is a tool you can use to provide EVIDENCE of risk and probability of death in any task. This can be measured in the form of a Micromort.

What the bloody hell is a Micromort?

In the 1970s, researchers at Stanford University developed the concept of the "micromort" to measure the likelihood of sudden death, yep what's the chance of dying!!! (Heavy shit)

The micromort is used by statisticians to calculate the probability of a one-in-a-million chance of experiencing sudden death.

There is a calculator you can google called "micromort calculator" funnily enough, and once you put in the details of any events, it can spit out a result for you.

Things like travelling on a plane, having an operation or skydiving are quick and easy to calculate. For example, jumping out a plane skydiving gives you 10 Micromorts. That is every 10 out of every 1 million jumpers will die from the event.

For me, that is a pretty good result as I like to think that 999,990 jumpers will survive. You beauty!!!!

I have always been able to see the optimistic angle and tools like this help.

The tool also looks at risks associated with everyday life, either acute or chronic and even relative to the actual situation. Results also vary from country to country, which would make sense.

For example, the Micromort for dying from a gunshot in America is 2.5 compared to Australia, which is 1.1; obviously, the difference between guns laws and the number of guns in the community proves significant.

There are millions of examples you can try and use to help aid with your Anxiety.

It also begs the question regarding using numbers or "gains and losses" to evaluate the situation.

Most people who suffer from Anxiety always swing towards the losses or dangerous aspect of the event, and their focus creates a spiral of Fear that is often more than warranted.

They also use the negative/losses mindset to stop them pushing forward with their Fear and reducing their opportunity to face Fear or anything that creates Anxiety.

If we can try and look at the optimistic/positive numbers as discussed earlier and focus on them, then it may go a long way forward to your recovery.

After all, I would instead focus on the 999,990 jumpers that survived than the 10 that didn't (poor bastards).[17]

WHEN THE STAKES ARE HIGH

It makes perfect sense that our Fear and Anxiety is at its highest when the stakes are highest. The possibility of failure or not succeeding can have a detrimental effect on us and create further production of our old mate Fear. It seems that the Worst Case Scenario and High Stakes go hand in hand, and it's all about perspective.

Right, let's pretend that you are practising shooting hoops in basketball and if you get a three-pointer then you receive $500,000.

When practising, the level of Fear and Anxiety would be somewhat low as the stakes are mostly small, and it doesn't matter if you miss.

However, if it comes time to shoot for the $500k and you only have one shot, then the stakes are high, and you have a massive influx of pressure.

What I am trying to explain is that most stakes we come across in our lives are not as significant as we often make them. There is not a lot of $500k three-point shoot-out competitions around in day-to-day life.

If it was a case of physical safety or significant danger, then, by all means, embrace the Fear and work with it to get you out of trouble. This is precisely the point of having a protective survival system in the first place.

What is needed, however, is a proper analysis of what the stakes are in our daily lives. Situations in sport, work or other performances may have particular significance to us or others but is it that extreme or high in the first place?

Kicking a goal after the siren in the Grand Final does have a certain level of High Stake about it. But what if you miss? In the grand scheme of things in life, it will wash away into the abyss and just be a goal that's missed. Although disappointing, it's still just a game.

Something for you to think about – gain perspective on what's important and that gains power over your Fear.

This is another angle of the Worst-Case Scenario and perception.

1) Ask yourself what the significance of this stake is?
2) What will happen if I don't achieve it?
3) What is the probability of succeeding?
4) How does it sit in the scheme of my life in one, two and five years from now?

STEP 2) RECOGNISING 1ST AND 2ND THOUGHTS (AUTOMATIC)

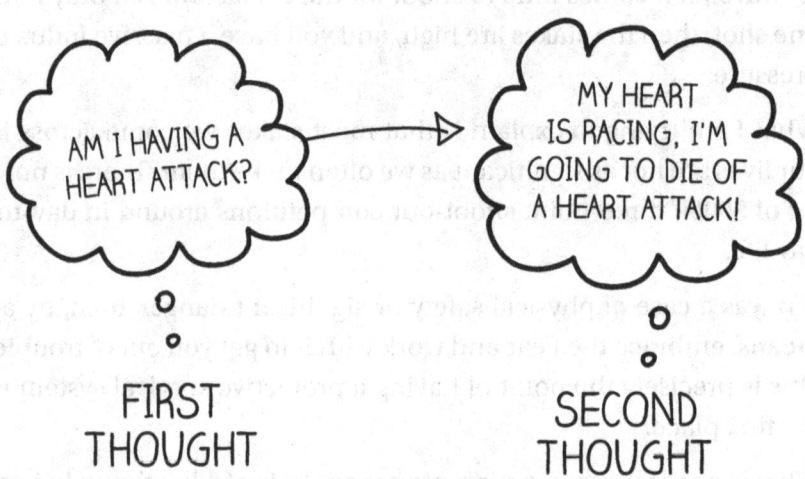

HELPING IDENTIFY YOUR AUTOMATIC THOUGHTS

Getting curious about what's going on in your brain is a great way to remove yourself from the shitty-thought-spiral. Asking questions allows you to look at what's going on in your brain with an outsider's perspective.

Here are some questions you can try:

1) What is the first thing that comes into your head when you start wigging out?

2) What are you scared of right now?

3) What is the worst possible thing that could happen to you?

4) What's freaking you out about how you feel right now?

Another handy thing to identify is your TRIGGERS. What sets off your Anxiety?

1) When you're feeling anxious, ask yourself what you're thinking.

2) Write down your thoughts as soon as possible – note the situation and your feelings. This will help you see patterns.

3) Try to remove yourself from the situation and observe what's going on (in your body and your mind).

4) Remind yourself that it's often the very first thought that sets off the Anxiety spiral.

Other stuff to think about:

1) Be aware that it's your unhelpful thoughts that create Anxiety in the first place.

2) Be more mindful of your thinking.

3) Live in the moment (stop and think about where you are right now, as opposed to what's coming up or what happened earlier).

4) Check-in on how you're feeling. Often, that will give you a direct answer to how you're thinking (for example, feeling anxious can mean you're having anxious thoughts, feeling happy might indicate having happy thoughts).

5) Meditation (merely observing what you're thinking without judgement and reaction ...you will be amazed how negative everything often is! We will address meditation later to help you out more here).

6) Write down your thoughts (it's very powerful and clarifies your thinking. Use the notes section on your phone to catch thoughts or carry a notebook with you).

7) Practise, practise, practise.

Don't freak out if this feels hard and slow, to begin with. You need to appreciate that change won't happen straight away. It takes practise and discipline. This concept of automatic thoughts and the first thought is the main hurdle to overcome because if you can't change this, nothing will change. Of course, if you miss the first thought, it's OK. Just aim for catching the second thought. *Simple!* [8]

THE POWER OF WRITING OUR THOUGHTS DOWN

Who would have thought that writing things down would be so powerful, or so useful? I'm not talking about typing on your computer or phone; I'm referring to writing things down on a piece of paper with a pen or pencil (old school).

The power of writing works in a couple of different ways with its effectiveness.

Firstly, it allows us to fully express our thoughts – that are often jumbled or confusing in our minds – giving us a clearer picture of what is being processed by our little brains in the first place.

There have been so many times when I thought I was fully aware of how I was thinking and processing things, only to be surprised that when I wrote it down the picture became so much clearer and more apparent.

It's like a mini decipherer of thoughts that provides clarity.

It's also a great tool to use when you're confused about a problem or situation, and you need to weigh up the pros and cons. Often, the answer just jumps out at you from the paper.

JUST A THOUGHT

The power of writing is super useful because it takes actual time to write things down physically. This slows down our busy brain and allows us time to absorb what's being written entirely. Handwriting provides our conscious and subconscious minds the time to process and understand what is happening with our thoughts.

This is an excellent tool for identifying unhelpful thoughts and retraining the subconscious mind to start responding more helpfully.

This skill is another cornerstone to overcoming our Anxiety and Fear because it actually pinpoints our thoughts, gives us time to process them and then allows us to document changes to our thinking that is needed to recover. [17]

So remember this:
if you don't write, it won't be alright!

STEP 3) DECIPHERING THOUGHTS & TRIGGERS

Now we are recognising our thought; the next challenge is to determine what's reasonable (or not) in our thinking. Our thoughts are potentially unhelpful and creating a world of Fear. Triggers are (weirdly) our friends because if we can work them out, we can come up with a solution AND understand where our Fear is coming from. You may be surprised to know a lot of us don't even know what it is we are scared of. This step gives us a chance to work it out.

A fair chance we have had a look at what we have been saying to ourselves and realised it was not great and possibly even a little (very) dodgy.

This is when we try to refute the hell out of our previous thinking with some new evidence gathering and problematic thinking. Mostly, this is trying to come up with different perspectives and a more realistic approach to our Fears.

At this point, I feel your frustration. *Are you kidding me, Chris? I've read this far, and now you're trying to convince me that Anxiety is bullshit and an illusion?*

Yes...and no. I think by now, we can all agree that Anxiety and Fear is very, very real. What it does to our body is very real. However, perception is just that – what we believe to be the truth. And yes, we can trick our minds...which in turn can trick our bodies. Stay with me here.

A quick, simple exercise you can do when a negative or Fearful thought or feeling presents itself is this:

1) What do I avoid doing because of my Anxiety?
2) Identify the thought, feeling or situation that makes you anxious.
3) Write it down with symptoms and outcomes (you can grade the intensity of the result from 1-10 if you like).
4) Identify the concerns, dangers and Fears you are thinking.
5) Ask yourself what a more helpful way of looking at this situation (I recommend coming up with at least three other ways to think differently about where you are at – x 3 rule) is.
6) Adopt another perspective.

I'll give you an example. Recently, I walked past a man whilst I was out with my sons. I thought it would be an excellent idea to say hello and show the boys; it's nice to be friendly to strangers. Unfortunately, the man stared and kept walking without saying anything back. Was I annoyed and a little angry at his rudeness when I was trying to teach my kids a beautiful lesson? Absolutely!

Then I adopted my approach of changing my perception x 3 and got the boys to help.

We came up with this:

1) He may have been deaf and didn't hear me.
2) He may be very shy.

3) He might not be able to talk.

4) He may be an asshole (but why waste energy on that, you can't change an asshole).

This helped alleviate the negativity and resolved, or at least reduced the emotion. You can try this with Fear as well.

You may need help from others in your life, like family and friends. They can be a great resource to help you out if stuck.

Let's look at another example of adopting a different perspective.

I wanted to go to a work function and celebrate my best workmate's going away drinks. My mate has been an excellent colleague. He's always had my back and was super fun to be around. I felt like I owed him the respect of saying goodbye at his farewell. The only problem is that my Social Anxiety is sky high with the work crowd, and I feel like I make a fool of myself in front of the Boss (especially after a few drinks).

Here are some different perspectives:

1) The working crowd might be delighted to see me there and include me in the fun as I don't go to many nights out.

2) There may be other colleagues that are quiet and happy to chat without making a lot of fuss. I can spend time with them.

3) My best mate will be with me and will make sure I am feeling comfortable.

4) Where is the proof that my thoughts are real and my concerns will happen at all?

Have you noticed that we are steering away from the heavy/negative thoughts of being judged or embarrassing ourselves at the function? It can be the simple practise of teaching and looking at other points of view that can propel us forward in our recovery.

You have to start somewhere and keep practising until it shifts.

STEP 4) LOOKING AT THINGS DIFFERENTLY

We have got to the point where it's time to take our new skills and give them a red hot go!

We have worked out:

- First and Second automatic thoughts and how they set up our Anxiety Spiral
- Analysed them to realise they are unfounded/negative and unhelpful
- Found that Worst Case Scenario is the root of our Fear and is a common symptom and thought patter of Anxiety Sufferers... therefore, we can pull it back
- Accept that if the Worst Case Scenario happened, we could cope (we did our visualisation, and we saw it was possible).

Now I've got to this stage; I need to start thinking in my new way about my Anxiety and the way I approach it. My new found perceptions are here to stay and become fully implemented.

Here are a few more questions to ask yourself:

1) How did I use to think about this Anxiety provoking situation before becoming Anxious towards it?
2) What is the most realistic outcome in this situation that makes me Anxious?
3) Is the most likely situation that intolerable?
4) What can I do to cope if it's the case?
5) Am I adopting my new way of thinking about my Anxiety?
6) What would someone who is not Anxious in this situation think?

JUST A THOUGHT

Now it's time to adopt a healthy, proper way of thinking when we are in the heat of battle and exposed to a stressful situation and we also need to remember to work on our thoughts and behaviours pre-exposure.

STEP 5) PRACTISE, PRACTISE, PRACTISE

Do it all over again. And again.

Man, that's a lot of information to try and workout!

Any chance of coming up with something to put it all together?

Yep, Bro got a little worksheet here as a one-stop-shop for any Anxious/Fearful situation.

You Legend!!!!

WORKSHEET FOR OUR ANXIETY / FEAR
(THE ONE STOP SHOP)

ANXIETY LEVEL	PHYSICAL SYMPTOMS	BEHAVIOURAL SYMPTOMS	EMOTIONAL SYMPTOMS
RATING (1-10)	(EG: SHORT OF BREATH / INCREASED HEARTRATE)	(EG: RUN / AVOID)	(EG: ANGRY / SCARED)

EVENT: _____

1. WHAT DO YOU THINK WHEN YOUR ANXIOUS IN THIS SITUATION?

_____

_____

2. ASK YOURSELF WHAT IS THE WORST CASE SCENARIO THOUGHT OR IMAGE IN YOUR HEAD?
(remember it is the core root of your Fear and also sets up our spiral of thoughts which are often automatic) - you can't fix what you don't know!!)

_____

_____

3. WHAT HAVE YOU BEEN AVOIDING OR NOT WANTING TO FACE?
(places, people, situations etc – Great working out triggers)

_____

_____

JUST A THOUGHT

Now we have to question our WORST CASE SCENARIO and argue/rebut the hell out of it!

REBUT BIT:
LIST 3 REASONS WHY IT COULD BE BULLSHIT/ILLUSION:
(SOME THINGS TO ASK YOURSELF):

1. WHERE IS THE PROOF/EVIDENCE OF THIS BECOMING REAL?

_____

_____

2. WHAT IS THE PERCENTAGE / PROBABILITY OF IT HAPPENING?

_____

_____

3. WHAT IS LIKELY TO HAPPEN?

_____

_____

4. WHAT ARE THE ACTUAL FACTS?

_____

_____

5. WHAT IS A MORE REALISTIC/HELPFUL WAY OF LOOKING AT IT?
(This is great for things like performance in sport, job, social, public events etc., Stuff you begin to realise is more Anxiety than fact)

_____

_____

OK, sometimes you have done all the work above and can't shift or change your way of thinking. I.e. generally stuck in thoughts, serious illness, death, serious accident and it's just pure fact that "WORST CASE SCENARIO" is apparent. Fear is a FACT!

TRY AND LIST HOW YOU WOULD COPE IF WORST CASE SCENARIO HAPPENS.

LIST AS MANY COPING STRATEGIES YOU CAN THINK OF?
Ask others if stuck what they would do? (E.G. visualisation tool, time, space, acceptance etc.)

_____

_____

_____

_____

_____

_____

_____

N.B. you can always utilise a therapist if you are unable to move forward.

JUST A THOUGHT

"DON'T WAIT TILL YOU REACH YOUR GOAL TO BE PROUD OF YOURSELF. BE PROUD OF EVERY STEP YOU TAKE." *(ESPECIALLY WITH YOUR ANXIETY).*

KAREN SALMANSOHN

CHAPTER 07

WHAT'S HAPPENING IN YOUR HEAD

We've looked at how managing our breathing is fantastic, and how observing and finally embracing the physical sensations that come with Anxiety can significantly calm our bodies. I've also asked you to recognise and question your thoughts, and to sit with your most terrifying thoughts on purpose (sorry about that one, but I promise you it's helpful).

Now I have extra strategies for you when it comes to our mind and thoughts.

These First Aid mnemonics are designed to nip anxious thoughts in the bud and deal with your sensations as well. They are the only tools that I have used and explored, and they aim to help you guide through an anxious moment or event.

You can come up with your own if you like as well.

They are:

L.E.T.G.O.E, the **5 D's, F.E.E.L G.O.O.D** or **W.H.A.T**.

By combining these strategies with **P.A.C.E** or **BREATH**, we can take one step closer to stopping these bastard sensations from ruining our lives and happiness.

Given that the goings-on in our mind AND body generate the Anxiety in the first place, it makes perfect sense to stop the Anxiety in the same way.

At any point during our Fearful experience, we can adopt these strategies time and time again until we gain empowerment.

WHAT'S HAPPENING IN YOUR HEAD

Here is how it looks like on a flow chart:

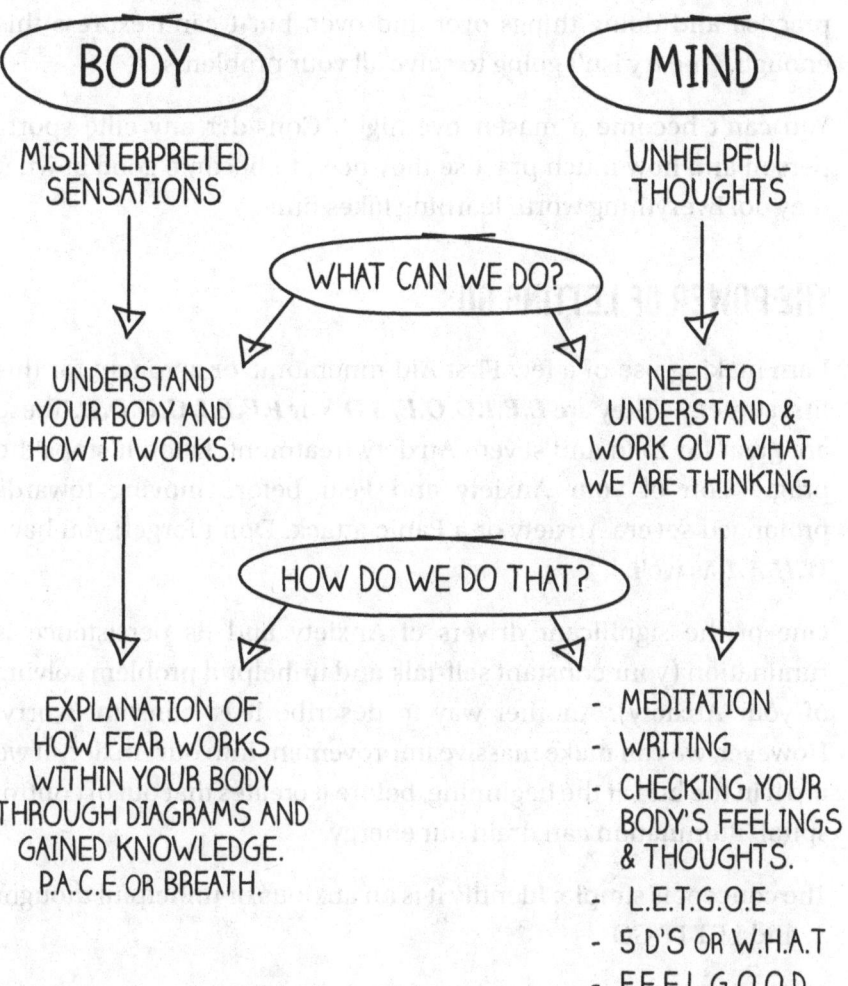

Understand that both thoughts and sensations are allowed to happen without resistance – fighting both will only empower Fear.

FIRST AID FOR OUR THOUGHTS

Before we start delving deeper into our minds, I want you to remember something fundamental. I know I keep banging on about practise and doing things over and over, but I can't express this enough. One try isn't going to solve all your problems.

You can't become a master overnight. Consider any elite sports person and how much practise they need to become good at what they do. Everything worth learning takes time.

THE POWER OF LETTING GO

I am making use of a few First Aid mnemonic or acronym for this first strategy - They are **L.E.T.G.O.E, 5 D'S** or **F.E.E.L G.O.O.D.** These are great for mild and severe Anxiety treatment. Often it stops the progression of your Anxiety and Fear before moving towards prolonged severe Anxiety or a Panic attack. Don't forget; you have **W.H.A.T** as well.

One of the significant drivers of Anxiety and its persistence is rumination (your constant self-talk and unhelpful problem solving of your Anxiety). Another way to describe it is 'constant worry'. However, we can make massive improvement into our Anxiety if we nip it in the bud at the beginning, before it creates that out of control spiral. Rumination can drain our energy.

The concept is simple: Identify it is an anxious or unhelpful thought ... and LET IT GO.

This is as hard as you think it might be at the start because you first need to be aware of your automatic thoughts and then also be able to acknowledge and LET GO.

The reason it is so powerful is that, by getting good at this, the Anxious thought will lose all its power and energy; reducing its impact on our Anxiety. The Fear Centre and memory in our brain; stopping it from attaching to an event or situation eventually becoming a distant memory.

To allow yourself the ability of being comfortable letting go of your thoughts, some background work has to be done first.

If you can identify thought and not buy into it without using this tool, then fantastic keep doing that. These tools are only a guide.

A lot of the same questions are covered in the last chapter, and as mentioned, these are other first aid tools you can use. I love em all.

Begin by writing down your specific Anxiety, and refuting it as much as possible until it is a helpful or more realistic thought.

Right. How do we do this?

1) Get a piece of paper
2) Write down your specific Anxiety
3) Ask any questions you need to try and improve the thought to be realistic and helpful.

Here are some examples:

- What is the percentage of probability of this occurring?
- What is the Worst Case Scenario? (I know you can do this one!)
- Even if the Worst Case Scenario happened, could I cope?
- What is a more realistic thought?
- What would someone who is not Anxious think about this?
- Is this just an Anxious thought?

This strategy can also be done with anger, other negative thoughts, things you can't control, and anything you're worried about in the future.

LETGOE

L. Listen

Your first/automatic thought sets up your Anxiety, the second thought starts creating the spiral. Pay attention to what that thought is.

E. Embrace

Accept the thought and roll with it. It has happened, you can't change it and your reaction to it the vital part. The action required here is NOTHING (easy, yes?).

T. Think

Is this an anxious thought? Is this an unhelpful thought? Is this a negative thought? Is this in the future? CAN I CONTROL IT?

G. Get Slow

Slow, deep breaths that is. This helps activate our Vagus Nerve, which in turn calms the body and allows for rational thinking before jumping to the worst-case scenario. Slow, deep breaths will also reduce overreaction to stimulus.

O. Observe

Imagine you are curiously watching – pay attention to your body's reaction, your feelings and symptoms. Don't judge, observe as they lose strength and power. Refer back to Chapter 4 and 5 and how the body responds to stress (this will help).

E. Envision

Imagine that deep in your mind; you are not Anxious. You are confidently coping and working through your Anxiety. As weird as it sounds, try to smile while you are doing this – it helps reprogram the wiring in your brain.

This is so powerful as it reminds the sub-conscious that everything is safe and OK.

WHAT'S HAPPENING IN YOUR HEAD

Let's look at an example when L.E.T.G.O.E. might come in handy:

You have an Anxious thought about a party you are invited to and socialising is tough for you at the best of times.

- Listen – "Shit, I have that party next weekend." (Anxious thought thank your Social Anxiety).
- Embrace – "OK, I'm not going to engage that thought and just accept it."
- Think – "Yep, it's an Anxious thought for sure."
- Get – Take some slow deep breaths to calm your mind and body.
- Observe – "This has triggered Anxious sensations in my body, and I'm going to just observe them without judgment."
- Envision – Visualise being at the party without being Anxious. You're coping well and enjoying yourself.

Because you have an understanding of your Anxiety and you have done your homework on this prior, there is no need to get caught in a spiral of Anxious through worrying and dwelling on the party. Let the thought go and continue with your day. You have realised that Anxiety gets fuelled by Anxiety but stops when accepted.

If letting the thought go is impossible, start by postponing it: "the party is in the future, I don't need to concern myself with that today. I will cross that bridge when I come to it. "

We want to get to a point where your conscious mind recognises, "ah, that's just my Anxiety. I can let that go."

THE 5 D'S

The 5 D's are similar in many ways to L.E.T.G.O.E, and this straightforward process might be more suited to you:

1) **Deep breathing** – take slow breaths and calm the mind. Allow yourself time before you react to your physical sensations and irrational thoughts.

2) **Determine** – consider what you are thinking and if it's helpful or not.

3) **Dispute** – replace unhelpful/negative thoughts with new helpful ones.

4) **Detect** – observe all symptoms without reaction or embrace them fully and encourage their severity (which, paradoxically, stops them).

5) **Dream** – visualise you being non-Anxious in the situation or event and *smile*.

Now you've got the rundown of both physical and mental strategies, here's one more First Aid mnemonic for you to take on board... something that combines all the strategy and reminds you of the space you want to be in (body and mind!).

FEEL GOOD

F. **Feel** sensations, understand symptoms and remember they don't harm you (the sensations are produced by a variety of chemicals in your body and are only activated to help, you don't need to Fear them).

E. **Expect** Amygdala – understand it's doing its job trying to alert you to Fear (it's the canary in the mine, shooting off messages and chemicals to the body and the cognitive brain most often subconsciously. It's always on alert using our senses ready to pounce being a protector rather than the enemy).

- **E. Establish** proper breathing by learning to breathe into your diaphragm (this gives you time to regroup, adapting your cognitive brain and also calming the chemicals released from the Amygdala shooting off before we have a chance to think about it).

- **L. Live** in the present – ask yourself if it needs to be dealt with now, today or at a later date. Also, do you need to control it? (Remember control of any situation is almost impossible, so why try and increase your stress about it).

- **G. Get** informed on your thoughts. Ask yourself questions (what are your unhelpful/Anxious thoughts? Are they Worst Case Scenario? Do I need to have control/certainty? Do I require approval? Do I have to be perfect or perform highly? Do I have to get it right? Do I feel Anxious about feeling Anxious? Why?).

- **O. Orchestrate** helpful thoughts (it's incredible how negative or incorrect our thoughts when on autopilot! Ask more questions: Does it matter if it's the Worst Case Scenario? Is it that bad? Do you have evidence that your thoughts are real? What's the probability of it happening? What would someone who is not anxious in this situation think? What is a more helpful way of thinking?).

- **O. Open** your mind to visualisation and project a positive vision about the outcome. (Flip the negative image in your mind to a positive result).

- **D. Delayed** sensations can be expected as the chemistry takes time to resolve from the body (you might have gone through all these steps and are still feeling Anxious. Give it a moment, your body takes time to readjust and the chemistry needs to settle. You are OK).

All these tricky little acronyms are here to make them easy to remember – especially at a time when your brain is a bit fried. All we are trying to do is cut the power and fuel from those unhelpful thoughts by using a few necessary tools and a strategic process to get your head clear. *You can make up your own if you like.*

A WORD ON WORRY

Worry is a tactic used by Anxiety and Fear and is a common trait with Anxious people. Anticipating adverse outcomes on future events and trying (unsuccessfully) to resolve this potentially terrible upcoming situation with countless, unproductive solutions.

The endless negative chatter in your head doesn't stop because your Fear is endlessly trying to work out a solution that is never productive.

The next time you find yourself worrying, think about this quote from the Dalai Lama, which works a treat for me:

"If the situation or problem is such that it can be remedied, then there is no need to worry about it. In other words, if there is a solution or a way out of the difficulty, then one needn't be overwhelmed by it. The appropriate action is to seek its solution. It is more sensible to spend energy, focusing on the solution rather than worrying about the problem. Alternatively, if there is no way out, no solution, no possibility of resolution, then there is also no point in being worried about it, because you can't do anything about it."

In other words, if it can be fixed, then spend your time and energy on the solution and resolve the problem without stress. This will prove productive. If you can't fix it or find a solution, then accept it for what it is and let it go. [8]

ARE YOU READY?

It's nearly time to throw yourself into your Anxiety. Get back on the horse.

Bloody hell, Chris, is it that time already? We're not even halfway through the book. I'm not sure that I am ready to tackle this mountain that I've Feared and stressed about for so long.

You know what? You are now armed with lots of new knowledge, and you have more understanding of your Anxiety than ever before.

WHAT ARE WE GOING TO DO?

First, come up with a plan, I reckon.

Write down a few things like:

You have an Anxious thought about a party you are invited to and socialising is tough for you at the best of times.

- What is my trigger or current Fear/Anxiety?
- When does it happen?
- What did I think about it in the past?
- What do I think about it now with my new way of thinking?
- What do I do with my physical sensations?
- Have I practised getting used to them?

OK, awesome! We have some new knowledge and understanding. It's time to give it a test drive. It is super important to start slow and work our way up in Anxious situations – don't go too hard, too soon.

We want to rev up the Anxiety to around moderate levels, allowing it to decrease over time in the situation, as this helps us learn we can empower ourselves and what we think when Fearful.

It's so essential to practise heaps and to expect perfectly regular stuff-ups.

There will need to be an increase in the exposure time. We are aiming for the Anxiety to start settling naturally over time.

You've got this!

> **"CHANGE THE BELIEF
> AND THINKING CHANGES.
> CHANGE THE THINKING
> AND THE ACTION CHANGES.
> CHANGE THE ACTION,
> AND THE RESULT CHANGES."**
>
> UNKNOWN AUTHOR

CHAPTER 08

PROMOTING PANIC

I've got loads more insights, tips and tricks to share with you but, before I do, there's something else I haven't delved into, and it's essential. Panic ATTACKS?

There are different forms of Anxiety, and the effects Fear has on us can be mild, severe and then ultimately Panic!

Mild Anxiety is something that is regularly felt by most people and generally can be dealt with by implementing useful or helpful thought processes that resolve after the event or when the situation has finished or completed.

It produces the same physical symptoms but a lot milder and easy to accept. It is mild because it's probable the Fear may be warranted to a certain level and the thoughts match the Anxiety. L.E.T.G.O.E., 5 D'S, and F.E.E.L. G.O.O.D work well for this.

Severe Anxiety is a whole new level of stress, Fear and worry. You are struggling to cope with the Fear and are suffering significant physical symptoms and thoughts that are almost unbearable and certainly not comfortable. L.E.T.G.O.E., 5 D'S and F.E.E.L. G.O.O.D are definite for this. You will also need to use both P.A.C.E. and BREATH simultaneously.

Panic Attacks are Severe Anxiety ramped up to the maximum level, and they're a horrendous physical and emotional disturbance that cannot be explained to the layperson. They generally leave you with a feeling of total exhaustion and very little to no ability to cope with the situation.

It feels like a full-blown assault of your physical and emotional wellbeing, and it's impossible to stop when in full flight. Remember, Panic Attacks CANNOT be stopped once they have started so please don't try and fight them. You need to let them run their course. The energy produced needs to be released and discharged from the body.

REMEMBER FEAR FUELS FEAR — CONSENT STOPS IT!

However, there is a couple of little tricks I have up my sleeve that may just turn this experience into a positive one! I know, I know, sounds crazy. But, if you're like I was, you're prepared to try anything (and, who knows, you might be pleasantly surprised!)

I mentioned in the first chapter that I gave my Anxiety a name. This was initially a bit of 'code' between my partner and me, but I've discovered from my research and experience that it's a beneficial tool. My naming it, it becomes more of an annoying (and stupid) friend, rather than a scary monster.

Mine is called 'Cyrus' because it rhymed with virus. Personalising my Anxiety allowed me to talk to it and that, in turn, settled my mind and body.

I would say things like: "C'mon Cyrus, leave those butterflies alone in my guts, they are far too beautiful for you", or "alright Cyrus, I know you're lurking around, but at the moment everything is safe, so piss off".

And, as I've also mentioned before, finishing with a smile does fantastic things to your nervous system!

WINNING BACK OUR EMOTIONS

The Anxiety Spiral is relentless.

Often, the Fearful thoughts and sensations are simultaneously arriving with the trigger or stimulus. This makes it incredibly hard to get on the front foot. Understanding the process and shutting things down BEFORE it all escalates into Panic is what we want to do. But how? Let's look at an example and tackle a few options.

PANIC ATTACK TEST CASE: *HAVING A PANIC ATTACK ON A BUS*

TRIGGER - *Bus*

(It is also essential to understand that although the trigger is the bus, it doesn't mean the bus causes the Panic Attack. Instead, it's the thoughts and memories activating the Fear Centre because something negative happened on a bus. This caused your Fear and made you alert for danger. This applies to any setting/situation/event. Understanding it's not the thing, it's the Anxiety or Fear surrounding the thing.)

FEARFUL THOUGHTS - Oh no! What if I have a Panic attack when I get on the bus.

SENSATIONS - Starting to feel short of breath.

INCREASED FEARFUL THOUGHTS - What if I can't breathe properly?

INCREASED SENSATIONS - Feeling even shorter of breath; heart racing.

INCREASING FEARFUL THOUGHTS - Will I die or suffocate? I need to get away from the bus!

INCREASING SENSATIONS - Tight in the chest; shortness of breath; heart racing; feel like hyperventilating.

INCREASING SEVERITY OF FEARFUL THOUGHTS – I'm going to die here, and there is no one to help me, HELP, HELP, PLEASE! I'm going to die!

INCREASING SEVERITY SENSATIONS - Really short of breath; now choked and suffocating; sweating.

RESULT - Panic ATTACK!

This is just an example of the spiral – how quickly it happens depends on how much you can counteract your Fearful thoughts and accept the bodily sensations.

So, what can we do to arrest this spiral of Anxiety and Panic and empower ourselves? Pretty much rebut the Fearful thoughts and accept our bodily sensations. I will use the same example as above, and we will look at two scenarios where we can nip the spiral in the bud before things get messy.

HAVING A PANIC ATTACK ON A BUS (NIP IT IN THE BUD #1)

TRIGGER - *Bus*

FEARFUL THOUGHTS - Oh no! What if I have a Panic attack on the bus?

SENSATIONS - Starting to feel short of breath.

INCREASED FEARFUL THOUGHTS - What if I can't breathe properly? Hang on a minute: the bus is my trigger. I know what to do if I start to feel short of breath, I just need one of those techniques (BREATH or P.A.C.E.), and I need to appreciate any other bodily sensations that I am feeling.

DECREASED SENSATIONS - Feeling a little short of breath, but decreasing.

DECREASED FEARFUL THOUGHTS - I can handle this. My breathing is starting to return to a more reasonable rate, along with my Anxiety.

DECREASED SENSATIONS - Normal breathing and feeling more controlled.

DECREASED SEVERITY OF FEARFUL THOUGHTS – I'm not going to die here. I don't need anyone to help me at all. I will continue with that BREATH technique and watch my thoughts that can fuel my Anxiety.

RESULT - NO Panic ATTACK!

HAVING A PANIC ATTACK ON A BUS (NIP IT IN THE BUD #2)

TRIGGER - *Bus*

FEARFUL THOUGHTS - Oh no! What if I have a Panic attack? As if. This bus isn't a problem. It's my Fear of Anxiety and Panic. I just need to address my thoughts and realise that my body will release chemicals that will make me feel Anxious, but they are not harmful. I need that L.E.T.G.O.E., 5 D'S OR F.E.E.L. G.O.O.D. Technique.

SENSATIONS - Slight increase in breathing rate and nervousness in the stomach but not significant.

NIL FEARFUL THOUGHTS, OR HELPFUL FEARFUL THOUGHTS - I'm glad that I am aware that my thoughts can create Anxiety and Panic because now I know I have the tools to deal with the Anxiety/Panic spiral if need them.

DECREASED OR MINIMAL SENSATIONS - Little bit of butterflies but otherwise quite comfortable.

RESULT - *Better get a seat, enjoy the ride and enjoy the day!*

NORMAL FEAR RESPONSE

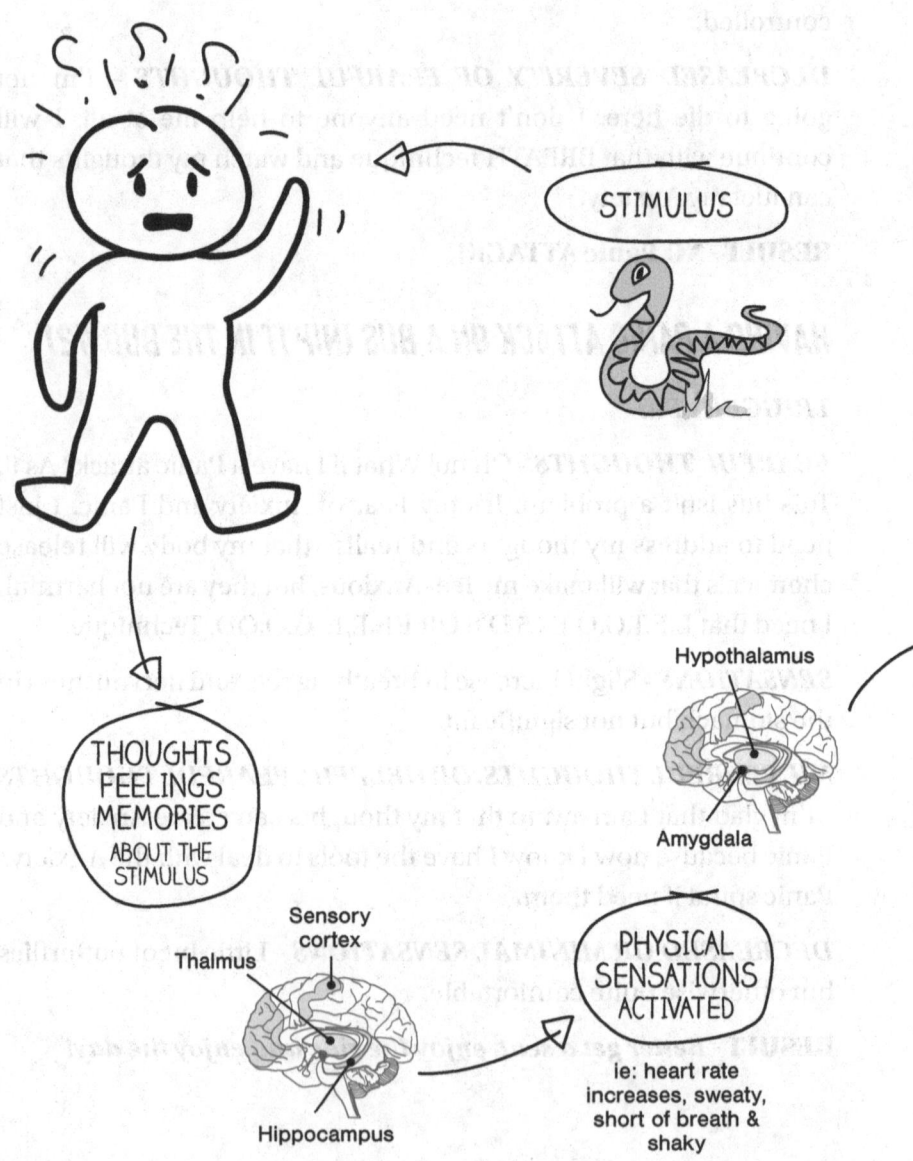

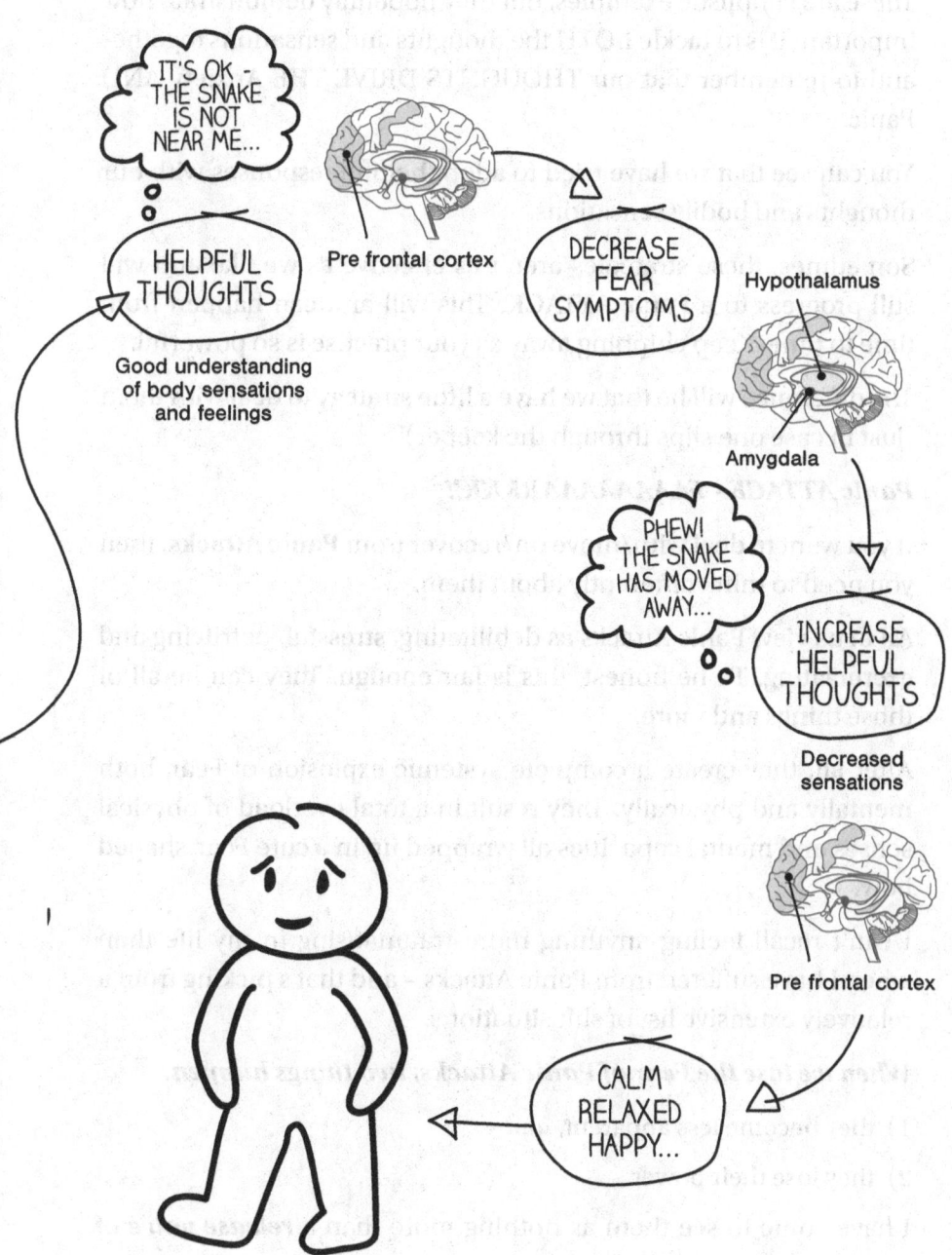

These are simplistic examples, but they hopefully demonstrate how important it is to tackle BOTH the thoughts and sensations together and to remember that our THOUGHTS DRIVE THE Anxiety AND Panic.

You can see that we have tried to adopt helpful responses with our thoughts and bodily sensations.

Sometimes, these strategies aren't as effective as we like and will still progress to a Panic ATTACK. This will and can happen from time to time. Keep chipping away as your practise is so powerful.

The difference will be that we have a little strategy to deal with them (just in case one slips through the keeper)!

Panic ATTACK - FAAAAAAAARKKK!!

If you want to deal with/move on/recover from **Panic Attacks**, then you need to think differently about them.

All of us view Panic Attacks as debilitating, stressful, petrifying and excruciating. To be honest, this is fair enough. They can be all of those things and more.

After all, they create a complete systemic explosion of Fear, both mentally and physically. They result in a total overload of physical senses and mental capacities all wrapped up in a cute Fear-shaped bow.

I can't recall feeling anything more traumatising in my life than when I have suffered from Panic Attacks – and that's picking from a relatively extensive list of shit situations.

When we lose the Fear of Panic Attacks, two things happen:

1) they become less apparent, *and*

2) they lose their power.

I have come to see them as nothing more than a ***release valve*** of ***stress***. Anxiety that needs to blow off pressure that has built up.

I have realised Panic attacks serve a positive purpose in releasing tension that potentially aids in reducing less stress-related diseases in my physical body.

I have also realised that they tend to be a real fucking problem if not addressed.

Remember, when we looked at our imagined Worst Case Scenario in Chapter 6? If you suffer from Panic Attacks and Panic Disorder, then often those Panic Attacks are your Worst Case Scenario.

What if we were able to dull, reduce and recover from them, so they drop down the list of Worst Case Scenario and eventually drift off into the background?

I have listed some experiences below that have helped me see them differently.

If you want to take the heat and Fear out of Panic Attacks, you need to know how they work, what they do and how to deal with them. Lets read some more.

PANIC ATTACKS EXPLAINED

As you now know, everything related to Anxiety and Stress and Panic results in a massive discharge of super-powerful hormones designed to speed things up, provide energy and tighten our muscles and bodies to defend and protect or flee. (Check out Chapter 3 if you need a revisit on the nervous system and all its various jobs).

Panic Attacks also mess with our breathing rate, which is something we want to use to settle Panic. People often get caught out on this alone.

We still apply the P.A.C.E. and BREATH but with one addition: total allowance and encouragement of all Signs and Symptoms.

HOW A BASE JUMPER SAVED ME

UNCONTROLLED PANIC CYCLE

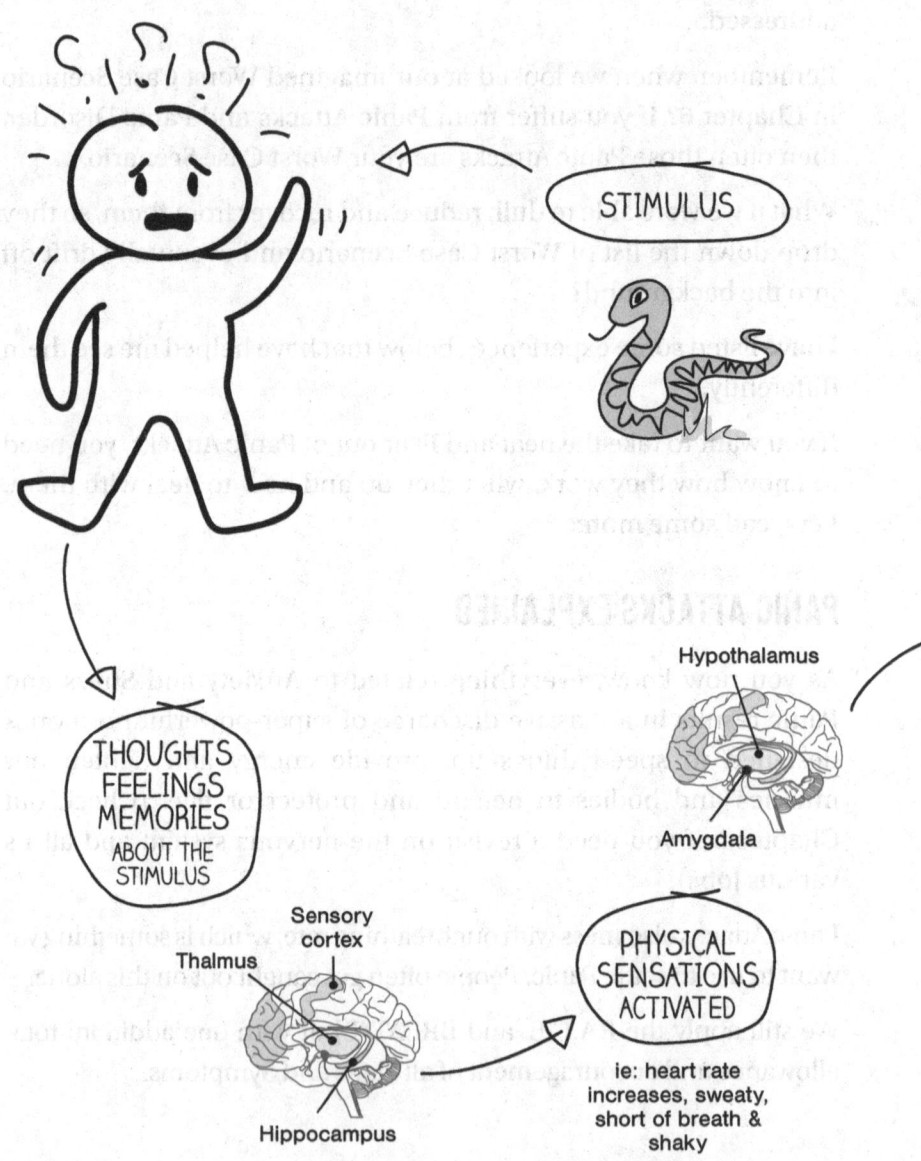

PROMOTING PANIC

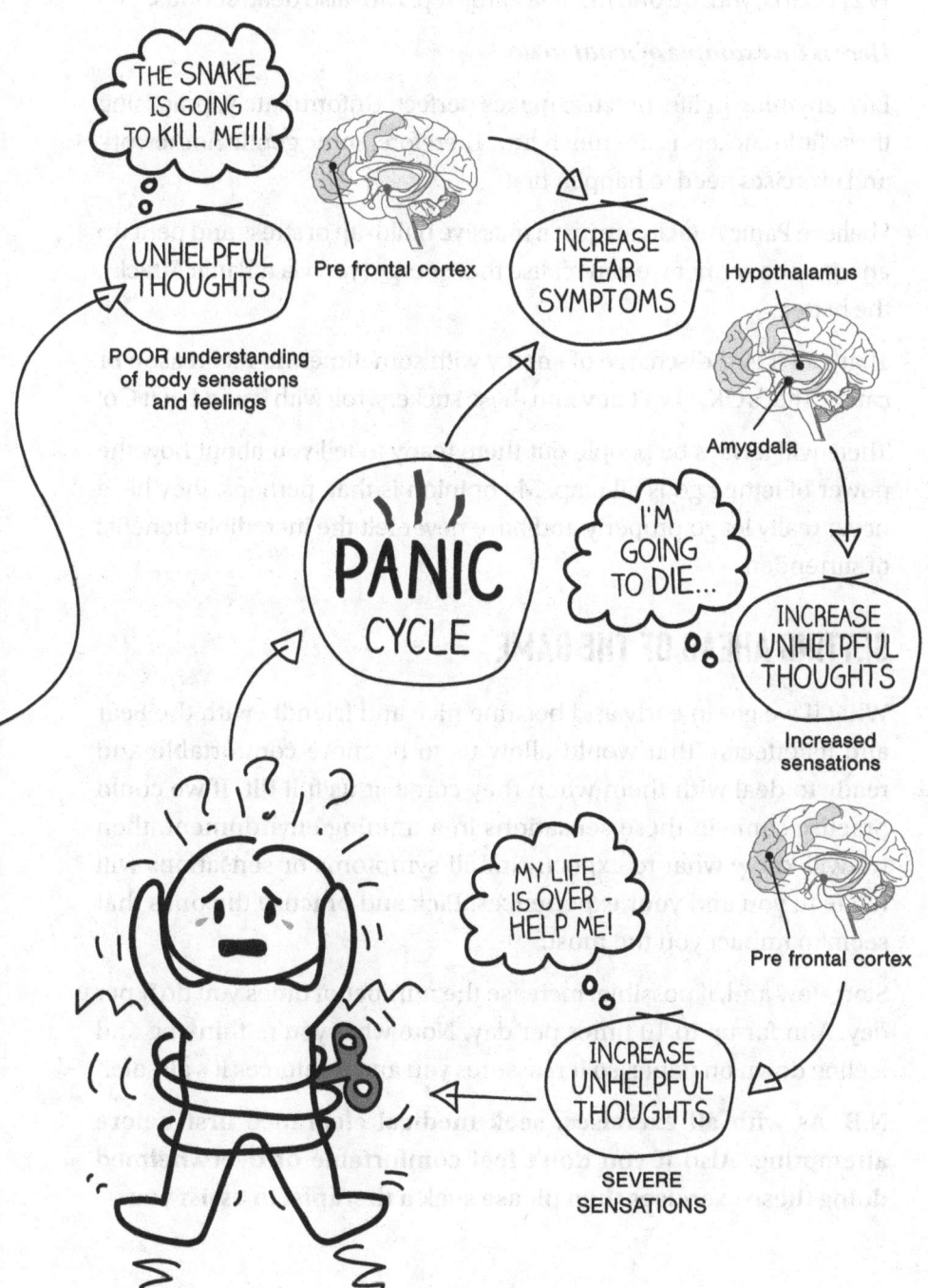

WTF! Chris, you are one mad bastard! Yep. I am also dead serious.

Here is an example of what to do.

Like anything in life, practise makes perfect. Unfortunately, practising these little suckers is not much fun. Therefore, some gentle homework and exercises need to happen first.

I believe Panic Attacks are just a massive build-up of stress and pent up energy. The sooner we can realise that energy (yes, via a Panic Attack), the better.

That's all it is: a discharge of energy with sometimes no real reason or cause. That's OK. Don't buy into these suckers, roll with it and Let It Go!

There will always be people out there ready to tell you about how the power of letting go is all crap. My opinion is that, perhaps, they have never really let go properly and have never felt the incredible benefits of surrender!

GETTING AHEAD OF THE GAME

What if we got in early and became nice and friendly with the Fear and its effects? That would allow us to be more comfortable and ready to deal with them when they come at us full tilt. If we could practise some of these sensations in a training environment, then we will know what to expect. Not all symptoms or sensations will relate to you and your experiences. Pick and practise the ones that seem to impact you the most.

Start slow and, if possible, increase the number of times you do it per day. Aim for up to 10 times per day. Note what you're thinking and feeling down on paper, so it reassures you and reinforces it's all safe.

N.B. As with all exercises, seek medical clearance first before attempting. Also if you don't feel comfortable or overwhelmed doing these exercises then please seek a therapist to assist you.

SYMPTOM INDUCTION EXERCISES

Here are some examples of symptoms we can produce in training:

1) Deliberately hyperventilate for 1 to 2 minutes creating a breathlessness, smothering sensation.

2) Hold your breath for 30 seconds, creating breathlessness and a smothering sensation.

3) Place a tongue depressor at the back of your tongue for 30 seconds. It creates a choking sensation.

4) Run-on the spot for 1 minute that creates a panting racing heart sensation.

5) Spin in a chair for approximately 1 minute, creating a dizzy, faint feeling.

6) Tense all body muscles for 1 minute, creating the sensation of trembling and shaking.

7) Breath through a narrow straw for 2 minutes, creating breathlessness and smothering sensation.

8) Shake head rapidly from side to side for 30 seconds, creating a dizziness and fainting feeling.

9) Stare continuously at yourself in a mirror for 2 minutes, creating a sense of being dreamy, dizzy or faint.[8]

I know—none of these sound like much fun.

The thing is, once you have been practising these for a while, there will come a time when you need to practise them for real.

To practise them we need to become Panic Attack chaser not dissimilar to storm chasers trying to create or produce one.

Some questions to ask yourself after doing the exercises to write down and review. Super powerful!

1) What are you experiencing?
2) What are you thinking /imagining whilst doing them?
3) How do they make you feel?
4) Is this similar to your Panic attacks, and why did you not have one?
5) What have you learned from your experience?

It is handy to write a list of situations and triggers.

TRIGGERS are significant because they help us identify where to find the fuckers, and then execute our plan of counter-attack.

The more you practise them and implement strategy, the less power they have because you begin to realise that the Big One never happens and you can deal or cope with the ones that come.

Remember it's the spiral of scary/unhelpful thoughts that create Panic as they build up our levels of stress and pressure, igniting the body into a Panic mode.

'Panic Attack' seems like a term that doesn't give the event much credit, and I think it almost reduces the severity by its description.

I think that petrifying sounds more worthy, as that's what it is at the highest degree. I had never felt more scared in my life than when I was suffering petrifying Panic events before I understood them better.

They are not something to take lightly.

Panic Attacks are so Fearful and significant; I believe they are often driven by a genuine threat of existence to you which leads to a catastrophic result. Sometimes our little brains and bodies go into overdrive, and it seems that no matter what, we are destined to cop an episode of pure Panic.

Guess what? Believe it or not, we can get on top of these Petrifying Panic events.

L.E.T.'S MEET THE ADRENALINE JUNKIE (THAT'S YOU)!

Well, I reckon we say to ourselves: bring the Fear on, and we can sit back and turn ourselves into an 'adrenaline junkie'.

Right, what is this guy talking about now? I haven't lost it, I promise you.

If you have ever experienced a Panic Attack, then you know they're impossible to stop. If we haven't been able to stop it before the ignition was turned on and the motor is running red hot, there is little choice at this point but accepting it.

I say stuff it then, man. No problem. Let's get a free hit of adrenaline and sit back and enjoy the ride! (After all, it's free and I'm a tight arse).

This is what I do when staring down the barrel of a Panic Attack:

ACCEPT – it's going to happen, and it's impossible to stop.

UNDERSTAND - your body and its sensations (as discussed at length previously) are snowballing out of control, ready to ignite. They won't hurt you.

PREPARE AND ASK - my brain to increase the levels of sensation in my body as much as possible (stay with me here). I want to increase my heart rate, the tingling, choking and any other symptoms, except for breathing. I'm going to do the opposite and either hold my breath or pursed lip breathing. (As discussed in Chapter 4).

I am essentially picking a fight with the Fear Centre.

While I'm doing this, I'm thinking about what is happening in my body with complete understanding. For example, as I recognise each sensation, I acknowledge it: yep, that's the adrenaline using the heart receptors to increase heart rate, chest tightness; or that feeling that I'm short of breath is the change in $Co2$ that makes the breathing centre change my rate and depth.

This is important. I believe it helps reduce the Fear because we are not worried about the reason for the symptoms. We understand our body now, and we see why it's reacting in such a physical way.

Once the Panic Attack is underway – that explosion where you get an intense rush of sensations – you need to let them shoot through your body without any resistance. Try and make it happen.

Understand the tipping point is when your mind is 100% petrified, and it feels like nothing will stop it! Let it happen. Don't read into the thoughts at that moment. Encourage Fear.

Now I want you to try and enjoy the intense feelings, just like an adrenaline junkie would as he leapt out of a plane mid-flight. Weirdly, it can feel pretty good.

Just like we practised in our visualisation and symptom induction exercises, I close my eyes and wait for the full brunt of the Fear, whilst picturing a state of combined relief, bravery, peace and, strangely enough, happiness.

The trick is to let it happen – this will not only speed things up, but it will also reduce the longevity of the attack. It also allows you to get a quick free hit of the good stuff with confidence. I have always enjoyed a little excitement, so absorbing the sensations works well for me and helps take away the Fear.

If you're not an adrenaline junkie, that's OK. Just feel the rush and don't resist the sensations to the best of your ability.

And remember Smile. It helps rewire the brain and body into tricking it that it's OK.

N.B. You will often get the urge to run or flee the situation; this is an inbuilt reaction from the Fear centre. It will pass, and my trick is to acknowledge when the urge comes and sit with it whilst it settles.

HOW I GOT HERE

When I first started suffering from Panic Attacks, I had no idea what was happening to me or my body. I was so scared that it took me to the point of a nervous breakdown in a brief period.

The turning point came in some different stages:

THE BASE JUMPER

The **FIRST** turning point came to me when I sat on a camp chair feeling horrendously scared, Anxious and on the brink of Panic. I was holidaying in the Lauterbrunnen valley in Switzerland, whilst backpacking around Europe. I was supposed to be relaxed and having fun camping. That particular day, I watched a group of base jumpers jump off this massive mountain in the Swiss Alps near the campground.

As I watched them mulling around at the top of the mountain, the thought occurred to me that they are probably feeling the same way I am in regards to Fear, but they seem to be getting a kick out of it. Being human, they would be producing the same stress/Fear hormones as I am except their situation is produced by a potential physical threat from jumping off a cliff and mine was because of a potential Panic attack. The thought occurred to me that if we feel the same physically, then how come they seem to be excited and pumped and I feel absolutely terrible?

This was evident once they landed – it looked like they were on a high and it lingered for hours (I saw them at the bar afterwards). This got me thinking; maybe I could turn my Fear into that of an 'adrenaline junkie'?

THIS WAS THE START OF ME CHANGING MY PERCEPTION TOWARDS PANIC ATTACKS

It had a huge impact on me and I couldn't get it out of my head that if I tried to be a base jumper towards Panic attacks and change my perception about them, then maybe it could be positive.

I also kept thinking that once they jump, they have to let go of all Fear and let it happen - that's how I come up with accepting the Panic and rolling with it!!!!

There were also other events or situations I started to realise about my Panic attacks and when I put them all together, it started to unravel a couple of things.

I RECOGNISED that I never stopped or avoided anything or any situation ever. I pushed myself to be where I needed to be and to do what I wanted. This knowledge still allowed me to travel through 25 countries and be out of my comfort zone with the awareness and understanding that Fear can't stop me (even though I often felt like shit).

Another turning point was when I was in the basement of an old flat we lived in Brighton, England, and I was in the laundry. It was so small; I couldn't stand up straight (I'm 6 ft and it was about 5 ft). It was dark, stuffy from the dryer running and I had this massive build-up of nasal congestion, along with general tension (stress) whilst attending the washing. It all became claustrophobic, and I had a Panic Attack.

The odd thing was, after the event, it fixed my nasal congestion as I could breathe clearly, and the general tension in my body had resolved. I also noticed that it 'reset' my mood by feeling like the release valve had been opened, leaving a sense of relief. This also gave me the thought that having a Panic Attack may not be the worst thing. It makes me feel better. Maybe it could act as a release valve to my built-up stress?

When I put all these experiences and thoughts together, I decided that when I had another Panic Attack, I would try to be an adrenaline junkie. Bring it on! Maybe afterwards, I would feel a little better?

Guess what? To my surprise, not only did I feel better physically and emotionally after my next Panic Attack, but I also gained confidence and empowerment that I had only dreamed of. Fear was decreasing.

The funny thing was, this curse that I had been dealt and tried to avoid forever was now the exact thing I was seeking to chase and experience with my new found strategy.

You wouldn't believe how hard it was to 'try' and have another Panic Attack once it seemed I had lost the Fear of them. It took several months before I experienced another one.

When I did, I adopted my strategies and will continue to do so for the rest of my life. I now get free adrenaline rushes without having to go on scary and expensive rides at the theme parks or jump off mountains!

It has become a case of 'whatever' when they appear and, these days, it's not that often. It is a fantastic feeling to have empowerment over what was once the most terrifying thing in my life.

The final realisation was that these bad boys are just a discharge of energy that needs to be released. This is just what I discussed earlier. Knowing this really allows me to completely let go when they are happening and feel a deep sense of relief when that incredibly unhelpful energy is gone.

SPONTANEOUS PANIC ATTACKS

Then you get those sneaky, out-of-the-blue ones that can't be explained. I occasionally get them in the middle of the night. I simply wake up for whatever reason and almost immediately develop a Panic Attack from nowhere.

As we have discussed in length about our thoughts and their ability to promote Panic Attacks (especially if those thoughts are unhelpful), I can imagine those of you who have suffered from what's known as Nocturnal Panic Attacks are sticking up your hand and shouting, yes Chris, what the fuck is happening here?

I'll tell you this: it's not that you've been overthinking because you're asleep.

I believe spontaneous and nocturnal ones are still related to a stress relief response in the body and are the work of the subconscious. I have given thought to the spontaneous Panic I have had, and they all tend to be after a stressful period or experience when I am unsettled mentally and emotionally. As always, it takes the body time to catch up with the conscious mind.

Given my perception on this, I still apply my strategy of becoming an adrenaline junkie (even if it's 2 am, we roll with it). I have learned not to get caught up in the 'how comes' and 'what ifs' and put it down to a simple case of your body needing to release that stress.

I know it seems almost too simple, but the fact is: your body knows its limits and your best interests and acts accordingly.

FEAR ABOUT FEAR

This concept or thought process is quite common in sufferers of Anxiety and Panic. It's one of the significant drivers into Panic.

It makes sense that it creates a much more harmful and severe situation as basically, it is creating more stress and Fear that only loads up that Fear response and eventually pushes the system into overload.

Thankfully though, something can be done about this, and it also is a significant driver in stopping our Anxiety and Fear from growing out of control.

I am sure you are familiar with the feeling: you're Anxious or Fearful in a particular situation and are unsure why you're feeling that way. You can't comprehend how you got to this point, and that surprise and confusion creates added stress and Anxiety. Suddenly, you're anxious about being anxious.

I suffered from this and generally didn't understand what it was, what was happening or even the fact I was feeling this way. That then drove up my Anxiety and Panic without me even realising.

So, how to fix it?

OK, so what do we need to do to fix this issue?

We already know, from the previous chapters, that our unhelpful thoughts and unexplained physical sensations can create a spiral of unhelpful thought producing a physical sensation that often generates another unhelpful thought which, in turn, increases the severity of bodily sensations.

We also now know the key is by identifying our thoughts, understanding why we are thinking them and understanding how Anxiety is physically produced.

HOW A BASE JUMPER SAVED ME

When I realise I'm Anxious about being Anxious, I first need to stop, listen and feel.

Because I had one of my first Panic Attacks on a train, I started feeling Anxious when I got on any train. My thoughts became debilitating and began to increase in severity, and my body became reactive and scared as I couldn't understand why I was so anxious about being on the train in the first place. It's just a bloody train, after all. I've used them my whole life.

Now I understand Anxiety and my Fear Centre. I know my mind and body are continually scanning the environment for signs of danger or threat, and the moment I identify danger, the system is activated to alert me.

If I get on a train now and feel my physical sensations increase, I know why I'm thinking so anxiously about the train in the first place. I can reassure myself that I'm not going 'crazy' or 'losing my mind'. It is merely my Fear Centre trying to alert me that we had a problem with trains before and to be aware. Just by identifying this as OK, can make all the difference.

TROUBLESHOOTING CHECKLIST

- [ ] Do you feel your understanding of how Fear works with both thoughts and bodily sensations is up to date?
- [ ] Are you able to apply PACE, BREATH, L.E.T.G.O.E., 5 D'S, FEEL GOOD OR WHAT forever?
- [ ] Are you being disciplined with your added background work?
- [ ] Are you continually writing thoughts down as it's the best, quickest route to recovery because of its power to see problem thinking and insert into the subconscious?
- [ ] Are you questioning thoughts every time you're Anxious?
- [ ] Have you identified the Worst case scenario? (The root cause of your Fear).
- [ ] Have you looked at and changed your diet (I will talk about this more shortly)?
- [ ] Are you practising exposure and practising often? It will fail when not done enough. You need to start somewhere and continue with it. Additionally, be aware brief exposure can have a negative effect because it increases your beliefs that your Fear is real.
- [ ] Are you avoiding or escaping thoughts and physical sensations because it only increases your Anxiety? Be aware it won't allow you to understand and accept them.

Although escape and avoidance are natural Fear responses, they're not sustainable in the long run. You will have to use strategies not to avoid. Avoidance is a short-term fix that will make things so much worse over time. It prevents Anxiety from declining naturally and decreases the quality of life because you're not living freely, and you feel like crap all the time.

☐ Safety seeking is when you try and prevent a scary outcome through thoughts and behaviours. The big issue is that you're not learning what's unhelpful in your thoughts to address them.

☑ Are you on the piss and telling your Anxiety to fuck off without using your manners? *Lol!*

NEEDING TO LEARN

As I've encountered more and more people suffering from Fear, Anxiety and Panic, it's become apparent that many people often aren't helping themselves (or their loved ones, if they have a friend or family member suffering). Parents, (including me) often do their children an injustice when it comes to dealing with Anxiety, and this isn't placing blame: Parenting is challenging at the best of times, and we just want to see our kids safe. Older people also do themselves a disservice by not taking the time to learn and understand what's affected them for a lifetime.

It got me thinking about what I do with my children?

I often avoided the situation or trigger in the first place with my kids.

As we have learned, this just reinforces Anxiety's strength that the situation is full of danger and stress, and this compounds Fear levels each time we have to come across it.

Instead, what I needed was a game plan.

I needed to Coach, my child, by explaining what symptoms or bodily sensations they may feel. Explain this is a normal response.

Help them think the right way by giving realistic, helpful thoughts to the situation and identify what they are thinking to correct them.

Allow them (kids) to experience the process of Fear and Anxiety by themselves, so they can learn what they think, what they feel and that often the Fear process settles and declines with time.

What makes things worse? When you avoid the Anxiety.

Of course, I'm not talking about danger here. This is about small things like walking to school without my wife or me, going to the shops alone or asking questions for themselves in different situations without intervening parents.

Give it a try; this is how they will learn.

WINNING LIFE'S LITTLE BATTLES

When we face our Fear and get a positive result, we can feel euphoric and a sense of achievement. The little battles along the way that you may have struggled with and then faced and watched them lose their power can make you feel excited. A certain level of confidence also sneaks in to help as well. As you climb the ladder of Fear and beating it, the little wins eventually turn into big wins and, before you are aware, the reward is right in front of you – a stress-free life.

It's a personal sense of achievement that no one else gets and probably won't understand but fuck it feels incredible when you beat your Fear and feel a particular situation has been conquered.

Start small and aim high: the thrill and excitement are waiting for you, and I promise, it's amazing!

GETTING THE BLOODY HORSE TO DRINK

OK, so you have probably been avoiding the shit out of certain things for a while. You've probably even made it this far into this book and not tackled anything yet. You will do anything to not put yourself in that position due to Fear.

Fair enough, I reckon. If you're here, you've likely had a crappy experience or experiences, and you're not exactly feeling great.

You've also had nil or little skill or tools to use to get back on track, let alone even understand what the hell is happening.

Well, now that you have some knowledge and strategy to have a crack back, we can begin to look at facing our Fear head-on in gentle little easy and manageable steps.

Once we have devised a plan of attack, we also want to give ourselves a little reward for accomplishing such a difficult feat.

Therefore, we need to come up with a bravery reward system because you deserve it. It can come in two ways and be charted that way as well.

First, make a list of things we would like to reward ourselves with when we have nailed our goals. It could be a monetary thing (each time you achieve a step forward, you put money away for something bigger, or shout yourself lunch, dinner or a movie ticket). I think you get the drift. We are aiming to create positive feedback that you can see with your actions and chart.

We can also chart how we want to feel emotionally (happiness, a sense of achievement elation or pride) for tackling the beast and defeating it moving towards freedom.

These need to be charted to give you a visual on how you're progressing as seeing that is incredibly powerful.

Once you have come up with a plan of attack with your thinking and physical sensations checklist covered, we can then start small with little things that cause Anxiety and Fear but only in small steps.

We may want to start with an Anxiety that is rated around 2 (refer to Fears and Worries List on page 160) and then go and face it.

The key is to experience the Anxiety and then let the Anxiety settle naturally, as that promotes confidence. It also teaches the Fear Centre that you're safe and it won't have to remind us that danger is there. Then chart your result and reward yourself!

PROMOTING PANIC

After completing that level, you're ready to move forward and increase your exposure to a higher level like 3-4 and repeat the same process.

Continue this process until eventually you can face your major Fear head-on and be comfortable with it. It may take time and patience but as long as you're planning, trying and rewarding you will get there and guess what? You are now a horse that has drank that bloody water!

Remember, if you don't try and face your Fears, then they won't change, and they definitely won't go away. Often, they just become worse. There will always be setbacks as well that will discourage you. That's something you will have to accept and understand this will pass.

It can be tough, but with a little coaching, knowledge and courage, you can do it.

HOW A BASE JUMPER SAVED ME

FEARS AND WORRIES LIST

LITTLE FEARS RATING (1-3)	BIGGER FEARS RATING (4-7)	SCARY FEARS RATING (8-10)
(1)		
(2)		
(3)		
(4)		
(5)		
(6)		
(7)		

BRAVERY REWARD CHART

LIST OF THINGS YOU LIKE - TO REWARD YOURSELF:

_____
_____
_____
_____
_____
_____
_____
_____

FEAR / WORRY (REMEMBER BUILD UP TO IT):

_____

1ST STEP TOWARDS FEAR:

REWARD FOR BRAVERY:

FEELINGS (E.G. HAPPY / PROUD / SENSE OF ACHIEVEMENT):

_____

2ND STEP TOWARDS FEAR:

REWARD FOR BRAVERY:

FEELINGS (E.G. HAPPY / PROUD / SENSE OF ACHIEVEMENT):

_____

HOW A BASE JUMPER SAVED ME

3ʳᴰ STEP TOWARDS FEAR:

REWARD FOR BRAVERY:

FEELINGS (E.G. HAPPY / PROUD / SENSE OF ACHIEVEMENT):

4ᵀᴴ STEP TOWARDS FEAR:

REWARD FOR BRAVERY:

FEELINGS (E.G. HAPPY / PROUD / SENSE OF ACHIEVEMENT):

5ᵀᴴ STEP TOWARDS FEAR:

REWARD FOR BRAVERY:

FEELINGS (E.G. HAPPY / PROUD / SENSE OF ACHIEVEMENT):

6ᵀᴴ STEP TOWARDS FEAR:

REWARD FOR BRAVERY:

FEELINGS (E.G. HAPPY / PROUD / SENSE OF ACHIEVEMENT):

7ᵀᴴ STEP TOWARDS FEAR:

REWARD FOR BRAVERY:

FEELINGS (E.G. HAPPY / PROUD / SENSE OF ACHIEVEMENT):

PROMOTING PANIC

8TH STEP TOWARDS FEAR:

REWARD FOR BRAVERY:

FEELINGS (E.G.HAPPY / PROUD / SENSE OF ACHIEVEMENT):

9TH STEP TOWARDS FEAR:

REWARD FOR BRAVERY:

FEELINGS (E.G.HAPPY / PROUD / SENSE OF ACHIEVEMENT):

10TH STEP TOWARDS FEAR:

REWARD FOR BRAVERY:

FEELINGS (E.G.HAPPY / PROUD / SENSE OF ACHIEVEMENT):

11TH STEP TOWARDS FEAR:

REWARD FOR BRAVERY:

FEELINGS (E.G.HAPPY / PROUD / SENSE OF ACHIEVEMENT):

12TH STEP TOWARDS FEAR:

REWARD FOR BRAVERY:

FEELINGS (E.G.HAPPY / PROUD / SENSE OF ACHIEVEMENT):

"BENEATH EVERY BEHAVIOUR,
THERE IS A FEELING.
AND BENEATH EACH FEELING
IS A NEED. AND WHEN WE
MEET THAT NEED RATHER
THAN FOCUS ON THE BEHAVIOUR,
WE BEGIN TO DEAL WITH THE CAUSE,
NOT THE SYMPTOM."

ASHLEIGH WARNER

CHAPTER 09

PUTTING IT INTO PERSPECTIVE

I've briefly mentioned Meditation, Visualisation and Immersion (remember me wanting you to focus on the Worst-Case Scenario in Chapter 6? That was fun) but now I want to go into a little more detail. The truth is, there's plenty of hard work that needs to go on behind the scenes that will allow you to understand and manage those pesky thoughts a little better. I want to give you a few 'tricks' that can make things clearer or simply offer some helpful perspective. Like everything here, read on and get a good understanding then have a think about what you might like to try.

CATASTROPHISING SCALE

This little sucker is a ripper of a tool used to put thinking – especially catastrophic or Worst Case Scenario thinking – into perspective. It can show us where our thinking maybe a little out of whack, and then rejig those thoughts into more realistic ones. It also helps us to question our thoughts – after all, you shouldn't believe everything you think.

We draw a vertical line or scale labelled from 0 to 100. The 100 represents the worst possible fact or situation that you could live with. The 0 is something not significant in your life and mostly harmless (none are meant to be related to Anxiety – really bad down to generally good scenarios).

Below is an example I could use for my catastrophising scale.

100 – family member murdered

90 – serious health condition like a stroke with an inability to use arms and legs

80 – the inability to speak

70 – divorce

60 – not seeing kids

50 – losing a job

40 – knee reconstruction

30 – an argument with the boss at work

20 – excessive bills

10 – losing car keys

0 – feeling healthy and happy.

The reason we do this without Anxiety examples is so we can compare them to our Anxiety to demonstrate how much they are often exaggerated and inflated, and that only serves to create more Fear.

Super powerful stuff.

Now once you have your scale set up and written down, put a mark where you think your Anxiety is and try and identify the reduced significance of where your thinking or Anxiety is. It is all another putting things into perspective. [8]

PUTTING IT INTO PERSPECTIVE

THE WORRY SCALE

This is good for you or others to gauge where you're at with your Anxiety. The visual component is again incredibly powerful.

This is different from the Catastrophising scale as this one rates your actual Anxiety and its level vs trying to change your perception.

Here is how we do it.

Write down 0 to 10 with 0 being no Anxiety and 10 being the most severe Anxiety and Fear you have experienced.

It might look like this:

10 – extremely worried (unbearable and super overwhelmed)

8 – super worried (almost losing control and on edge)

6 – worried (feeling upset and concerned but able to just manage)

4 – concerned (worried and upset but dealing with it)

2 – a little stressed (feeling low stress but relatively good)

0 – relaxed and chilled out (sweet as).

This helps you work out how shit you feel by giving it a number and labelling it. The reason this is good is that it can help by giving you the confidence to deal with whatever level you're at.

If you keep a record where you sit on your Worry Scale, you will soon see that even at the worst or highest level of Fear, you survived. Although horrendous things were felt, they settled and went away.

It's impossible to suffer at extreme Anxiety all the time as it eventually changes and settles. Nothing lasts forever!

Another excellent reason for using the scale is that it helps promote confidence to say to yourself: OK, I have been at this level plenty of times, and I can cope or handle this, and I have belief in me handling this especially if it's at the lower end of things.

Remember coping, or the thought that you can't cope is a significant driver in your Anxiety.

This tool is great for your Bravery chart as well.

I also like to make it a game by taking on my number of Anxiety and challenging it. This alone tells the Fear Centre that you're not that scared and helps bring that number down lower to reduce your Fear. It also makes you question your thoughts about Anxiety and determine if they are helpful or realistic. For example, if the level is rated at 8, I like to try and ramp up my Fear and aim for a level of 10. This has a paradoxical effect on my Fear often switching off the Fear and reducing it.

Seriously, try it and see what happens. [19]

GIVE A SHIT METER (AKA OPTING OUT OF THE TRIVIAL STUFF)

OK, now let's get the Give-a-shit meter (G.A.S.M.) out and give it a go. The G.A.S.M. is a simple tool you can use when you find yourself caught up in the trivial things in life and those ongoing stressors that seem to be bothering you.

The problem with getting caught up in everything in life's journey is that it starts to take its toll on your health, happiness and, of course, Anxiety. All stressors slowly ramp up the levels of stress in you pushing the body to that hyper-aroused state we often talk about and want to reduce.

This is another form, or tool, to nip things in the bud early before they gain momentum and spiral out of control.

Start by drawing a line and marking it 0 to 100. 0 represents not giving a shit at all and 100 represents massive shit issues to concern you.

Then mark where you think this situation or problem sits in life to see if it's worth pursuing or releasing. If the score is small and low, then it generally means it's trivial, and like all trivial situations, they pass unless you get caught up on them. This is when stress and angst can build, which in turn helps ramp up our Anxiety.

Ask yourself these questions:

1) What is the exact problem?
2) Do I have any control over it at all? (If not, stop – there is nothing you can do except accept there is nothing you can do, apart from let time pass).
3) If I can control it, what productive strategies can I do to change it?
4) Is it worth giving a shit about and wasting my energy? (If not, let it go).
5) Will this be a problem in 12 months? (If not, let it go).

If the problem or stress can be addressed, then do so and move on. 99% of things we get our knickers in a knot about are so trivial and often mean stuff all in a few days. My advice is: acknowledge it's not very pleasant, identify its significance, and let it go.

Even if it's still a problem in 12 months (rare), then time does two things. It allows you to shift your attitude towards the problem or the problem changes. Both results end up with the initial worry not being a problem!

No more shit.

Win-win, if you ask me.

MEDITATION

Everyone keeps talking about it, right?
For a good reason, actually. It's a fantastic tool that is free, easy and super effective. It might come across as a little woo-woo or wanky, but I beg you: please don't buy into the negative 'this is only for alternative kale-eating-tree-hugging-people' because the fact is, they're on to a good thing, and they know it.

We all know or have heard that meditation is right for you, and it has some incredible benefits. It is a broad term that covers a variety of different practises which vary in their approach to the mind and its function.

I have experienced the amazing benefits of this simple but ever powerful tool, and it's worth you having a crack at it.

Several studies have demonstrated the many different benefits that meditation brings including (but not limited to): improving ones focus; increased immunity; less worry and Anxiety; less stress, Fear and depression; increased self-esteem and self-acceptance; ability to be resilient against adversity; increased optimism, relaxation and awareness; improved memory retention; improved cognitive and creative skills; improved decision making; reduced blood pressure and heart rates; enhances empathy and compassion; decreased inflammatory disorders; and increased prevention of arthritis and fibromyalgia. Overall, it's a little ripper!

Physically, it can increase the size of grey matter in areas related to memory (hippocampus) and thought (frontal area) and increase brain volume in areas of emotion mainly positively related and self-control. It is also recognised that it increases the size of the cortical region of the brain.

It is proven that people who practised mindfulness meditation for eight weeks were able to decrease the activity in the Fear Centre of the brain (amygdala). Meditation can physically reduce the number of neurones firing off in the brain's Fear Centre.

You don't have to be a genius to work out that this simple tool with all its benefits listed is impressive for everybody but especially sufferers of Anxiety, Panic and high stress. It is our medication via a technique rather than a tablet that is another keystone to our recovery and ability to turn down the Anxiety volume.

There are 1440 minutes in a day. How many do you waste on social media, the T.V. or your phone? Don't you think it's worth giving a few minutes to your mind?

Meditation can come in many different forms – it's not just the old 'sitting in a chair, using a mantra and observing your thoughts' style although that works too.

There are many ideas for meditation that may help calm the brain and work better for you.

Some things that can work are:

- exercise (in the form that needs full attention. For example, a boxer who is solely focused on his opponent and in the moment, not in his Anxious thoughts outside of boxing ring).
- becoming focused on a puzzle, a card game, sudoku or any other activity that detracts from your Anxiety and forces you to focus purely on the task at hand.

You may have activities you enjoy that seem to take you to another place and give you a break from your problems and stressors (fishing, bike riding, painting, dancing, bird watching, you name it). Utilise these activities as often as you can because they only serve to calm your mind and help reduce your stress.

The idea behind meditation with regards to helping Anxiety is to try and slow and calm the mind from its endless chatter from Fear and Anxiety.

That means not spending so much time focusing on what is stressing you in the first place.

Meditation will help you unlock your unhelpful, Anxious and stressful thoughts as you train yourself to observe them. It will also set you up for the practise of visualisation and the dramatic effects that have on our Fear or reduction of.

This focus is our pre-season training. The first step in helping get us back on track and reprogram our brains.

A little something to remember when you delve into an activity meditation exercise: you might not have experienced the feeling and sensation of being truly relaxed for a long time. So, this practise of meditation will be challenging for you merely because you're not used to it. Feeling comfortable is a new skill you will have to learn and therefore, may take time. Bear with it, and things will get easier as you go. If you feel Anxious, remember to use your tools of P.A.C.E. or BREATH and of course L.E.T.G.O.E., 5 D'S or FEELGOOD or WHAT (head back to Chapter 5, 6 and 7 if you need a refresher on these).

You can do it, I promise! [20,21,22]

RIDING THE (BRAIN) WAVE

I'm about to get a little technical again for a bit. You know how necessary knowledge and understanding is now, so let's look at the brain's activity – specifically brain waves – to understand better what we are trying to do and potential it has.

Brainwaves are the electrical activity that is produced in your brain from millions of neurones (brain cells) that communicate with each other. We can read these brainwaves through a particular machine called an electroencephalogram (E.E.G.). The more neurones firing, the higher the level of activity that can be detected. One of the things we are trying to achieve with meditation is to reduce the level of activity, or neurone firing, to decrease our Anxiety and Panic. The good news is, we can train our brain to change the brainwaves to lesser, quieter levels for calmer, more peaceful minds.

There are five categories of brainwaves which are **Beta**, **Alpha** (our goal), **Theta, Delta** and **Gamma**.

BETA BRAINWAVES *(14 - 32 Hz alert and focussed)*

Beta is our most common waveform and is our default brainwave pattern for everyday life when fully awake, alert, active and engaged in mental activity.

BENEFITS

- This is the brainwave involved for the fight/flight response (Fear).
- Increases concentration and alertness.
- Improved logic, reasoning and logical thinking.
- Feelings of Anxiety, stress and difficulty concentrating.
- Can also be a key feature in insomnia.

ALPHA BRAINWAVES *(7 - 14 Hz relaxed and calm)*

This is the brainwave we are aiming for through the powers of meditation and visualisation. This brainwave is slower and assists in helping analyse complex situations, memorising things and performance.

It can also help release beta-endorphin, norepinephrine and dopamine that are linked to feeling happy, mental clarity and positivity. These brainwaves are consistent with relaxed states like meditation or daydreaming. They are known as the bridge between the conscious mind and the subconscious, which is incredibly important when we perform our visualisation to alter the level of our Fear.

BENEFITS

- Brain hemispheres become synchronised.
- Relaxed and a calmer mind.
- Increases receptiveness to casual and autosuggestion.
- Increased memory, focus and concentration.
- Decreased Anxiety, stress and depression.
- Reduction in pain.
- Decreased blood pressure.
- Increased motivation, energy and happiness.

THETA BRAINWAVES
(3.5 - 7 Hz deep relaxation and twilight state)

Theta brainwaves are the 'trance' like state where the mind feels as though it has gone to sleep although it can be conscious of what's happening around it. There can be a feeling of loss of time and prolonged daydreaming. Theta waves can aid in creativity, visualisation and hypnosis (direct suggestion) with this waveform also synchronising the brain hemispheres.

BENEFITS

- Deep relaxation.
- Improved memory.
- Increased sense of inner peace and emotional stability.
- Heightened intuition.
- Decreased mind chatter.
- Increased physic ability and spiritual connection.
- Improved sleep and mental fatigue.
- Reduced Anxiety and stress.

DELTA BRAINWAVES *(0.1 - 3.5 Hz Deep sleep)*

This is the slowest waveform that is produced when we are in a deep sleep which is incredibly beneficial for the body to recover, restore and repair. Delta is the place of most profound relaxation, healing and spiritual connection along with a connection to the subconscious mind.

BENEFITS

- Release anti-ageing hormones including melatonin.
- Release of Human growth hormone (HGH) that maintains the skin, bone density, joint repair and asset in healing.
- Creates an environment of advanced compassion, empathy and understanding for others.

GAMMA BRAINWAVES *(40 Hz or higher Zen mind mastery)*

Gamma waves are the quickest and most rapid form that can be detected. They are linked to having the ability to process information and large quantities in short periods. They are brainwaves that upgrade the brain's ability to perform and efficiently. This waveform is challenging to reach and generally achieved by Zen mastery.

BENEFITS

- Higher levels of intelligence.
- Higher compassion.
- Higher amounts of self-control.
- Higher levels of happiness.
- Increased awareness with the five senses.

So how do we meditate and which one is best?

I have always used mindfulness meditation because it has allowed me to realise what thoughts and images are produced when thinking about specific topics. It increased my awareness about my negative thought patterns and imagery that created a spiral of Fear and Anxiety that I wasn't aware of before meditating.

I was astounded at how the majority of my thoughts were geared so destructively and obviously to the detriment of my health.

Mindfulness meditation allows you to sit back and listen to the endless chatter that happens in the background. When your awareness of your thoughts is placed in front of you, it can be quite surprising and confronting but is also the starting point to understanding how your Anxiety is so ingrained in your thinking. It also gives you hope that it can be rewired, reprogrammed and redirected to more helpful, more fulfilling thoughts.

We can't recover until we understand what we are thinking, so we then can stop and process those thoughts effectively. This tool assists in our automatic thoughts which encompasses that first and second Thought Spiral of Anxiety that I talked about in Chapter 6.

When you start mindfulness meditation, the results come straight away because those maladaptive, negative thoughts and images that have been fuelling your Anxiety and Stress have been working overtime – putting you in this situation. Think of it as a discovery about yourself that you didn't know and now are ready to tackle with grit and determination.[23,24]

A SIMPLE GUIDE TO MINDFULNESS MEDITATION

1) Get yourself in a comfortable position that is upright and relaxed. This might be with legs crossed on a cushion, on a chair, or the edge of your bed with both feet firmly on the floor. You just want to make sure your back is straight, but you are relaxed. Rest your arms and hands on your thighs – either apart or cupped together.

2) Simply focus on your breathing (if that makes you anxious focus on an object, sound or sensation or use a word "mantra") – go in at your own pace, then slowly out again. This will bring you and your mind to the present moment.

3) Because you want to do this to help your Anxiety, you need to identify your thoughts. To do this, simply observe (like outside looking into your brain) the thought, and then let it go without reacting as you bring your mind back to the breath or whatever you're focusing on.

4) At this point, your mind will be like a cat on a hot tin roof, jumping around everywhere. This is when a lot of people stop and say meditation isn't for them. I want you to know; this is not only normal, but it's also totally fine. You just want to note what you're thinking and practise letting go without any reaction.

5) When starting, it's super hard to stay focused and relaxed. It takes practise. Start with five or 10 minutes and build up to 20 minutes overtime.

6) Remember, there is no right or wrong way to do this.

7) Try to find a regular time slot and a quiet place to do this. Also remember doing this for five minutes a day is much better than doing it for two hours on a Sunday. It's all about practise and training.

MINDFULNESS & MINDLESSNESS

There are two other tools you can use to create calmness in your mind and body. As you know now, your mind activates the stress felt in your body so if we can turn down the amplitude coming from the brain, then our body and mind will feel better.

The result of this is a reduction in our Anxiety and Fear. Sounds pretty good, I reckon.

MINDFULNESS (NOT MEDITATION STYLE)

Mindfulness is a buzz word these days that relates to being present, in the moment and essentially taking each moment step by step. Appreciating what is happening in any given second allows you to feel, smell, touch and taste that exact experience by purely focusing on the moment.

It's fantastic for reducing your stress and calming the old brain because it's only taking one job or experience on at a time without getting too hooked up on the past events or the Anxious person's favourite problem: future events.

It is harder than how it first appears, but with practise, it can become more of a habit and way of thinking.

All Anxious people are stressed and projecting into the future with the What Ifs and potential dangers that lay ahead. They're so good at this; they've developed this as our default mode for thinking.

When you first start practising mindfulness, it will seem almost impossible because you are not used to it. My advice is to take it step by step and remind yourself that change takes time, and with persistence, anything can be achieved.

So, how do we do this mindfulness stuff?

Here's a simple example that you can start with and explore along the way:

STEP 1) Focus on the current task you are doing at the moment, for example, cleaning your teeth.

STEP 2) Focus on putting the toothpaste on the toothbrush and observe the amount applied.

STEP 3) Focus on the taste of the toothpaste in your mouth and the areas you are brushing.

STEP 4) Focus on the clean feeling and the freshness achieved by cleaning your teeth.

STEP 5) Focus on spitting out the toothpaste and rinsing your mouth with water and the feeling it has (perhaps cold, warm or refreshing).

PUTTING IT INTO PERSPECTIVE

STEP 6) If you find yourself moving away from cleaning your teeth with other thoughts, simple, bring yourself back to the cleaning.

Wow! You have successfully practised mindfulness.

Have you noticed that all the steps ask you to focus on each aspect of your task?

The reason for this is that you are not getting caught up in a thousand other thoughts and concerns relating to the future or past. You are just present.

You will naturally wander off from time to time to other thoughts whilst applying your mindfulness strategy but just bring yourself back to the original task, nice and gently.

In essence, this mindfulness is a form of meditation that helps calm and relax your mind and reduce your Anxiety.

My favourite mindfulness exercise is one that I practise with my kids: eating a piece of chocolate. To watch them savour a small piece swirling it around their mouths, taking on the texture, taste and smell and the pure bliss of eating such an amazing thing is lovely to watch. Grab a piece and try it for yourself.

You will be blown away how long it takes to eat a small bit of chocolate when you're focusing on the moment. It lasts longer and is fully enjoyed. My kids average around two minutes per piece and have an absolute look of satisfaction when they're done.

It often gets me wondering why we rush things like eating our favourite foods because we should be doing the opposite: appreciating every little taste and flavour for as long as possible to embrace it.

It would make more sense to eat the foods we don't really like quickly.

Food for thought? *Pun intended!*

MINDLESSNESS (ONE OF MY TRICKS)

Mindlessness is different from mindfulness as we are trying to not engage in any thought. We are trying to limit thinking as much as possible but still producing the same results as mindfulness in reducing our stress and calming the mind and endless internal chatter.

Mindlessness is achieved by not engaging in any thoughts at all and just observing our surroundings. We can also do this with mindfulness, but the difference is there is limited thinking.

I know it sounds a bit weird and initially hard to do, but with practise, it can happen quickly.

One of the main benefits to mindlessness is that you are not linking up any emotion with any experience. You're just basically taking a break from thoughts and feelings, which is sometimes just what we all need.

This is how we achieve mindlessness:

STEP 1) Be present in the moment and just observe.

STEP 2) Observe your surroundings and sensations.

STEP 3) Reduce thinking or limit your thoughts to your surroundings and sensations by not buying into them.

STEP 4) Quieten your mind by moving away from deep thought and engagement.

STEP 5) If you find yourself thinking deeper, slowly bring yourself back to observing without judgment or analysis.

Mindlessness and mindfulness end up with the same result but work on two different pathways. They are little stepping stones to freedom from the Fear that eventually makes room for a big, fat surge of relaxation and happiness.

VISUALISATION - A PICTURE PAINTS A THOUSAND WORDS

Visualisation is also a simple tool that has been used for long periods and for various reasons to help us.

It is so powerful in helping Anxiety as it helps integrate the conscious mind into the subconscious mind (amygdala) where the Fear Centre lives, fuelling the power of Anxiety.

Your thoughts have a massive impact on Fear, Stress and Anxiety, and through the practise of positive visualisation, it can change the subconscious's idea of what's Fearful and stressful and what's not.

It also helps the subconscious mind 'turn down' its overzealous Fear response, which we all know is super ready to explode at any given time. This hyper-arousal can be tamed.

How often do you hear people say to you, I can see you in that role, or I can picture you doing well in that situation?

That's because we are always using imagery in our minds to create networks and wiring for our brains. Have you heard someone say: if I can see you do that task physically, then I would remember how to do it"? This is what we do all the time without even realising it.

It is often used by athletes to enhance their performances and other people who are lucky enough to have discovered it to improve their mental clarity and psychological desires.

Meditation is helping with our thoughts, and visualisation helps with our imagery.

There are two methods of visualisation you can try.

The first is the PROCESS METHOD.

This little method is a ripper that requires you to focus on the process or technique in a particular performance and rely on getting the desired result. This works by reducing your Anxiety or stress about the result or outcome, and instead just taking one step at a time to get to the end. This helps to reduce your overall Fear.

Let's look at an example. Say you're playing a game of football (Australian Rules) and are required to kick a goal from the 50-metre line to score after the siren. Suppose you spend your time focusing on your technique and process, things like hand placement on the ball, correct angle towards the goals, the right amount of effort to kick the ball into the air and the middle of the goals. In that case, there is little time to stress and get nervous about the outcome (which is getting the goal). Providing you practise your process, there is less interference from your Anxiety and to perform under pressure.

The second is the RESULT METHOD.

The second method is also excellent, but this time it concentrates on purely focusing or visualising the result or outcome wanted.

If I use the same example as above in regards to the football game, I focus on kicking that ball through the goals over the line. I watch it leave my hand and hit the line. I rely on the fact that my technique is sound and that my inner voice is that of confidence. I am totally convinced that the kick will make it and I block out all the other outside noise like the crowd, and the pressure to kick the goal.

Both methods rely on plenty of practise and training before you become confident at using them. Either way, they aim to reduce your Fear and Anxiety or inability to perform under pressure (I know, helpful stuff. This bloke is a genius!)

The beauty with visualisation is that it is easy to do, potent and I have also found it to act fast.

I first started using visualisation because it became apparent to me when I was meditating that I often conjured up images in my head of adverse outcomes when I was thinking about my Anxiety.

Then I got to thinking about how my mind worked and realised why visualisation is so powerful. I also realised that I continuously use visualisation all the time, in my day to day living, without even knowing it. For example, let's say I need to get a new pair of pants at the shopping centre and I visualise what type of pant I want: the colour, style and even the price. I also visualise driving there and where I would park. This is something we do all the time but don't pay a lot of attention to it.

I then discovered that when I am Anxious or in a Panic, I visualise without realising how powerful it is. Unfortunately, it's often from a negative aspect with the Worst Case Scenario playing images in my head that creates a little circuit of Fear and stress. This makes things so much worse and without me genuinely understanding or having the ability to identify its destructive power, it's an ongoing cycle of negative feelings.

When I am visualising, try and be as realistic as possible with things like smells, the energy around you, sounds and body sensations. This will make it more believable to your brain.

Let's say I was asked to be the MC (Master of Ceremonies) at a wedding. What I would do is visualise the whole speech going poorly and embarrassing myself. I can see how stupid or weak the speech was in my mind's eye, and it creates such negative images that it produces so much more Fear and Anxiety and a horrible feeling of dread.

Then, the usual cascade or spiralling of Anxiety kicks in, and between thoughts and images, it's almost impossible to get off the roundabout.

Of course, when the actual event took place, there was little confidence, and high levels of stress and that make the job even harder to do than if you were feeling calm and confident.

We then go ahead and add that to the memory bank for future public speaking occasions, and the cycle continues. By recognising and acknowledging this, we can help rectify the problem.

I adopt three strategies with my visualisation: Worst-Case Scenario, Realistic Scenario and Positive Scenario. The Worst-Case Scenario allows me to feel the sensations and emotions quite strongly, and that enables me to become comfortable with them. (Discussed in chapter 6) Eventually, all the negativity subsides at even the worst case. This can take time, but eventually, it works.

NEGATIVE IMAGE

LOOKING AND FEELING EMBARRASED

POSITIVE IMAGE

I HAVE NAILED IT! I FEEL AMAZING

The second stage of visualisation is a Realistic Scenario where, although not perfect, promotes uncomfortable sensations and emotions but certainly more tolerable. This allows me to not set higher than required expectations on myself and aids significantly in depressing my Anxiety.

The third scenario of visualisation is a Positive Scenario, and it's flooded with pleasant emotions and sensations, which then help the subconscious rewire to a positive bias vs negative.

A few things happen with these approaches. Firstly, I have desensitised the Fear through negative imagery, become realistic about my actual performance and then started rewiring the circuitry to positive bias.

What I've found is that when the thoughts arise about being an MC (if we revisit that earlier example) instead of the circuitry going directly to a cynical and Anxious spiral of emotions and sensations, the opposite starts happening. I feel more pleasant sensations and emotion, along with realistic thoughts and beliefs. It takes time, but with dedication, it is a potent tool.

Let's take the same situation and apply a positive or more realistic outcome of events and images:

I am asked to be the MC at a wedding. I understand the power of visualisation and move from negative imagery process and understand the effects of positive or realistic imagery.

I look into my mind's eye and see me standing in front of all these people, being viewed as slightly nervous for making some errors along the way. Although not incredible, I give a reliable performance which reflects a realistic outcome.

I often adopt a realistic outcome first in my visualisation. I then move towards positive imagery – in this instance, it might be calm and relaxed, sounding articulate or funny, being comfortable and embracing the moment.

What this does is stop the negative cycle of Fear and Anxiety and helps produce positive and helpful thought processes. When the wedding happens, you have spent so much time imagining a realistic or positive result; it generally happens the way you have viewed it. It's like a type of mental training.

I was amazed at how I always looked at things so negatively and how it seemed to be the default system my mind would go into – I would still play pictures of disaster and Fear.

So that you know, it's perfectly normal not to have a positive default system with our thoughts. If we are in Fear or on edge, then our chances of surviving are a lot higher.

However, we can override this evolutionary protector in most situations because most situations we face are not life-threatening and nothing to be Fearful of.

Now that I have a good understanding of how visualisation works and its power, I have become very disciplined at being aware of my thoughts or images. As soon as they become negative, I flip the images from negative to realistic and then positive.

Even if it doesn't turn out exactly the way you pictured it, it at least stops the ever-evolving cycle of Fear, and that's a great thing. That's why visualisation is an essential cog in the wheel to gaining freedom from your suffering. [21]

MORE PRACTISE PLEASE

To help strengthen the wiring and power of visualisation, there are a couple of things you can do to enhance its effectiveness.

Firstly, you can practise it anytime and anywhere for short little mini bursts of visualisation whilst doing any activity. You know, imagining positive and helpful images at the traffic lights, in the shopping centre, walking to school or riding your bike.

It's a replacement for the negative or Anxious ones in 10, 20 or 30-second bursts at regular intervals.

This is exactly what Anxiety can do to us all the time. I say: "Stuff you, Fear, we are going to do this my way!"

This just allows you to become tuned in with your thoughts and images and become disciplined to them. It also just plugs away at the subconscious, replacing negative to realistic and positive. Fantastic stuff! I do it all the time.

PUTTING IT INTO PERSPECTIVE

The second way to speed up integrating your conscious mind to the subconscious is by taking some time out to focus on what you want to achieve.

Say you want to be confident and calm in dealing and coping with a petrifying episode or Panic Attack whilst on an upcoming plane ride:

STEP 1) Get comfortable in a quiet place and start to relax your body.

STEP 2) You can do this by following the breath in/out or working through your body, relaxing all the muscles from head to toe. It doesn't matter what you do as long as you can relax your mind and body as best you can. We are aiming to achieve that Alpha state of brainwaves and that requires settling of your mind.

STEP 3) Once you feel that you are comfortable and relaxed, start to visualise what you hope for or want to achieve. In this case, it's feeling confident, calm and able to cope in the event of having a Panic Attack on the plane.

In our anxious, non-educated minds, we would imagine lots of Fear while in the seat of the plane, an image of wanting to get off the plane and needing someone to help me. Additionally, pictures of me embarrassing myself and making a scene losing control and, of course, having this huge, life-threatening episode that scares me so severely. In my visualisation practise, I simply envisage the opposite.

I start imagining I'm on the plane and am currently experiencing a Panic Attack. Still, unlike the previous example, I am sitting in the seat, feeling confident that I am in control, not needing to get off the plane quickly or embarrassing myself.

I also imagine that Panic Attack's pass quickly with a strong sense of resolution and a decreased feeling of Fear.

It's not the most significant and worst event of my life. I imagine small things like the smell of the plane, or the perfume of the lady sitting next to me, the temperature in the cabin and the noises from various people chatting throughout the nearby seats.

You're trying to visualise the event as if it's happening now and in as much reality as possible.

I continue to do this for 5-10 mins and slowly bring myself, when ready, to a pleasant relaxed state and then continue with my day.

This needs to be done every day to be effective and powerful. It does not have the same impact if done occasionally once or twice a week.

However, you may find that the more you do it, the quicker the results, and that will encourage you to do it often.

You can do this skill for anything in your life: sport, work or relationships. The concept is still the same, and that's projecting positive, helpful images instead of negative ones. Go right ahead and start right away, trust me, you will love it!

IS YOUR GLASS HALF FULL, OR HALF EMPTY?

I want you to think about a time when you were anxious.

What images did you see in your mind? Were they positive? Or negative?

I want to bet they usually are always negative and full of Fear. They're also generally in the future, and this is what is creating that spiral of Anxiety and Fear.

However, what if we changed those images to positive or helpful ones? Doing this not only leaves you less stressed but also stops the Anxiety and Fear cycle.

PUTTING IT INTO PERSPECTIVE

It's important to understand that when we project into the future, it's an illusion or a make-believe story because it hasn't happened yet Anxiety sufferers tend always to picture Fearful images, which then compound into negative thoughts and constant stress and Anxiety.

So why do it?

You have a choice. You always have a 50/50 decision as to how to view things.

I choose positive or helpful images because the knock-on effects are enormous. Even if your positive projection doesn't become a reality, it will have stopped significant stress and Fear.

My glass is half full thanks.

IS YOUR GLASS HALF FULL OR HALF EMPTY?

> "IF WE HAVE NO CONTROL
> OF THE SITUATION
> AND IT DISTRESSES YOU,
> THEN CHANGE HOW YOU SEE IT
> AND WATCH THE DISTRESS
> MELT AWAY."
>
> — CHRIS BREEN

CHAPTER 10

RETRAIN YOUR BRAIN

Well, that's all well and good, you're saying to me now you've read that last chapter. But I can't help it! That's just how my brain works.

It's true; some people are more wired towards positivity than negativity. Perhaps you've spent your life surrounded by people who are just naturally quite happy with their lot, which makes you feel like your everyone else's Tigger.

The fact is though, our minds can be tricked and changed, and there's plenty of ways that, although we might not get you to Tigger status, you could at least make it to a Winnie The Pooh mindset!

THE SUBCONSCIOUS MIND

The subconscious mind's only function is to do precisely what you tell it to do: for better or for worse, it remembers everything and keeps every memory you will ever have. *(Pretty cool, hey!)* It makes up approximately 80—90% of your brain, depending on what literature you read.

The thing is, the subconscious mind doesn't know the difference between what is real and what is imagined.

It's not creative and doesn't get the jokes you tell it (which is a shame, because I'm pretty funny!).

Your conscious mind is comprised of the remaining 10 – 20% of your brain and is tasked with interacting in the physical life.

Your conscious mind has no memory at all (that's the subconscious mind's job). Instead, the conscious mind is responsible for working out information through your five senses (sight, sound, smell, touch and taste) and making decisions based on what is relevant to you.

The job of the subconscious is to obey your commands and bring them into the physical world, which is called manifestation.

Our thoughts are like an energy that the subconscious mind converts into physical energy.

To put it another way, whatever your consciousness plants are exactly what will grow in the subconscious.

Your subconscious mind is continually being programmed and conditioned through thoughts, habits and beliefs.

Given this, it's easy to see how important our thoughts are in generating how we feel and what drives us.

It's also easy to understand that we can change how we feel physically by repeated positive thoughts, affirmations and imagery.

If you look at your current life, circumstances and state of affairs, it is merely a mirror of reflected thoughts patterns. Therefore, if you don't like the now or your current situation, change your thought patterns and watch the incredible change develop and prosper.

So, if we know positivity is the key, how do we get that message through to our subconscious? [25]

ACTIVATING THE SUBCONSCIOUS

First, we need to do a little house cleaning and identify all the negativity in our lives. How we think via thought patterns, how we see our world (imagery) needs to be adapted to more helpful positive beliefs instead of negative ones.

This may mean flushing out negative people or influences in your life because as we are starting to realise, negativity breeds more negatively, and the spiral continues to grow and grow. We can often begin taking on their thoughts and beliefs, which weirdly enough become our own.

Once we have done our house cleaning, it's time to activate that subconscious energy generator into more positive energy.

Now you may have had some practise identifying your negative thoughts, patterns and beliefs with meditation and visualisation, we need to ramp up spying on our thoughts like a parent watching a toddler near a pool.

The sooner we can identify our thoughts and correct them if necessary, the quicker our advancement and success will come. Old negative thoughts (which is negative energy) will be replaced and **bang** – it can help change the body's energy and vibe, and a sense of lightness starts to appear as your not loaded up with negatively.

It can be challenging to monitor all our thoughts all the time. After all, we can have up to 70,000 thoughts per day or 35-50 per minute. (27) That would be exhausting. Another way to help with the process of converting negative into positive is through how we feel.

If we are feeling flat, tired, cynical or frustrated, take a moment and stop! Ask yourself what you're thinking right now and then address the thought patterns.

The more you practise, the easier it gets, and after a while, you won't have to monitor your thoughts as closely. They will eventually be trained to be of more positive than negative, but the easiest way to check it is always through how you're feeling.

WHAT DO YOU WANT?

Have you ever noticed that happy people think and talk about what they want, where unhappy people think and talk about what they don't want?

Our thoughts so often determine our feelings.

One great way to activate your subconscious is by goal setting. The secret to achieving what you want or desire is first knowing what you want or desire.

What better way than doing that then by writing down a very clear goal in every detail. This will tell the subconscious precisely what you want and this, in turn, will help manifest it.

Say you want a new bike. Try writing down the exact brand, size, dimensions, colour... rather than just a writing 'new bike', give as much detail as possible.

This added information helps you adopt a game plan to achieve that goal. Next, you need to break this plan down into smaller steps or short-term strategies. For our bike, it might be breaking down how much per week you need to put aside to afford, and how many weeks are realistic to make that happen.

It's easier to convince the mind that you're getting there as every success breeds confidence and belief and that it is possible. The more small steps you take and conquer along the way produce positivity and effective outcomes when aiming for your goal.

It would be a little challenging to aim straight for the top in one go, and you may find it challenging to achieve your goal due to the inability to see the final result.

Next, you need to list everything that you will need to do actually to get the goal achieved. For our bike, this might be looking at places where that particular bike is sold and looking at how long it might take you to save money to buy it.

This will help strengthen your desires and beliefs.

I find that I ask myself what I can do today to work towards my goal. There is no rocket science here, just small steps that have a powerful impact. Some days the actions might be small and almost meaningless, whilst other days may be full of vigour, excitement and productivity.

Once you're up and running, it's essential to review your progress. This helps keep you focused on reaching your goal.

SPEAK NICELY PLEASE

Isn't it interesting how we often say things to ourselves that we would never, ever say to a good friend or loved one?

You may think 'positive affirmations' are a load of crap and a waste of time, but auto-suggestion and self-talk fast track the training of your subconscious.

I am tipping, with all your Anxiety, that you've not said a lot of nice, helpful positive things to yourself for a long, long time. Maybe it's time for a change.

This is a potent and easy tool to use, and it's incredibly useful.

It is simply a matter of deliberately talking to yourself in a helpful, positive manner – feeding the subconscious some good stuff and directing it into the place you want to be: turning your body into a beautiful bundle of energy with sincere belief and spirit.

You can write down your affirmations (emotional support or encouragement) and read them regularly, or speak positive self-talk, out loud, on any topic you wish!

Here are some simple examples:

"*I am*" ready to achieve success.

"*I am*" worthy of love.

"*I am*" a beacon for abundance in my life.

"*I am*" a kind person who attracts happiness.

"*I am*" ready to accept opportunities that are golden for me.

"*I am*" worthy of having space to live, breathe, relax and entertain.

I use a simple starting point with my affirmations with the words "**I am**" at the start of the sentence. Then, the words that follow "**I am**" are what I want to follow me.

Like "**I am**" worthy of love and happiness. It's the love and joy I want to attract and follow me.

You can google thousands of great affirmations or make up your own.

They are a fantastic replacement to the negative affirmations we often say.

"**I am**" useless, "**I am**" never going to succeed, and "**I am**" not enough will never help you. (28)

SEE IT & BELIEVE IT

Vision boards are a series of actual pictures of the goals you want to achieve. The images can be accessed from anywhere: newspapers, the internet, magazines, books or drawings. It does not affect where they are sourced. If you don't want to cut things out, have a look at an online board, you can check in on regularly – like Pinterest.

They work on the subconscious through imagery on something real and hard copy versus visualisation, which is in your head.

As I mentioned earlier, the subconscious can't differentiate between real or imagined, so this practise is useful because it can demonstrate your goals in a literal way, very specifically. Looking at our earlier bike example, you might find a picture of the bike you want (colour, size, brand etc), and pictures of people happily riding bikes in the kind of places you'd like to ride yours someday.

You can place as many pictures as you like on the board and place the board in a spot that you can frequently see, reminding and transferring the thoughts and images to the subconscious.

It is thought that the subconscious is 30,000 times more powerful than the conscious mind. It is our source of energy, and if harnessed and trained appropriately, it can deliver some fantastic result to oneself and positively affect our general wellbeing and physical and mental health.

The exciting thing is that it isn't rocket science and difficult to do. You need to be shown, educated and enthused (and give it a go!). The rest is nothing but bliss and fulfilment. [26]

WIRED FOR EMOTION

We are learning more every day at uncovering how our brains work, and science has started to establish which aspects of our brain are involved in emotions, and what gets triggered during these emotions.

The prefrontal cortex, which is found in the front of the brain, helps us think (we discussed this earlier in Chapter 3) and it also affects our emotions.

Scientists have discovered that if the left prefrontal cortex is activated regularly, you are more relaxed, happy and satisfied. Pretty cool, hey!

On the other hand, if the right prefrontal cortex is predominantly active, you are more stressed, depressed, unhappy and Anxious. Safe to say this is the area that is activated for us Anxiety sufferers.

Additionally, research has discovered that people who are depressed or Anxious appear to have an underactive left prefrontal cortex.

This makes the problem twofold and hits your emotions twice as hard because there is not a lot of positive, happy feelings being generated from the left side.

Scientists also suspect that when the Amygdala fires up the Fear Centre, it actually can shut down the left side of the prefrontal cortex.

This can explain why we are flooded with Fear that leads to helplessness and despair, and there's not a lot of happiness going on.

We've also discovered that severe emotional stress over a long period, can cause damage to the brain, it's cell's and structure, along with connections between brain cells.

Stressful events can flood the brain with cortisol. Low doses alert us and organise our behaviour, so we make sure we protect ourselves. However, large amounts of cortisol can make us feel stressed out, inattentive, disorganised, depressed and Anxious as mentioned earlier in the book.

Bloody hell, right? So some science tells us the wiring is predominantly swinging to the right side of the prefrontal cortex, creating heaps of Fear and stress whilst at the same time, reducing our ability to be happy and relaxed.

That is a tough pill to swallow, but of course, there is a reason why I am telling you this. Yep, I have a little exercise you can do to swing the wiring back to the left side of the prefrontal cortex. Woo hoo!
(13,29,37,38)

TRAINING THE LEFT PREFRONTAL CORTEX

We can activate the left prefrontal cortex through the skill of visualisation. Believe it or not, we can learn to be happy by visualising our two buddies in the brain called the Amygdala. Yep, those are the little dudes that activate our Fear (see Chapter 3 for a refresher).

Picture the two Amygdala in your mind (I've given you a cracking little image to help you out – remember they're about the size and shape of an almond and are located on either side of the head between the eye and the ear – about an inch inside).[21]

Now, visualise a switch on each one with the click back position turning on the Fear feelings, and the forward click position turning on feelings of pleasure.

Picture yourself purposely clicking this switch forward.

Do this exercise for 5-10 minutes aiming at keeping the switch flicked to 'on' for feelings of happiness and pleasure.

THE SWITCH

Another tool you can use to stimulate lighter and happier feelings is by visualising yourself tickling each Amygdala with a feather.

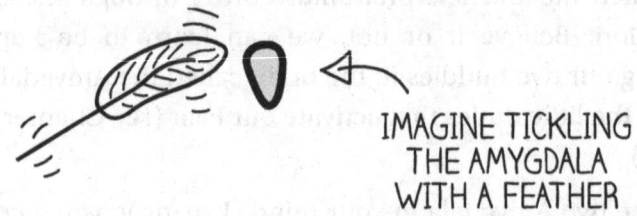

IMAGINE TICKLING THE AMYGDALA WITH A FEATHER

You can directly elevate your mood through behavioural changes like laughter, or physical exercise, or you can lift it through mental stimulation with these amygdala exercises. So, get out your feathers and switches and let 'em rip.

These exercises have been shown to stimulate the connections between the limbic (Fear) part of the brain, and the more evolved left side of the prefrontal cortex to develop habits of happier thought and feelings. That's exactly what we want, more left side than the right.

Many people could learn to be happy by regularly repeating thought and visualisation practises like these. It's a matter of reprogramming happiness vs pain.

Studies are now demonstrating that if we use our ability to see things in a lighter, happier or positive way, it can reframe the event to decrease the limbic (Fearful) response. That's why I am always trying to get you to smile with all the exercises we have discussed – whether it's using L.E.T.G.O.E., 5 D'S, or FEEL GOOD in dealing with your Panic Attacks or Anxiety.

A SMALL REWIRING JOB

Are you starting to see now that our wiring and pathways can be altered? This begs the question: can we repair or reverse damage to the neural circuitry without using drugs?

Well, yes. We can! This is called NEUROPLASTICITY!

This idea would have been laughed at not so long ago because scientists believed the brain was a very inflexible organ. We now know the brain is malleable (adaptable) – even more so in our early years of life but also as we get older (so there's still hope for me).

Our brain is continually changing and rewiring – both physically and functionally. It was often thought that the older, adult brain is somewhat set in stone and only deteriorates as we get older. However, it turns out that the brain is continually changing with cells, both dying and being reborn all the time.

The notion of plasticity within the brain is evolving incredibly, making it possible to relearn and reprogram even as we get older. This is a great thing to have been discovered.

We know this because of improved technology that improves our ability to see the brain changing via a diagnostic machine called Magnetic Resonance Imaging (M.R.I.) and more specifically, functional M.R.I. (fMRI).

That's all very interesting, Chris, but what's all that got to do with me and my Anxiety?

Well, with the right conditions and approaches, we can relearn and program our Anxious circuitry to a calmer and happier one. One that brings back our ability to live in harmony and fulfilment once again. Just like some of the tools we used activating the left prefrontal cortex tickling the Amygdala.

It isn't full of overwhelming, hardcore science or powerful drugs, rather smart and informed techniques and approaches.

The critical point here is that we've developed a world of Fear and stress that has taken control. We are now taking back the power and directing things more positively.

Here are some tips on how we go about reprogramming for the greatest success:

Tip 1) The brain wants complete focus, attention and involvement to generate neurochemicals that aid in rewiring (that's why visualisation is so powerful).

Tip 2) Practise, Practise, Practise will help the connections of neurones firing together. Remember that this creates strength in the connections. Think about playing an instrument like the guitar or piano over and over again and how certain cords or notes only strengthens the connections of your fingers and the correct placement.

This is relevant to both negative and positive thoughts regarding our Anxiety. The more something is practised, the stronger it becomes: either good or bad.

Tip 3) The brain likes to predict what happens next by connecting neurones from particular moments that occur one after another. This helps the prediction of future events (again, visualisation of you overcoming your Anxiety in a story helps immensely with the prediction phase).

Tip 4) The brain takes a while to adjust and change its wiring entirely. It will only do this if the experience is worthwhile, and the outcome has meaning, whether good or bad. It also remembers the good and bad attempts at slowly making adjustments. Visualising, or imagining good or fun things can help this process.

Tip 5) You can rewire purely through mental rehearsal as well as physical exposure (just like I mentioned earlier with sports people – it's proven that visualisation of a particular event and rehearsal is as effective as actually doing it).

Tip 6) The brain wiring can strengthen new connections or skills and weaken connections that are used during that precise moment. For example, if it is learning new non-Anxious neuronal connections in a particular situation, then the Anxious old connections are getting weaker.

Tip 7) The brain has a 'use it or lose' it mentality. The more something is used, the better off it will be in regards to strength. In other words, if it's placed out the back of the brain, then it becomes not important and loses all power and status.

This my friends is why practise is so important. The more something is done, the stronger it gets. [30,31,32]

THE CHEMICALS IN OUR BRAINS

There is a field of science called **Psychoneuroimmunology** that studies the effects of how every thought produces a chemical reaction in the brain that releases chemicals in the body. One of these releases is called a Neuropeptide (nerve proteins).

Now, these little suckers are pretty cool. Neuropeptides are chemicals that help cells communicate with each other, connecting our mind and body – and of course, emotions. They are produced in the brain, and the body allowing us to feel good and also help regulate our metabolism.

We know that our thoughts can create an emotion that, in turn, can change our physical health, especially if the thoughts and emotions are of a negative and unhelpful perspective.

When we have a negative thought, it produces a negative feeling and that then negatively affects our nervous system.

The neuropeptides help the communication between mind and body with the nervous system continually informing each other of the current situation. An example of this is when our emotional wellbeing is out of whack; neuropeptides assist in generating those annoying physical symptoms in the body.

A Neuropeptide has a certain emotion that is affiliated with it, so if a particular emotion is experienced, then that neuropeptide will be apparent.

This is the reason why we can get physical symptoms or illness through negative or unhelpful thinking – there is a scientific reason why this happens.

This then allows us to choose which way we want to think and now understand that a helpful, more positive way of thinking helps in reducing illness in the body versus thoughts of negativity.

Our body reacts better to thoughts and feelings of happy, pleasant emotions, and this is almost like a particular 'medicine' for good health and wellbeing.

This may also help to explain why bottling up or suppressing our emotions can harm our physical health, creating illness.

If your negative thoughts aren't dealt with, they still get recalled and remembered via the subconscious mind, and they can often remind the person through illness as an alert that things need to be addressed.

With this knowledge, we now know that our thoughts have an effect on our emotions and, in turn, affect our physical wellbeing.

Can I give you any more reason to start changing your thoughts?

An example of a Neuropeptide is Neuropeptide Y (N.P.Y.). This little gem is excellent for Anxiety sufferers because it's our natural tranquilliser that reduces Anxiety. It also helps with appetite, learning and memory. It tries to help out the 'thinking part of our brain (prefrontal cortex) by keeping it active for longer, allowing us to make better decisions. Especially during high stress.

There have been studies during special forces training that has found these guys have naturally higher levels of N.P.Y. compared to regular troops, allowing them to be calmer and think clearer. It's thought that training your brain via visualisation may help increase the production of N.P.Y. and therefore increase its calming effects. (34,35)

USE IT OR LOSE IT

We are creatures that have this fantastic brain, something that processes information and enables us to think and create beautiful things.

Because our brains gather so much information, it sometimes finds it difficult to have space to keep all the data for use. Therefore, it utilises a filing-type system and mostly weeds out information that isn't used much and either store it in a long-forgotten file, or eradicates it.

In some ways, this is what we are trying to achieve in regards to our Fear and Anxiety. We want to train our brain, over time, to not create Fear (or at least minimise it) in the first place by making it almost unimportant – becoming a file that doesn't need to be used regularly.

This, in turn, creates a sense of what you don't use, you lose... as our Fear loses its power and strength, eventually making it redundant.

NEURONS THAT FIRE TOGETHER, WIRE TOGETHER

On the flip side to 'what you don't use, you lose' is the opposite: neurons that fire together, wire together. This relates to the fact that the more something is utilised similarly, then a natural circuit is created with our wiring. If used often enough, it becomes quite engrained in our processing.

It's a bit like sheep following the same track and wearing a path into the ground, making it more noticeable and more substantial. If they continue to walk on the same path, it will never alter.

In regards to Anxiety and Fear, if the same patterns of behaviour and thoughts towards a particular trigger or stimulus are regularly activated then that circuitry is thicker and more robust, making it even harder to break and stop the spiral.

The brain works on getting rid of old neurons that aren't firing together, which is called synaptic pruning. There are cells called microglial that play this role.

The best way to get neurons firing together is to make it a regular practise to think differently, along with visualisation of thoughts and actions. I think you're starting to see what needs to happen to create a new you.

Let's say you're always Anxious about dogs, and it creates a Fear response in your body. This starts to develop a circuit of thought: Fear response- thought – Fear response, etc. that grows in power and strength.

Even if it started with one particular dog in a specific situation then over time, if not corrected, seems to spread like wildfire to different dogs and other cases involving dogs.

It can become so ingrained that you feel helpless about the circuitry of power, and it's almost impossible to correct. Those neurones that fire together and wire together become so familiar that it can feel like the norm.

This can happen in any situation of trigger that causes Anxiety and Fear.

This is why it's so important to identify our thoughts, correct them, observe our bodies responses without creating a Fear or Anxiety attachment to the Fear Centre.

The L.E.T.G.O.E., 5 D'S or F.E.E.L G.O.O.D strategies (in Chapter 7) stop the neurones firing together, thus halting the wiring process and of course the circuit of Fear.

We can rewire the already wired for a more favourable result in any situation with patience and practise. [31]

BAD HABITS

They say it can take up to six weeks to break a bad habit and create a more healthy or happy one.

If we can appreciate this time frame, then it will help understand that it takes time and discipline to change our neurones and thought processes that have been wired together and relate to Fear.

When on the road to recovery, you may have addressed all the appropriate strategies, began to believe that your Anxiety and Fear is just a big fat illusion (or total bullshit). However, you still can't work out why the hell you're still having periods of setbacks and old responses.

That's because it takes time for the process to rewire to the new, improved and healthier version. Change takes time, and so does your ability to break bad habits in the form of Anxiety and poor thought processes.

Understanding this concept alone can ironically help you become less anxious about the fact that it's taking a long time to feel better, and less Fearful even though you have taken control of your Fear. Be patient peeps. Remember, change takes time. [39,40]

> "YOU WILL NEVER SPEAK TO ANYONE MORE THAN YOU SPEAK TO YOURSELF IN YOUR HEAD, BE KIND TO YOURSELF."
>
> UNKNOWN AUTHOR

CHAPTER 11

DRIVERS OF ANXIETY

Something that drives people suffering from Anxiety crazy is the frustration of 'why'. Why me? Why does MY brain work this way, and no one else's seems to?

Some of this can be genetic and simple dumb luck, but sometimes our Anxiety and Fear can be driven by our beliefs and our values. This might be in the way we've been raised, or in how situations and events have built up over time and become part of our personal story.

When we are looking at all this positive self-talk, setting goals and visualising our fantastic future that is free of Anxiety and Fear, we've got to recognise and get past the demands that we insist upon before we're able to move forward.

DEMAND FOR FLEXIBILITY, CONTROL AND CERTAINTY

Most of us who suffer from Anxiety and Panic become, over time, very inflexible and controlling with our thoughts, actions and external environment – often this happens with a lot of conscious thought.

The reason for this is because our modern world is full of (triggers) Fear and Anxiety. As we often concern ourselves with the outcome of particular events (whether that be the result of a performance, social interaction or general Anxiety or Panic), we want to be able to control them as best as possible to reduce our suffering.

It makes sense if you think about it: if the environment or specific triggers can be controlled, then so can our level of Anxiety and Panic. The world becomes safer to us; we feel a sense of power over the Anxiety and try to lead a somewhat normal existence. This is fine to want this and achieve it if you can. We generally have less stress and pressure if we can control and organise things in our lives to maintain balance. It's in our DNA to achieve control and have some sort of plan in place.

However, what if I were to tell you that our need to control things and have limited flexibility can fuel our Anxiety. It can disempower our ability to recover and live in everyday existence, the very life we are so desperate to lead.

We require a constant understanding of every outcome. However, our whole life and world are full of unknowns and inability to control anything externally. Therefore, with this realisation and learning, how can we possibly try and control it.

We can't control the environment; when someone gets sick; when we get sick; what others think of us; other people's opinion; or even catastrophising events like earthquakes, storms or the death of loved ones.

If we can appreciate that, then why try and control our worlds? It simply sets us up for failure, heartache and Anxiety because it shouldn't be this way or that. A feeling of 'I can't control this situation' actually fuels the one thing we are trying to stop: Fear!

We need to shift perspective and appreciate that everything changes from moment to moment. By being flexible, and not controlling, allows us to be less caught up in the spiral of Anxiety and basically take each event, moment or experience on merit and deal with it individually each time.

I am guilty of trying to control my external environment as much as possible to reduce any potential threat. Sure, it worked from time to time, but sucked a lot of energy from me and also produced a higher level of Anxiety and stress when I realised I couldn't control it.

When I first started to suffer severe Panic attacks on the Tube whilst living in London, I would often try and get on a carriage with only a few people, so there was plenty of room. I'd wait for peak hour to subside to reduce delays or being stuck underground with the busy commute.

This worked sometimes but trying to control three million commuters per day on a public train system was bound to prove futile. When the train become packed and delayed, I would feel a lack of control over the situation, and it would drive up my Anxiety tenfold, often leading to Panic.

My external environment was chaotic, and I was powerless. Admittedly, back then, I had zero intervention or any sort of strategy in dealing with my Panic.

Now that I have both an understanding and strategy, I've learnt to accept whatever comes my way and deal with it – no more trying to control the non-controllable.

The same goes being flexible. How often do plans change, or external factors shift without warning?

By being flexible, we have the freedom to take on anything that comes our way, on its own merits, and deal with it then and there. Being flexible also reduces our stress levels, which we know can increase the stress levels in the first place. I once was given a nice bit of advice from my grandmother, Mona, who would always talk about trees.

She would say that a tree that is stiff and inflexible will always snap and break in a storm whereas a tree with trunk and branches that are flexible stays strong and able to withstand any storm. *Thanks, Nan!*

DEMAND FOR PERFECTION

Perfection or trying to be perfect is Anxiety and Panic's best buddy. It loves the person with a mind that needs to be perfect because it's like food for the condition.

The reality with perfection is that it's impossible to be perfect. Even if you come close with one thing (in who's mind?), then the probability of making something else perfect becomes even more challenging or difficult to obtain.

This, in turn, drives up your stress and activates our body, making it hyper-aroused and ready to act. This state of stress – trying to achieve the impossible all the time – has our bodies and minds on the edge and can contribute to exacerbating our Anxiety.

We would all love to be perfect. To look fabulous, present amazing things at work, be amazing friends and family members, be exceptional at our sporting achievements but, in reality, there are always going to be times when we just suck. Embrace being Mr or Ms Average at times. Appreciate that perfection can't happen all the time and you might have to be just like the rest of us: average but contented.

How do we break down the perfection mindset and relax a little? I found that I work on an 80/20 cut. That is 80% awesome and 20% as best as I can.

Sometimes it is purely a time constraint thing where I run out of time and have to make do with the product I have and the effort I've put in.

This still allows me to feel proud of what I have achieved but takes off the stress and pressure of being perfect. Others may prefer a 70/30 cut or some may have to start at 90/10 cut and work down to 80/20 before they become comfortable.

The realisation that the 80/20 cut is still just as productive and plausible in any given situation and will aid in reducing your stress and Anxiety to more manageable levels. Trust me!

Of course, I'm pretty perfect in the looks department. It's a straight 100% there. I'm sure everyone agrees. *Lol!*

DEMAND FOR APPROVAL AND JUDGEMENT

Good old approval and judgment, hey! We all want to be loved and liked and, of course, approved. We are hardwired to feel a sense of community and wanting to be part of a group, and this comes with a need to be wanted.

In most cases, we are loved, accepted and approved by the people we love, respect and care about. The problem is the people we don't get that from, or when we don't feel approved by anyone no matter how hard we try. It can often feel as though we are always being judged and often unfairly.

We know Anxiety is all about increasing stress and pressure in our lives, thus ramping up the Anxiety/Panic spiral, putting us in a knifes edge ready to flick off at any moment.

The constant Fear and feeling of not being approved, or judged, for some people can be quite overwhelming and drives them to the nth degree to find that satisfaction. Sometimes they will stop at very little to achieve it.

The desire is fair and reasonable considering we have a level of hardwiring going on that is designed to help us procreate and live in groups, or communities, imperative for our survival.

In healthy levels, this can be advantageous as it can govern our behaviour, actions and treatment of others in the hope of acceptance.

The problem comes when our self-esteem is so low; our actions exceed our energy and stress levels. This puts us at constant risk of inflaming the Anxiety.

It can be difficult if the people around you are inflexible or harsh, but it will still always start with you, not outsiders.

Once you learn to love yourself, than being loved by others can often follow. How do you expect others to love or approve of you when you don't approve of yourself?

You may need to seek professional help, confide in close family or friends and even be bold and ask them to help you out by demonstrating what they love about you. Either through physical (hugs, cuddles, physical touch), verbal (kind words, notes, letters) or emotional (acts of kindness and love) expression.

Whatever it is, sometimes this exercise rocket ships you forward in your emotional journey and helps provide a sense of approval.

It might also be a timely reminder even to see the beautiful qualities you have and can give to others, thus promoting your sense of worth.

There is also the fact that not everyone is going to love or approve of you. This is something that can't be changed, but merely appreciating this is the case may be enough to shift the pendulum to move forward.

You may ask yourself the question: do I approve of everyone in my life? The answer is probably 'no', and that's OK. Acceptance that we can't all be loved or approved is all part of the big picture, and the simple fact is, we can't win them all.

We can't control others judgement of us. It is impossible, and they will think what they want regardless of your best efforts to please them. Just remember that you are a sum of all your experiences and traumas and have done a fantastic job to get to this point. So be proud of who you are, and fuck those who judge you. Others have no idea what it is like to be you or how you've got here, so don't get caught up in their views – it is simply based on speculation. The same goes for you towards others: they all have a story, and it may be best to practise compassion before judgment.

COPING (& THE INABILITY TO THINK WE CAN'T)

Coping and Anxiety have a unique relationship as most of us who suffer from Anxiety have a strong sense or feeling that we won't be able to cope with what life has in store for us or any situation that generates a significant amount of stress.

The fact of the matter is, this is simply not true! We can and do have the ability to cope with whatever our Anxiety throws at us and deal with it appropriately.

The reason I know this is because you are already proof that you can cope. You have been coping with your condition for as long as you have had it, and although you may be tired and weary, you are coping so far, and you are living proof of that.

The reason we feel this way is generally related to fatigue and those feelings of being always overwhelmed.

As you may be starting to realise, our anxieties and future illusions often don't become a reality.

These illusions of negativity and the often disastrous conclusions we anticipate, suck our energy and put us in this vulnerable position of feeling we can't cope!

Even if the Worst Case Scenario that we conjured up in our heads actually did happen (even though it's doubtful not to), we will find that there is an inner strength and resource that can and will be found and this enables us to deal with it and cope. So next time you get a feeling or sense that you can't cope, STOP. Say to yourself: "yes,

I can cope with whatever life throws at me, yes I will find the resources required, and the reality is this is my illusion of Anxiety playing Worst Case Scenario and sapping my energy, and that is contributing to this sense of helplessness".

As we move forward into our recovery, you will find that your energy improves, your understanding of Anxiety and its illusions of negativity are false, and your ability to cope is just fine.

SHOULD'S, MUSTS, DEMANDS AND EXPECTATIONS

The should's, musts, demands and expectations of our way of thinking are considerable drivers in our Anxiety and Fear.

When we think to ourselves 'should' or 'must', we are placing an expectation on that current situation, event or thought process.

The expectation is crucial because it provides hope. With hope, there is positive energy and drive towards what we are wanting. This energy often turns into success or achievement of our goal or expectations, because that's what we are putting all our energy into by trying to get to that point.

If expectations and demands didn't exist, then progress wouldn't be achieved, and we would all sit around in the same spot not progressing. Overall, expectations can be a good thing.

But what about when our expectations are not met?

Glad you asked, mate.

I have a simple motto: ***Aim high to achieve, but you can't win them all.***

If you can accept that there are times when the situation or expectation isn't met and be comfortable with that, then you don't set yourself up for feelings of failure or extreme disappointment. You have a little disclaimer in place to buffer the negative result.

Sometimes, our expectations can be out of whack – a little too high or non-achievable. It's good to learn to recognise these moments.

When you hear the words 'should', 'could' or have a certain level of expectation, it's time to stop and re-evaluate.

I discuss this concept with my children all the time when it comes to their sporting and academic abilities.

For example, I asked my oldest son, at ten years old, how he felt when he played a game of Aussie Rules football. He told me he thought he played poorly and had poor skills.

Now, I know for a fact that his skills are quite good for a 10-year-old, and when I watched him play, I thought he had a great game. The reason he appraised himself so poorly was that he felt he 'should' have kicked the goal from 20 metres on a tight angle and 'should' have marked the ball in the pack of five or six players in slippery conditions.

His expectations of himself, at such a young age, was to emulate that of his heroes that play in the AFL and kick those incredible goals and take strong pack marks.

He couldn't see that he had probably over calculated his ability at this point in his playing career and placed huge expectations on himself, thus concluding that he had a poor game.

When we broke it down, I discussed with him a few critical points in his evaluation. Firstly, the goal was challenging for any player of any level to kick given the tight angle.

Secondly, the ability at his age to kick the distance was probably at his limit anyhow in regards to taking a pack mark with a slippery ball, once again difficult to do especially when wet and amongst five or six players.

I suggested that even the best players miss goals regularly and often miss pack marks also. We discussed percentages with low percentage shots at goal versus a high percentage being directly in front with a limited angle.

Once it was broken down and discussed, he re-evaluated his game and felt he had a relatively good match with a couple of near misses and difficult marks.

He was able to change his expectation more to the level he was at, and this allowed him to see his game in a much lighter, positive way. We can continuously reassess our 'should's', 'musts' and expectations that reduce and minimise our stress.

He could also take the approach of 'aim high to achieve but accept he may not always get the result' and consider, 'at least I tried', and we move on to the next opportunity.

The same process can be applied to your ability to view relationships, business, personal achievements, sporting ability or general wellbeing.

So, STOP and think next time: what are your expectations of yourself (or others) in any given situation?

Next, try and come up with a more realistic perspective of that situation, and you will find that often your expectation is far too high and resulting in nothing but increased distress and negatively.

Alternatively, adopt my motto, aim high to achieve, but you can't win them all. This only works if your prepared to accept failure and not being able to reach your desired goal from time to time and move on.

Some questions you might like to ask yourself if you find yourself thinking 'should' and 'must' a little too often:

Is my expectation of my partner's actions or behaviour warranted?

Am I expecting too much?

Is my ability that good, or am I still learning the appropriate skills needed?

Have I dedicated my time to this skill long enough to become an expert in it?

Should I perform this well in my new job considering I have only taken the new role recently?

Should other people, or the world, see things the same as I do?

The answer to all these questions may show you some readjustments need to be made, and you may be projecting a little high. This doesn't mean that you can't aim high to achieve, it just means that if you are realistic in where you and others are at, the less distress you will feel.

There is also a saying that has been widely used that helps me deal with other people's behaviour and my expectations of them or myself: "Past behaviour best predicts future behaviour".

What does that mean?

Well, think about it for a minute. It generalises the fact that we are creatures of habit and tend to show the same behaviours time and time again. It makes sense because we have specific ways and styles of living and thinking that makes us, us. Think about neurones that fire together, wire together to help explain this.

If you live a healthy lifestyle, then your behaviour would be that of eating healthy often, exercising, and continually working on your wellbeing because it makes you feel good. It becomes a pattern of behaviour and allows us or you to predict future behaviour based on past behaviour.

The same theory could be applied to self-sabotaging behaviours such as excess alcohol, drugs of poor diet and lifestyle. You can predict what that person will do with themselves in the future.

The reason for making this point in regards to expectation is because it can help us deal and accept other people's behaviour (and our own), which then allows us to understand and accept their actions.

This, in turn, reduces our stress or angst. For example, let's say you have a friend who is always late or cancels at the last minute, and they are annoyingly unreliable. Remind yourself: this person has a history of doing this, so my expectation of them should be low as I will predict they are going to behave the same way in the future (cancelling or not turning up).

Another example may be that your partner always seems to abuse alcohol, regardless of the event, and ends up drunk.

It would be foolish to think they may do the right thing and not get so pissed time and time again because that's their history of behaviour and it will continue.

The best way to deal with this is to accept you can't change people, and if you stand back and observe, the pattern will be distinct. You may have some influence on changing some actions, but the fact is, it needs to come from them internally if they want to change especially if it relates to self-sabotaging behaviour.

THE FUTURE IS BULLSHIT

We all hear the old phrase about 'living in the moment', and probably all realise that it would be so beneficial if we did.

Why then, is it so hard to do? Why can't it just be automatic and easy?

You see, our brains like to predict the future and therefore always conjure up a circuit of images, thoughts and possible outcomes. This can help with future events and results. However, it does not help the Anxiety sufferer. I know from experience that if you practise trying to live as much as possible in the moment, then the benefits are a pleasant reward for all your hard work. It's a challenge for sure, though.

Us Anxiety and Panic sufferers are not only not living in the moment but stuck in the world of living in the future. Remember earlier in the book when I said that Fear=Unknown? Our Anxiety skyrockets because we don't know the outcome because (funnily enough) it's unknown! When living in the future all the time, we project our

DRIVERS OF ANXIETY

thoughts into the unknown. We try to plan, control and at times, avoid the result well and truly before it has happened.

Here's a rhetorical question: do you think that is good for your Anxiety?

No way, man.

Here's what you need to remember: it is impossible to predict the future and the outcome of our lives. The future, and our Anxiety, is an illusion. Or, if you want to make it clear: it's all bullshit. It's make-believe and generally based around negativity. Our brains need to create this full circle or loop in a story because there must be a conclusion. It's the way our brains operate. So, from now on, let's not make the illusion negative and full of Fear, but instead try to create a more helpful, positive one.

What we can do to help is plan and be prepared for future tasks or events and then leave it there. Concentrate on the present as best as possible and tackle each moment on its merits at one step at a time. Doing this leaves little room for Anxiety to take hold and control your thoughts.

It is an essential cog in the wheel of Anxiety, and many of us never even realise that it is a habit of ours. I began to learn a few things that make a huge difference in my stress and Anxiety levels:

I realised that the past is gone and I can't change it, but can learn from my mistakes or success.

The present is something I can alter or change my perceptions and thought processes.

Finally, you can plan for the future in order to be prepared. Then you can deal with anything that comes your way, but you've got to leave it there.

In my profession as a paramedic, I attend cases or scenes that are potentially career-ending due to the horror or devastation that I am witnessing. It's a job that can create reasonable stress which, in turn, is likely to affect my mental wellbeing. I have seen plenty of colleagues have this happen and I'm sure it will continue given the nature of our job.

The reason for sharing this is because most of us have strategies we may or may not even realise we have to deal with our role.

If I was to live in the future, I could easily conjure up all sorts of horrific images of the potential scenes I could witness. I could be creating those scenes in my mind before being at work or even whilst at work, and I would probably need to read this book lots and lots.

The fact is, if we did this from a negative angle, our mental health would be severely affected and all because we terrorised ourselves by living in the future.

The way most of our cases are approached is by one job at a time. Not concerning ourselves about what's up next and the ramifications and dealing with it when it happens. The old saying 'cross that bridge when we come to it' always works well.

We do, however, plan for future cases via study, clinical discussion and example scenarios but we don't live with them. Instead, we wait until they happen and then go in as prepared as possible.

HYPER-AROUSAL, STRESS & DANGER

Hyper-arousal is closely linked to stress.

When we are stressed, for whatever reason, our body starts to identify that it may need to be ready for action. Our breathing becomes faster and shallower, hormones are released to get us ready to respond with increased heart rate, increased blood pressure and general vigilance. This, of course, can be a good thing. If you need to perform in a particular work environment or performance, being 'heightened' actually sharpens skills and thoughts to achieve the best outcome.

DRIVERS OF ANXIETY

During this hyper-arousal, the HPA axis (Hypothalamic Pituitary Adrenal Axis) is activated and the production of cortisol keeping us going – increasing energy stores for us to maintain our level of stress. But when this stress goes on over an extended period, there is a considerable cost that our bodies and minds pay.

Our sugar levels increase along with an increase in lipids (this promotes an increased chance of diabetes, stroke, heart attack and peripheral vascular disease). We also find hyper-arousal causes serotonin to be reduced, making us potentially more depressed.

Additionally, increased stress can cause brain shrinkage, especially in the Hippocampal and Prefrontal Cortex (PFC) region, decreasing our ability to think clearly and make new memories. There are also stronger neuronal connections built with the amygdala and PFC that creates greater vulnerability to Fear and Anxiety.[13]

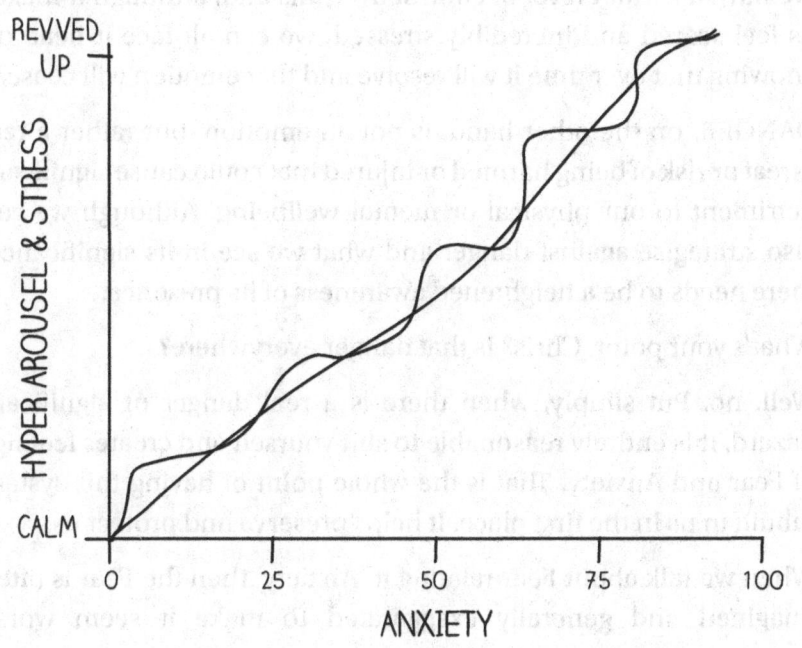

HYPER AROUSEL & STRESS VS ANXIETY

When we are always stressed, we become stuck in this spiral of stress and hyper-arousal. The body and mind are ready to pounce. You're on edge, ready to tackle what comes your way. However, this state of hyper-arousal and Anxiety creates a perfect platform for more Anxiety and Panic because the OFF button is so far from the ON switch that it's hard to stop. To help us have an opportunity to tackle our Anxiety and Panic, it's vital to reduce our stress levels as best as possible. Doing this is hard work and takes lots of practise.

But Chris, I hear you say, the Fear is real! I have every reason to feel this stressed all the time.

OK, let's discuss the difference between Fear vs Danger to clear a few things up.

Fear is an emotion that is created when we are in threat, pain and, of course, danger. It can be imagined or real, but it is something that we can use strategy against and use perception to move it up the scale from high to low or vice versa.

We have a certain level of control over this and, although it makes us feel scared and incredibly stressed, we can all face it head on knowing that over time it will resolve and that emotion will cease.

DANGER, on the other hand, is not an emotion, but rather a real threat or risk of being harmed or injured that could cause significant detriment to our physical or mental wellbeing. Although we can also strategise against danger and what we see in its significance, there needs to be a heightened awareness of its presence.

What's your point, Chris? Is that danger everywhere?

Well, no. Put simply, when there is a real danger or significant hazard, it is entirely reasonable to shit yourself and creates feelings of Fear and Anxiety. That is the whole point of having this system inbuilt in us in the first place. It helps preserve and protect us.

When we talk about Fear relating to Anxiety, then the Fear is often imagined and generally exaggerated to make it seem worst.

DRIVERS OF ANXIETY

The same messaging and physical sensations are released as in danger, but the difference is we can reduce and conquer our Fear through our thoughts and perceptions. This, my friend, is why Fear can be overcome and danger cannot.

Let's say you are walking home down the back alley at night and hear some noises in the bush that resemble a person lurking around. Someone that may attack or ambush you. It creates a feeling of Fear and Anxiety. Fair enough, I say.

On further investigation, you realise it's nothing more than the wind in the bushes. The Fear is tamed, processed, and you're back to normal.

Using the same example, walking home in the alley, but this time someone is lurking in the bushes. This is Danger and Fear is warranted. Those sensations of fleeing or fight are there to keep you alive. My advice is to use them and protect yourself.

So, when you're feeling Fearful in the future, ask yourself this question: **is this feeling of Fear imagined and exaggerated, or real danger?**

This may aid in allowing you to put things into perspective and work through your Anxiety if you're not sure.

"HAPPINESS IS LETTING GO OF WHAT YOU THINK YOUR LIFE'S SUPPOSED TO LOOK LIKE & CELEBRATING IT FOR EVERYTHING IT IS."

MANDY HALE

CHAPTER 12

THE MAINSTREAM BUDDHIST

I often wonder what type of rooster I am. Especially regarding how I think and act. Like many men out there, what you see is not always what you get, and we have layers. I like football, socialising, having a few frothies (beers) and talking a lot of shit. The other side of me is a lot deeper and tries to understand the complexities of life. This is where I am more attuned to philosophy and spirituality in my quest for answers. I reckon it's a ripper balance as I can sort of have my cake and eat it too.

This chapter, I want to get in touch with your inner Wayne Dyer and look at some of our more profound thoughts and emotions, and what they might have to do with our old mate's Anxiety and Fear.

FAILURE

Bloody failure, man. It can be a dirty word that can have such a strong emotional impact on us. I know: I used to write down my failures and successes to work out how fucked up my life was and if the ledger was even or not.

I even gave the failures and successes scores from 1-5, depending on what level of intensity they were and probably what level of emotional pain. How efficient of me.

I look back at my list of failures now and view them in a different light. Some of my faults, although not great at the time, emotionally seemed to have a somewhat positive effect or fateful rationale. There were times when I felt I'd failed because I didn't get the result I wanted, but in hindsight, those 'failures' worked out for the best.

An example of this was me busting my arse in Year 12 to achieve good scores to get into a course called Human Movement – it had a little buzz around it at the time, and it was what I wanted more than anything. Unfortunately, I narrowly missed the cut-off score and ended beginning a course in Nursing ... something I didn't even really want to do.

Anyhow, this Nursing has ended up being a blessing. I met my wife and some best mates which i still have at the university I attended. I was able to travel overseas and find work easily in London, and it gave me a great stepping stone into the world of Paramedicine. This is a profession I love, and one I would never have ended up doing had I 'succeeded' back then.

If I hadn't failed, then who knows where I would have ended up.

My point is that failures are simply a door closing, allowing you to be available for another one to open — one that potentially will lead to bigger and better things.

Failures are learning points along the ladder to success. They give and provide you with the opportunity to grow and move forward.

If you are not failing, then there may be little or no growth.

Failure is also something that is predominately in your head and created from your perceptions. Although you think that you have failed, remember it is your own beliefs and values that are driving those thoughts, not necessarily anyone else's.

One thing I admire in people is when I see them having a go at something. Regardless of if they fall short or not, they are at least not left wondering and regretful. This is magic in itself.

Failure should be rebadged as 'learning opportunity', or 'growth', because, without failure, we would stay stagnant in our worlds.

Don't be scared to fail because it doesn't exist; it's just a stepping stone to succession.

If you think of every successful person, you've ever met. They will all have a story to share about their numerous failures on the road to achievement. It's a weird gift from the universe.

So next time you think you have failed, don't be so hard on yourself. Try changing your perception to that of an opportunity to learn.

Learning from the experience is the first step in the ladder you're trying to climb.

Yep, I am most wise. The Dalai Lama could learn a thing or two from old Chriso! *Lol!*

THE NON-PERMANENT NATURE OF LIFE

The world of emotions is full of ups and downs. They can come and go quickly or take a little longer. A minute, hour, day or week.

Identifying this has been a tremendous advantage in dealing with my own emotions and making sense of my world. The realisation that nothing in my life is permanent means a situation like a fight with my wife, money stressors, a feeling of sadness, sickness or the full range of emotions eventually change and often melt away like soft butter through my fingers.

The point I'm trying to get across is that if we can be patient, observe and work through our problems with the confidence that it will shift, it has a powerful ability to lessen the blow and provide hope for both now and the future.

Right, let's say you work in sales. Your first three customers show little or no interest in you or your product one morning. It can quickly get you a little down, and the monkey in your head can start its negative talk. However, if you can keep focussed and continue with the afternoon work confidently and with the understanding that nothing is permanent, then you may find that sales swing the other way Who knows, there may be four sales that day.

Other examples may be something that lasts a lot longer like the separation from your partner or a relationship breakdown.

Something this major will be emotionally tough and take a long time to heal. However, with the knowledge and understanding of emotional ups and downs and remembering that nothing is ever permanent, it is a sweet comfort that over time things will improve and the fog and heartache will lift.

I have found this to be a psychological winner in tough times as it essentially provides a sense of hope that, in the toughest of times, can take the edge off just enough to get to the next little stage in you're suffering.

We all experience emotional ups and downs every day. That knowledge reminds you regularly that, good or bad, this will pass and nothing is ever permanent.

The best thing you can do is to observe the emotion and recognise simply. See that it is anger, sadness, frustration, guilt, worry... fully feel it and sit with the discomfort, and then allow it to move on. If you can actually sit with an ugly emotion and just observe, you will find that physically it's tolerable and often not as significant as you think.

Sitting with the discomfort, feeling the feeling, also allows you to deal with the current issue and not sweep it under the carpet.

Pushing it aside or ignoring it means it sits there in your periphery, always waiting to rear its ugly head in the future via your mental or physical health and wellbeing.

It's OK to be not OK. Give it a go! You are encouraged to acknowledge and embrace your Anxiety and Fear. Life and pain pass guys, please remember that.

SHIT IN THE PIPE

Everyone has troubles in their lives – sadly, there's no such thing as perfect. The thing is, you have two choices. You can sit, sulk and dwell on how unfair the world is; or you can work out how to make a problematic situation work in your favour.

Have you ever heard the expression 'shit in the pipe'? (No because I made it up!)

This is when life, its struggles and all those frustrating little annoyances just always seem to leave a bit of shit in the pipe!

These are things like the rude person at the shops, the stain on your shirt whilst at work, the nagging of children, the drip of a leaking tap or the constant ache in your hip that keeps you awake at night.

Whatever it is, these issues all have a common theme: they are relatively constant, will always be part of us and as soon as one is resolved, another appears and create yet another low level of frustration in our lives.

Now, I know I have provided lots of little solutions in this book so far, but I am afraid I can't help you with this one. It's impossible to resolve all of life's little frustrations.

However, it is our ability to deal with them constructively that make all the difference. It is acknowledging they will be part of our lives, and tolerance is the key. Being able to tolerate these annoyances as minimally as possible will also help with your Anxiety.

The reason being is that if all this starts to mount up and become more significant than what it needs to be, then it becomes a stress or stressor that as we all know fuel that pesky Anxiety cycle. Revisit the strategies mentioned earlier once again — it's an excellent method to help move forward and accept lives little challenges.

Otherwise, get the old GASM (Give a shit meter) out.

GUILT AND GRIEF

One of the fun things that come along with a mental illness or chronic condition is good old-fashioned guilt and grief. If you are anything like me, it came on thick and fast and generally because of no one else's issue - just mine.

I used to feel so guilty that I was letting family, friends or other people I care about, down which — of course - made the guilt worse. I was always able to continue living my life, but lots of yucky feelings behind the scenes. I can remember that I was so fixated on my Anxiety that it seemed to take up the whole conversation. Everything and every topic was an issue, and if I wasn't able to verbalise it, then it was fairly evident in my body language. I was a constant pain in the arse (so I thought).

I knew I didn't want to be a burden or affect other people around me, but when your brain is wired full of Fear, it's challenging to sit and smell the roses, if you know what I mean. You try and do your best but often end up with a certain level of guilt about not being the person you want to be (how I felt)

I am here to tell you that guilt is a nasty, non-helpful little prick of emotion, and it needs to be eradicated.

The fact of the matter is this: you have a medical condition that alters your life and the way you can enjoy it. It reduces your ability to have fun and relax. So instead of feeling guilty, feel proud that you not only acknowledge this, but you also have the inner strength to live as best as you can in a shitty world.

Often, once you've pushed past guilt, your left with his mate: grief. Grief is a real part of Anxiety and the life you have slipping by you that is filled with so much Fear and Panic.

It's OK to grieve for all the beautiful memories and experiences that you have lost. It's OK to grieve for the time wasted on crap that you know isn't right, but you've struggled to fix or resolve it.

Take the time to feel your grief and understand that you have missed out on lots of beautiful experiences either through being not being present or being worried about Fear holding you back. Then pick yourself up and challenge the world you live in. Never give up because one day you will be free from this world of Fear and suffering.

ACCEPTING YOUR CONDITION

The sooner you can accept Anxiety as part of who you are and your makeup, and remember that the condition loves nothing more than resistance from you and it's symptoms, the better.

If you can learn to accept its nasty little unwanted and unrealistic thoughts, physical sensations and challenges whilst congratulating yourself along the way, the quicker your recovery will be in your quest for peace and healing.

It's a bitter pill to swallow but a reality. Anxiety will eventually need to become a friend, not a foe, to win your life back. When you achieve this result, look out – it's a little rocket ship to freedom.

It takes time to achieve this weird romance towards it but eventually, acceptance will prevail.

ACHIEVING BALANCE IN LIFE

One of the things I often see when I observe my peers, family or work colleagues who seem stressed, Anxious or unhappy is that they have very little balance in their lives.

We've all got a lot to deal with: family, work commitments, money, social life, exercise, diet, kids — just to name a few things.

The problem seems to come from the fact that too much time is spent on one or two particular categories, and little time is left for the rest.

This can happen to all of us, and often work is the biggest culprit. There is also the issue that it can't be avoided due to the demands of any particular industry and the hours required to complete your role.

However, there can and is a solution to this problem, and with a little thought and planning, we can get more balance into our lives and a reduction in stress, Anxiety and unhappiness.

The first step in getting our balance back into life is to make a list of everything we do and the time constraints it has.

You may find that there are some activities that can't be changed like work, school or specific family requirements. However, there may be solutions to some of these as well.

There may be a possibility that you could have more flexibility from work by either working from home or starting later. This seems to be gaining popularity recently, especially given the benefits and advances in technology and attitude.

There may also be the revelation that work, or your current employment is not where you want to be or have a passion for such as changing job or focus could be an answer. A potential to study or either step-down or up in your role is a possibility.

THE MAINSTREAM BUDDHIST

Once you have got your list sorted and you can see in black and white where your time goes, look at what you can alter and change (or even scrap for a while) that has been part of your life and probably become a massive habit.

You would be amazed at how much we are creatures of habit and go on autopilot with our behaviours and actions.

If you can see that you spend time with people or things you can avoid, then do it to free up extra time.

Ask yourself if you need to go to the party of a colleague you don't like or a function with a sporting club that is irrelevant. Then simply say No respectfully and let it go.

If you look at a particular day and break it down in terms of time, then we are looking at 24 hours.

Of that 24 hours, eight is spent sleeping (I hope we will talk about that soon too!) And 8-10 is spent at work. That can be a total of up to 18 hours. That is pretty much standard for most of us.

Therefore, we only have 6 hours left to fit in family, friends, socialising, exercise, time out and anything else. If you have a family, then you can often feel as though you're stuffed!

As a husband, I have a wife and two children that need help with dinner, cleaning, driving to sport and training, household chores and everything else under that umbrella.

This has not even taken into account time to yourself, exercise, socialising with friends and general wellbeing.

There simply aren't enough hours in the day to attend to the demands of everybody or everything. This is why it's essential to stop, assess, plan and prioritise: what is essential and what is not.

There are going to be times where you will feel bad, or even rude because you have said no to certain social or employment events, but for a time, it is necessary if you want to get some balance into your life.

HOW DO WE SPEND OUR TIME?

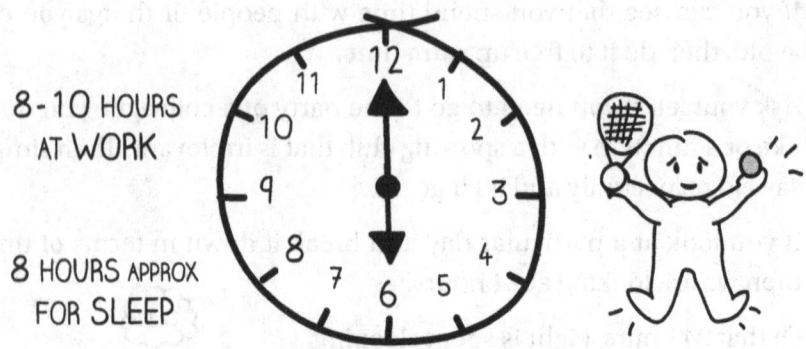

8-10 HOURS AT WORK

8 HOURS APPROX FOR SLEEP

6 HOURS REMAINING: FOR FAMILY, FRIENDS, EXCERSIZE

The other type of balance I want to talk about is moderation. If you can achieve moderation in most aspects of your life, then it will give you a fighting chance against the perils of an ever-demanding world.

Moderation in alcohol consumption is an example. *(And for those of you thinking: Oh no, please not an alcohol example... it might highlight a flaw... That's another book, mate. No judgement here.)*

If we drank moderately during a night out, then it would reduce the likelihood of a hangover, which then in return will reduce the chance of sitting on the couch, eating junk food and not moving too much the next day.

Then, if we woke up feeling a little fresher, we would feel like doing things with the kids, eating healthier, being more active and getting the extra balance we need in life.

This example can be extended to diet and the moderation of healthy and unhealthy food intake. If you ate some crap or junk food, then follow it up with a healthier diet and exercise, you have the best of both worlds, and you won't feel like you're missing out.

Other examples could be late nights, exercise, and finding time to rest and recharge. Think about it; you can't have it all!

Time is precious and valuable. It's worth investing the time to make time.

THANK YOU VERY MUCH

Gratitude. This fella is such a good mate of mine now; I like to refer to him as "Grattie".

Being friends with Grattie makes you feel thankful and appreciative of the things in your life. Things like your health (both physical or emotional); family; friends; and materialistic stuff. It is also appreciative of other people's generosity and kindness.

The point of practising gratitude to help with our Anxiety is that it allows us to flick into a more positive mindset and trains our brain to look at the good in our lives versus all the negative things.

The fact is, in all our lives, it is good and bad, and it's impossible to have a life that is only positive and blissful. It is the power of seeing things in a lighter way that assists in reducing our stress, resentment and other negative emotions that generally drive up our systems and put us in that state of a hyper-arousal and ready to fight or flight.

The reason we (as Anxiety sufferers) are not that good at doing it naturally is that we've learnt that most of our lives and experiences are marred with crap, and we feel that there isn't too much brightness in the world.

That's all about to change, and with the practise of gratitude and continually revisiting what's right in your life and people around you, you will find this is another excellent tool you can use to keep Fear at bay.

Simply writing a list daily (remember, we know the power of writing into our conscious and subconscious minds) or consciously practising your gratitude will make a difference. You just have to try.

And if you don't believe me, here are some proven benefits that academic types have learned about gratitude:

1) It makes you happier because you are focussing on good things in your life, versus the negative, unhappy things.

2) It increases your emotional wellbeing by reducing envy about 'The Jones": what others have and what you don't. Instead, you are focusing on what you do have.

3) It creates optimism that, in turn, increases happiness and general wellbeing.

4) It decreases stress by not comparing yourself with others (primarily materialistic stuff). This stops you thinking that you have failed and not achieved anything in your life.

5) It aids in improving self-esteem because looking at what you do have offers a sense of achievement.

6) It promotes sleep by reducing your worries about things in life you don't have, instead focussing on what amazing things you've already got.

7) It improves your health because as we know, negative thinking promotes illness in the body; therefore, positive thinking only serves to produce a tonic of calmness and relaxation for your body.

8) It makes you a great friend or family member because you are appreciating their efforts to help and not just always expecting more from them. Expectation often turns people into being ungrateful and bloody rude (and you'll be the last to notice when you are).

9) It also helps your mental health and eases frustration because you're looking at things from a helpful positive way instead of negative all the time. For example, let's say your sister buys you a gift for your birthday, that is nice but not you. When you're in a negative mindset, you will be thinking: "Stupid sister buys me a stupid gift that's useless and a waste of money." However, when you are practising gratitude, you are thinking: "Although the gift isn't exactly what I need or want, I am so appreciative she bought me a gift in the first place and took the time out of her busy schedule for me. I feel loved. Thank you!"

Only you get to decide how you think. The choice is yours, watch the difference and see the results!

PHILOSOPHY

Being philosophical and looking at the "Big picture" can help when all else fails or at least an addition to your critical thinking and revised helpful/realistic thoughts.

It is my go-to when all else has failed, and you are stuck!

Sometimes, s#*t happens, and there is bugger all we can do except accept the situation and where we are at in any given moment.

There may be times where all the strategies we put in place, and effort seems irrelevant or not helpful.

So, I have decided that providing some of these quotes may help with your journey along the way. I know they certainly helped me when things looked bleak and tragic.

It can mean the difference between pure suffering and allowing yourself some room to breathe a little looking at things that you may not be able to change differently. Hope they help and inspire!!!

You can Google hundreds of them as well!

"Happiness is letting go of what you think your life's supposed to look like & celebrating it for everything it is". *Mandy Hale*

"If this problem is in the future, then I plan how to tackle it and then park it." *Chriso Breen*

"If we have no control of the situation, control our response to it." *Chriso Breen*

"Life will only change when you become more committed to your dreams than you are to your comfort zone." *Chriso Breen*

"Beneath every behaviour, there is a feeling. And beneath each feeling is a need. And when we meet that need rather than focus on the behaviour, we begin to deal with the cause, not the symptom" *Ashleigh Warner*

"You will never speak to anyone more than you speak to yourself in your head, be kind to yourself." *Unknown Author*

"Don't wait till you reach your goal to be proud of yourself. Be proud of every step you take" (especially with your Anxiety)

Karen Salmansohn

"I learned that courage was not the absence of Fear, but the triumph over it" *Nelson Mandela*

"The brave man is not he who does not feel afraid, but he who conquers it" *Nelson Mandela*

"Forgive others, not because they deserve forgiveness, but because you deserve peace." *Unknown Author*

"You only have control of 3 things in your life: the thoughts you think, the images you visualise, and the actions you take" *Jack Canfield*

"Change the belief and thinking changes. Change the thinking and the action changes. Change the action, and the result changes." *Unknown Author*

"If you don't like something, change it. If you can't change it, change your attitude" *Maya Angelou*

"Worrying is carrying tomorrow's load with today's strength, carrying two days at once. It is moving into tomorrow ahead of time. Worrying does not empty tomorrow of its sorrow; it empties today of its strength" *Corrie Ten Boom*

"One day the people who never believed in you will brag about how they used to know you." *Unknown Author*

"Success is normally found in a pile of mistakes" *Tim Fargo*

F-E-A-R (Has two meanings - it's your choice)

Forget Everything And Run

Or

Face Everything And Rise *(Unknown Author)*

OUR BLEMISH

Or should I say stigma'?

I found a quote recently, and it sums up exactly how I feel – how you should never judge someone until you've walked in their shoes:

THE MAN IN THE ARENA

"It is not the critic who counts; not the man who points out how the strong man stumbles, or where the doer of deeds could have done better. The credit goes to the man who is actually in the arena, whose face is marred by dust and sweat and blood; who strives valiantly; who errs, who comes short again and again, because there is no effort without error of shortcoming; but who does actually strive to do the deeds; who knows great enthusiasms, the great devotions; who spends himself in a worthy cause; who at best knows, in the end, the triumph of high achievement, and who at the worst, if he fails, at least fails while daring greatly, so that his place shall never be with those cold and timid souls who neither know victory or defeat."
Theodore Roosevelt

Stigma is when someone sees you in a negative light because of your illness and then puts you in a particular category or stereotype because of what they think you are.

This negative, and often ill-informed, view leads to discrimination and sometimes poor treatment against you because you have been pigeonholed into a particular 'not very good' category.

This leads you to feel shit about yourself. Shameful, guilty, wrong, depressed, weak and hopeless. It also makes you think that you're not good enough to be accepted by the 'general population' because you're somewhat different. And suddenly, we are placing the stigma we hate on ourselves.

I fell into this category. I felt weak, ashamed and often saddened because I had a 'mental health condition' and that the consensus of the population is that mental health is either not an issue or a severe deal.

I've come to realise, though, that being weak was far from the truth. When i was at my worst, walking down the street was a super effort as opposed to a relaxed, easy one. I also learned that until you have been in this situation, no one can comment or judge.

If I could swap with any critics out there for one hour of living with my Anxious mind at its worse, I bet they would give it back within one minute.

Over time (a very long time)! I've accepted that my previous mental health issue (Anxiety and Panic attacks) is not something to be ashamed of. I'm super proud of me and how far I've come.

I am proud of the fact I didn't turn to self-sabotaging behaviours like excessive drugs, alcohol or violence. I am proud I still turned up for work and contributed to society, and I gave a shit about my friends and family despite running at a level of 100% distress.

I also started to see my mental health as a medical condition like hypertension or diabetes. I have to manage it just like other people suffering those conditions do: with diligence. I would also note that they don't cop crap for having diabetes and are not judged or ridiculed because of the things they have to do to make life easier.

Therefore, I am not going to judge either! Not me, and certainly not you.

The next time you feel anything negative about yourself regarding your Anxiety and any stigma attached to that, I want you to tell yourself you're reliable, amazing and doing a great job at the moment. Also, remind yourself that critics wouldn't criticise if they had Anxiety because they would know how it feels and instead, they would have empathy.

THE EMOTIONAL PIE

I have never seen one of these at the bakery before, are they expensive?

Relax, I'm nearly at the end of my woo-woo chapter, but yes...here's a little more about feelings.

This concept is another simple tool that can be used to determine where your emotional wellbeing sits, and sometimes it can help establish why you are feeling a particular way, especially concerning negative emotions. It can help you find and fix, or at least understand, your emotional status.

I learnt this many years ago when I first started my studies in Paramedicine.

The pie can be made up of as many slices as you like, but for this example, we will use a total of eight pieces.

Let's hypothesise you are feeling sad and upset but not sure why (it's become a habit now, right? So I am sure these moments roll around regularly for you).

Let's also assume that a full eight slice pie means that you are full of health and happiness and with minimal stress and care in the world.

When I'm feeling a bit flat or sad, I go to my emotional pie and see what's happening.

I might have started the morning with a full pie: I felt good, healthy and happy.

THE MAINSTREAM BUDDHIST

Then my wife yelled at me for not putting the bins out. This may sneakily sneak away one slice of pie.

Then I get to work and find problems with a colleague who has been speaking poorly of me for reasons unknown. Potentially another slice of the pie taken.

Then I get into my car for lunch, and the battery is flat, and the cost of replacing the battery is not in my budget due to excessive bills. That hit cost me maybe two slices. What a day!

But then I get praise from my boss for how well I handled my colleague, which replaces a slice of pie after lunch. Woo hoo!

The end of you're working day comes, and you get into the car and feel sad and flat but can't understand why? You remember being praised for your excellent job, and you know you handled your colleague professionally and diplomatically, so why are you still feeling shit?

This is when we go over the whole day and reflect on what's happened.

You started with an emotional pie of eight slices which is feeling good and happy.

Then you lost one slice with your fight with the wife. That now makes it seven pieces.

Then you found out about your colleague speaking poorly of you. Another slice gone — making it six.

The battery and replacement with costs nailed another two slices, meaning your down to four.

However, praise from your boss replaces one slice bringing the total to five slices. An increase, but still nowhere near full.

You are down three slices from the start of the day — no wonder you're feeling sad and flat.

HOW A BASE JUMPER SAVED ME

It sounds ridiculous, I know, but it does help you determine why your mood isn't what you think it 'should' be. It's quick and easy to do and effective at identifying what the problem or problems are.

This way you can address them (or acknowledge them and move on), and get the slices back up to seven or eight.

Go on, give it a go and watch the results. Become emotionally in tune and healthy by eating emotional pie. I promise you won't get fat either!

CHAPTER 13

A GUT FEELING

In chapters 3, 4 and 5, I talked about how Anxiety works on a physical level – what happens in your body when your mind is highly stressed.

I want to revisit some of that here, but in a different context. This time, I want you to see that you have some control over how your body reacts (and this time, I am not talking about meditation or mind tricks).

This is some practical stuff, and it's all about what we put in our mouth.

ENTERIC NERVOUS SYSTEM (ENS)

I touched on this earlier in the book, but I want you to understand it again – because this is a part of the body that we often take for granted.

The Enteric Nervous system (ENS) is part of the Autonomic Nervous system (ANS). It's located in the gut of humans stretching up the lining of tissue in the oesophagus, stomach, small intestine and colon and it has an estimated 100 million neurones in it.

You might recall that the ENS is dubbed the 'second brain' as it can work independently to the brain in our heads. You might also remember me talking about the CNS (Central Nervous system) and how that evolved so we could make choices – like who we wanted our sexual partner to be, or what we felt like for dinner.

The CNS and ENS are pretty tightly connected because, as it turns out, they were initially formed together in the embryonic stage.

They started as a mass of neural tissue called the neural crest and then split in two, developing the CNS and the ENS.

These two systems can communicate with each via the Vagus nerve (do you remember me talking about this previously) and how often it fires off. This is known as the gut-brain axis.

It can send, receive and respond back and forth emotions to the brain via its nerve cells, which are full of neurotransmitters called serotonin, dopamine, glutamate and norepinephrine.

90% of serotonin (that's the happy hormone) can be found in the gut, and dopamine (the pleasure hormone) levels are equally found in the brain and the gut.

While this seems like a convenient little system we have going on, things can get a bit out a hand when something goes wrong. We have the ENS working basically on its controlling digestion, sorting out muscle contraction and movement of fluids and wastes.

Its receptors detect sugars, protein, acidity and other chemicals that monitor the progression of digestion and gut function to work this stuff out.

It also is the region in our body that our immune system is located. Approximately 80% of our immunity is made up of gut flora or gut microbiome (this is the bacteria found in the gut – more on this shortly). It helps protect us from foreign invaders like bacteria and viruses that enter the body.

The ENS influences the brain significantly as up to 90% of signalling from the Vagus nerve come from the gut and listened to by the brain. It is set up with a full range of receptors and systems to help it work out it's overall 'health' and reports it back to the brain.

There is also the effect the brain and its emotional wellbeing has on the ENS, and if we are stressed and emotional, then it creates unhappiness in the gut as well. The guts response to stress is the release of histamine and prostaglandin, which in turn create an increased inflammation in the gut lining. You can see it's a two-way street going on here.

Stress and Fear can ramp up the 'firing' of the Vagus nerve and serotonin production, causing the gut to become overstimulated with diarrhoea and cramping as a result. Nerves in the oesophagus when overstimulated create a 'choking' sensation and can create a sense of making it difficult to swallow.

This tells us that the gut is incredibly influential in providing information to the brain. Therefore, the health and wellbeing of your gut can have a significant effect on our moods, emotions, our levels of stress and Anxiety. Something to keep in mind when you're up for a day of piggin' out on fast food! [13, 42,43,44]

YOU ARE WHAT YOU EAT

We've all heard the expression 'you are what you eat'. It seems to have some truth in it as science presents findings backing ideas eastern medicine has known for years that whatever we put into our body impacts mental and physical health.

If you think about it, when you have a night out with too much boozing, and lousy food like kebabs and pizza at 3 am, you tend to wake up feeling reasonably s#&t.

You have no energy, feel sick and nauseous, and have nil or little ability to cope with much stress and emotional situations because you feel so terrible until your hangover and body recover.

This seems a little extreme as an example, but it highlights the truth. On the flip side, if you are eating healthy, have plenty of sleep and exercise, you feel terrific. This is the point I'm trying to make.

Our lifestyle choices can alter how we feel, and below you will see how our dietary choices affect our mental wellbeing.

However, if the gut is unhappy, there can be strong signalling and information sent to the brain that can influence our emotions and, in particular, our Anxiety.

Let's see what we can do to keep the gut or ENS happy and try only to send friendly, complimentary messages to the brain.

The answer to this is via our diets and the status of the guts natural ecosystem that is full of gut microbiota (previously named gut flora or bacteria in the gut).

These bacteria weigh up to 2 kgs and can there are around 1000 different species of bacteria. We have so many of these little suckers in our gut, and of them, 30% are standard in most people, and 60% have our unique little makeup making our collection of bacteria incredibly individual.

We are born without any bacteria in our gut – this is termed 'sterile' – and our accumulation of bacteria grows as we do. We get it from our mothers (vagina, faeces, skin, breast milk, etc. From before we are born, through the birthing process and in the months after our birth), our diet, and our external environment.

Our gut microbiome could be affected from early in life or throughout our lives. Exposure to antibiotics, or perhaps things like gluten intolerance, external toxins, reduced breastfeeding, increased stress and infection are all part of the recipe for success or disaster when it comes to wellbeing.

The gut lining acts as a barrier to reduce toxins being released from the digestive system into the body. When your gut microbiome is out of whack and unhealthy, the gut lining can become leaky (you may have heard of leaky gut) allowing large protein molecules to escape through the lining. This creates a variety of symptoms discussed below, affecting both physical and emotional wellbeing.

There is 'good', and 'bad' microbiota and one can take over the other, creating an imbalance if our diets are poor and the factors listed above are present. If the bad bacteria start to outweigh the good bacteria, then we begin to activate both physical and emotional symptoms.

We must fix the 'leaky gut' to allow healing to take place first.

Obvious tummy problems like bloating, reflux, diarrhoea, constipation and pain can be a result of conditions like inflammatory bowel disease, allergies, obesity and even diabetes. Other conditions such as arthritis, hyperthyroidism, crown's disease, multiple sclerosis and chronic fatigue have been attributed to this.

One of the leading causes of "leaky gut" is Candida overgrowth that is essentially a yeast that throws the balance of "good" and "bad" bacteria out of whack breaking down the walls of the gastrointestinal tract penetrating the bloodstream releasing toxins into the body. The symptoms listed can be attributed to this and is often overlooked.

Emotional symptoms like sadness, feeling scared, agitation and frustration can be a result of depression and Anxiety. All this from the stranglehold that harmful bacteria or microbiota has.

This microbiota does a lot of great stuff within our tummies, like help with our digestion and metabolism; maintain the lining of the gut walls; assist the health of the immune system. We can also get as much as possible out of the foods we eat by extracting vitamins and nutrients that are needed to power us.

As mentioned earlier, gut microbiota helps produce hormones like serotonin that alone can play a huge role in how we feel (mood) and also the regulation of our gastrointestinal tract.

Not all is lost, though, as we can help alter and change the bacteria in our guts by adding or subtracting certain foods and making use of probiotics.

We must mix up the types of foods we eat within a well-balanced diet that will provide a diversity of different microbiota. Different foods harbour diverse microbiota, and eating a variety also increases the variation of this.

Apart from a varied diet full of healthy vegetables and fruits with limited processed, packaged and sugar-laden foods, we also add in two foods that have a super-strong influence on the good bacteria. They are prebiotics and probiotics.

I can't stress highly enough the importance of eating as clean as possible.

Also, if you think these symptoms are what you have experienced, it may be worth looking at starting a "Yeast-free diet" that aims at avoiding all sugars, carbohydrate-rich foods and vegetables high in starch.

This diet is pretty challenging and best to perhaps seek out professional help in a dietitian and Integrative GP, which I discuss later in the book. [13, 42,43,44,45,46,47]

A LITTLE NOTE ABOUT PACKAGED STUFF

Processed and packaged foods are full of hidden impurities like additives and preservatives as well as sugars, salts and fats. This only serves to feed the harmful bacteria in your gut which then sends with love messages to the brain that we are unhappy down here, and that increases your chance of feeling shit.

I have deliberately not put any recipes or advice in this section as I feel it's important you spend the time thinking and researching your diet and food consumption. It's a fascinating journey, and by making your discoveries, you're more likely to stick to it as a way of life.

Maybe start with a diary for a week or so, just to get an idea of your diet and the food you're eating, and analyse that.

I am fully aware that it's bloody hard and almost impossible to eat 'clean' all the time and let's face it, a bit of chocolate, a few beers and some pizza is gold! However, being aware of how processed and junk food makes you feel it is a fascinating exercise. Sometimes, you might decide that a block of chocolate isn't worth being emotional for the next two days.

I suggest aiming for an 80/20 cut on healthy food options and diet. This way, your fuelling your gut microbiome with a majority of healthy opportunities and reducing the bad bacteria's chances of thriving, but it's also more realistic and achievable. This is what I aimed to achieve.

The 80/20 diet may be beneficial after the **"yeast-free diet"** and is something to think about.

PREBIOTICS

Prebiotics, or fermented fibre, assist the gut microbiota by selectively promoting the growth of certain bacterial species. They can be found in natural foods like garlic, onion, leeks, asparagus, artichokes, tomatoes, bananas, plums and apples.

They also come from bran and almonds. Mostly, we are after a diet that is high in fibre. This promotes fertile and nourishing playgrounds for that good bacteria. Pretty much essential for feeding the good stuff in your guts. [48,49]

PROBIOTICS

These babies are live microorganism that promotes the health and wellbeing of bacteria.

Most probiotics come from fermented foods and processes. Fermentation with food increases beneficial bacteria, vitamins and enzymes in foods. It has been used for thousands of years to preserve foods, and now we realise the benefits of them. Some fermented foods include kefir, sauerkraut, kimchi and kombucha.

Fermented foods are readily available from supermarkets and health food stores and can also be made at home.

There are hundreds of recipes and tips online or in books to peruse to either make or source your own. It's pretty easy!

It is also essential to take it slow at the start when introducing these foods as you may struggle to tolerate them initially, remember everything moderation.

Supplementing probiotics via a capsule is another way to increase your intake, and again, there are numerous options and availability in pharmacies, health food shops and your naturopath.

Taking your probiotics is best at night before bed so your body has time to digest overnight to aid in increasing its effects.

Although still in its infancy, the science of gut health and the microbiome is undoubtedly exciting. Perhaps someday we may be able to treat Anxiety and depression with a course of probiotics and diet changes as opposed to anti-depressants.

There have been numerous studies on mice, more so than humans, on the effect of probiotics have on their emotional wellbeing. It seems to be evident that mice had an anxiolytic impact on certain bacteria being *Lactobacillus rhamnosus* and *Bifidobacterium Longum* when colonised with these demonstrating a direct effect on their Anxiety. Numerous studies have identified these two bacteria species as future prospective treatment options.

There are also recent studies on patients who have had a faecal implant to help treat *clostridium difficule* (an infection in the bowel) and the benefits of this. Faeces from a donor who has a healthy bowel (yep I know!) is implanted into the patient with the infection, and there have been positive results with the health of the patient suffering from the condition. Interestingly, what has also been observed is that the recipient had also taken on other features from the donor. For example, if the donor had depressive symptoms, then the recipient would also develop depression despite not actually suffered depression before. This is the hidden power of our gut bacteria. There are also cases where the patient began to put on weight post-transplant despite being slim all their life. It was often noted that the donor was either larger, or obese, passing on that particular bacteria to the recipient. This has to lead to studies beyond mental health and into and potential obesity treatment. (48,49,54,55,56)

IT'S ALL IN OUR GENES

As I mentioned earlier in the book, several factors can affect our Anxiety and our probability of being in the firing line. Along with our gut health and the exciting potential for treatment for mental health conditions, genetics also seem to be proving they may have a significant role to play as well.

Although in its infancy, there is some evidence and studies that are identifying some key genes that are playing with our heads.

We know and have known for a long time that many physical conditions are hereditary and relate to our genes or mutations like Huntington's disease, Progeria, Cystic fibrosis, Sickle Cell anaemia and Down Syndrome to name a few. This has been well studied and evaluated.

We also know that parents can carry a genetic mutation and, if combined, create physical conditions in their children.

Our parents give us two sets of three billion letters of DNA which make up the human genome. Your DNA can be affected by various factors such as direct sunlight, stress, smoking and drug intake, alcohol, poor diet and even emotional traumatic experiences. Our DNA is fluid, and it replicates and degrades over time. [13]

Recently, there has been some fantastic new science and intervention into altering these mutations in our DNA and enabling us to reprogram our genetic makeup literally. This would have been impossible five years ago.

We can edit mutations in our genes called point mutations through a process called **Base Editing**. It allows us to change our genetic DNA sequence by changing the base in our DNA that creates disease. Scientist use a process called **CRISPR** that are essentially molecular scissors that search, bind and cut specific DNA sequences and then allow for the base to be edited, thus eliminating the disease. It's all a little technical (you don't say, Chris!) but the science is growing at a rapid rate that will hopefully see changes to our physical wellbeing. [58,59]

IS THERE AN ANXIETY GENE?

Yep, it seems there are a few. There have been some gene mutations that have been identified as a link to Anxiety and mental health. One of the most popular is the MTHFR (Methylene TetraHydrofolate) gene. These mutations may not have to be treated in a complicated way like the Base Editing mentioned previously, but only by taking specific vitamins and mineral supplements. Good news, right?

The MTHFR gene mutation is quite prevalent in the population with up to 50% of people having this problem. However, there has been some exciting treatment and studies for this gene mutation and how it affects us. The MTHFR gene has two mutations which are the C677T and the A1298C which can affect our Anxiety and also depression.

C677T MUTATION - If you have this bad boy in your set up, it decreases your ability to convert folate into active folate. Becoming deficient in folic acid creates symptoms of Anxiety, depression, shortness of breath and poor memory.

Decreased folate levels also create vitamin B deficiency with B1, 2, 3, 5 and 12 being affected. Deficiency in these B VITAMINS produce symptoms of irritability, nervousness, Anxiety, fatigue and depression, to name a few. You can see how it can play a significant role in our mental health.

A1298C - This mutation affects our ability to produce neurotransmitters that help make us feel happy, relaxed, calm and relaxed. Yep, you might have been able to guess Serotonin and Dopamine are the two main ones.

If you have both mutations, Einstein doesn't have to be present to work out that things are not going so well, and these genetics are creating havoc in our systems.

These gene mutations are only determined via genetic testing and currently seems to be fairly expensive. The science is relatively new, and I would imagine as time goes on, more evidence and knowledge will shed light on treatments and ways we can help ourselves.

There is evidence of a female who suffered significant Anxiety and Panic attacks in Adelaide, Australia and her life-changing experience was documented when she became aware of her MTHFR mutation. A physician treated her with Folinic acid, and that essentially cured her condition.

You can google her story and see for yourself.

Other genetic mutations to note include:

FAAH, CBS, COMT, MAO, MTR/MTRR, BHMT AND VDR. [60,61,62,63]

HOW A BASE JUMPER SAVED ME

At the time of writing this book, the best practise for treating our Anxiety is still CBT (Cognitive Behavioural Therapy) understanding our body sensations and exposure therapy. It has worked for me to date. The thing that gets me excited is the fact that science is continually advancing and developing new ideas and treatments.

I do not doubt that gut health and gene therapy will be part of the big picture as the science continues to improve, and there is no doubt that future discoveries will aid in our recovery, making it a lot quicker and easier. Whilst that's not a helpful, quick fix today, there's comfort in knowing that what you are tackling is a common enough problem that scientists are actively seeking answers.

CHAPTER 14

L.E.T.'S GET PHYSICAL

I've talked about changing your thinking, working with your mind, eating better and how science is trying to help us.

There will be those of you out there who are itching with all this long-term, mind mumbo jumbo stuff… what can I DO to fix it, you might be asking.

There are quite a few things you can try that will make a big difference to your Anxiety levels.

10 SECOND BREATHING TEST

So, looks like he wants us to breath for 10 seconds and then what?

Well, not exactly, I want to try a simple test to see how you breathe.

It goes like this: when we are relaxed and breathing; naturally, we tend to breathe into our belly, slowly with gentle expansion. When we are not comfortable or continuously on the edge and Fearful, we often breathe into the top of our chest – that's permanently shallow and faster breathing. The problem with this is, that shallow breath activates the Fear centre by sending messages that we are ready to run or fight. This causes your already hyper-aroused Fear centre to be even more on edge, and the spiral continues.

Here is an easy 10-second test to see where you are with your breathing behaviour.

Sit or stand, and place one hand on your tummy and the other on your chest.

Breathe in and out regularly and take note which hand is raised more.

It's either the one on your chest or tummy.

Chances are if you're suffering from Anxiety, then the hand on your chest is going to be moving more than the one on your tummy.

We aim to retrain breathing deep into our belly and not up in the chest. This is a gentle exercise, not forced when your breath in.

To help aid this try more NASAL breathing (Breathing through your nose) than your mouth as it aids in breathing deeper rather than shallower.

Like anything, it will take time and practise, so give it a go and see if breathing deep calms down your body and mind.[13]

THE POWER OF TONE

We have all experienced or observed a moment when someone yells or screams at us. It can often create feelings of fear, stress, or even dismissal, as we tune out what the person is saying because it is so powerful.

We have also experienced the feeling of calmness, safety, and reassurance when someone talks in a soft, gentle manner to get their message across.

L.E.T.'S GET PHYSICAL

I have noticed in myself, both as a Parent and Paramedic, the power of using my tone of voice and the positive (or negative) effect it has. Particularly softer tones concerning stress.

So why is this?

Anecdotally, I can tell you that there is a direct correlation between using a calm tone and the ability to calm yourself and others around you.

My job as a Paramedic can find me in very high-stress situations where there is a lot of emotion and Fear released by both me, wanting to do the best job possible, and the patient or others at the scene.

My role expects me to be able to act calmly and effectively under pressure without losing my cool or control of the job.

One of the most effective tools I use is to speak calmly, use softer tones and be as gentle as possible with my patients. Not only does it have a direct impact on their wellbeing, but it also creates a feeling of safety and reassurance.

Being calm also helps me by sending messages to my brain that everything is safe and relatively controlled. This impacts my stress levels immediately, lowering them to a tolerable state.

It seems that if my tone is one of anger, aggression or Fear, it activates my stress response. However, if the opposite is applied in regards to speaking calmly, softer in tone and slower, it doesn't seem to trigger that fight and flight response.

Next time you're feeling stressed or anxious, try speaking in a slow and calm tone and watch the effect it has on you and your body. I guarantee that you will feel a sense of calmness and safety, with added reassurance in whatever you're doing. [70]

MUSIC TEST

First, he wants me to check out my breathing... now I have to listen to music too?

There is a rationale behind my ingenious tests, I promise.

When we're wired with Anxious thoughts and thoughts that unsettle us, it can be tough to break away from them as they seem to want to stay in that cycle of Fear and distress.

It is also hard to think of other things when we are solely focused on these unhelpful thoughts. Remember, Anxiety creates a fixation on threats and Fears (even if they are just thoughts).

What if I were to tell you we can train our brains or minds to shift thoughts and, in turn, decrease our distress and Anxiety?

When we are meditating mindfully, we allow our thoughts to come in and be observed without judgement and let them go. It's excellent for helping us move or shift our focus.

Another way we can help shift our focus is by replacing our unhappy ones into happy ones by gently shifting our concentration.

I have come up with a test for you to prove that it can happen, and with ease.

We all know that experience of getting a song stuck in your head – an earworm. It starts to drive you nuts and never wants to leave no matter how hard you try. It's like a cracked record going around and around again.

One day this happened to me, and I tried a million ways to get it out of my head with no success. Then, like an angel out of nowhere, my wife came past singing a different song. It was one of my favourites and a great tune as well. *(Ironically, Peaceful easy feeling-Eagles for your reference)*

I started to sing with her, just for fun, and we laughed. After she left the room, I noticed that the old annoying song had gone and the new one had replaced it. It was blissful and refreshing.

I now apply this strategy whenever songs get stuck in my head. I change the song to one that is more enjoyable and pleasant without force...just a gentle nudge.

Initially, it starts as a battle of two songs, but eventually, the old song becomes replaced with the new one, and that earworm is a distant memory.

This might be an approach you can use for dodgy songs, but also unwanted Anxious thoughts. Gently bring in new, pleasant, helpful ones and slowly watch the difference.

Go on, try the music test and see for yourself how easy it can be and of course liberating also.

While we are on the topic of music, I have found listening to music to be incredibly powerful. If I am feeling down or a little out of sorts, I tend to listen to slower, softer songs while I contemplate my emotions and allow myself to feel them entirely. It helps me delve into myself and experience this negative emotion.

The beauty is, I notice that I start to feel a change or shift in my mood, and it starts to become lighter. Along with this shift, I initiate a change in the song genre and shift the energy to something more upbeat. I have done this subconsciously since I was a young boy not realising the powerful effects it has in helping me feel, shift and change my emotion from low to high.

This is something you could try if you're stuck in any emotion and struggling to move forward.

POSTURE

Did you know that walking upright with a straight back and shoulders open (like you have a stick up your arse) helps send messages to the brain and everyone else that you are confident, in control and also helps reduces your stress?

Having an assertive posture increases your testosterone levels by up to 20% and decreases your cortisol levels by up to 25%. This is pretty amazing, considering it's such a simple thing we can all do with ease.

Another advantage of sitting or walking upright is that it allows more natural breathing that promotes increased oxygen flow. If we are hunched over, it requires more effort because our breath is shallower. This then creates extra messages of stress to the brain and the body.

So, remember to breathe gently into your belly with your back straight and shoulders open and see if you can notice the difference.

Put that invisible stick back up your arse, guys! (There's some advice you never thought you'd take on board, hey?) [71,72]

STRETCHING YOUR MUSCLES

What has stretching got to do with Fear and Anxiety?

As you already know, Fear gets the muscles primed for fighting or fleeing – becoming full of energy and oxygen. When the energy is used up the way it's designed, everything works correctly, and the muscles soon return to a relaxed state.

If that nervous energy is not exhausted or expelled because you are sitting in a chair in your office full of Fear about an upcoming presentation, then your body becomes contracted, stiff and tense.

Therefore, that tension needs to be released so the muscles can find a relaxed state again. In chronic stress and Fear, there is often a constant state of stiffness (no not that type of stiffness, you dirty buggers!) and contraction that becomes the norm and you don't even realise the point you have got to.

That's when all the physical signs develop in regards to headaches, stiff neck, back, shoulders etc. as they are not as supple as they once were (or should be).

Introduce passive stretching regularly to help aid relaxation and flexibility of your muscles. It is a great tool that's easy to do; it's free and helps relax your body and system in the fight against Fear.

Any time of the day or night is fine, although I find it works exceptionally well before bed. Releasing tension in your muscles, especially the tighter ones, brings an enormous sense of calmness and wellbeing.

Exercises found in yoga and Pilates has undeniable benefits for your physical and mental wellbeing. Here are some extra benefits to stretching:

- Stretching promotes better posture by keeping your muscles and bones in correct alignment. We have discussed the benefits of having a power posture and the added benefits it has on reducing our Anxiety and stress; it also supports your posture.
- Stretching increases stamina and circulation in your muscles because then they're not always full of tension (requiring extra energy and blood flow).
- Stretching aids to decrease the risk of injury, pain and soreness as it promotes greater nutrient supply through improved blood flow to the working muscles.

Here's a comfortable stretch for you to have a go of right now...

Stretch your neck muscles by moving your head side to side, front and back. Now stretch your arms out side to side, pulling the triceps and biceps. Lift your arms up and down passively. Move on to stretching your upper and lower back bums, hips, legs and calves.

I think you get the picture, the more muscles you can passively stretch the better. Take your time and appreciate the extra calmness once you're done. [13,73,74]

PSOAS MUSCLES (SO—AS)

While on the topic of stretching your muscles, how about some interesting information regarding your Psoas muscles. They are the muscles near your groins on both legs, which are attached to your spinal cord and have a role to play in activating your Anxiety. (I'm not bullshitting you, stick with me here.)

When we are in a state of Fear, our muscles contract ready for action, and the psoas muscles are partially responsible for getting your legs activated and become contracted.

This sends a message to the brain that we are ready to go and act if required. If these muscles are consistently tight and contracted, then it continues to send a message to the brain that it's game on, activating your Anxiety.

Therefore, we need to deactivate these muscles by stretching them regularly to turn off that stimulus.

Remember, the body is continuously accessing sensory information to aid in assisting a detection for danger, and this is one of those signals. Stretching will help reduce this signalling. [75]

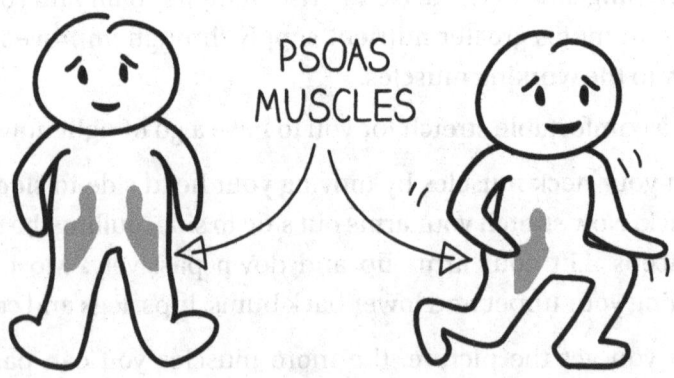

EPSOM SALT BATHS

Epsom salts are salts from Epsom in England that have unique properties thanks to the minerals found in them. One of the main minerals helpful to us is Magnesium (Mg) and salt.

What's so good about Magnesium, Chriso?

Well, Magnesium aids in calming and relaxing our muscles and nervous system. It's an essential mineral required to achieve the proper function of these elements within the body.

Stress often depletes our stores of Magnesium, and we need to increase Magnesium (or Mg) in our diet via food or supplements to be effective in raising the levels.

Another way of increasing our Mg levels is by having a bath of Epsom salts that contains plenty of Mg and can be absorbed into our body through the skin.

Not only does a standard bath promote calmness and relaxation without Epsom salts, but it can also be supercharged to increase those pleasant feelings by adding Epsom salts.

All you have to do is run a bath and add the dose stated on the packet into the water. Easy peasy.

Then simply lay or sit in the bath and allow the Mg to be absorbed into your skin. If this is done at night, you will undoubtedly feel the calming effects it has before going to bed, allowing for a restful sleep. It is also fantastic for your skin.

If you don't have a bath, then simply get a large bucket and add Epsom salts into that and place your feet in. It will still help your body absorb the Mg.

This is also an excellent tool for detoxing your body from all the impurities that have accumulated.

On the topic on Mg. A good Mg supplement is also very useful in helping relax the nervous system and muscles that have been flogged to death by your Fear and stress.

They are readily available in most pharmacies, supermarkets or health food shops. If you're concerned about taking an oral supplement, speak to a medical professional for advice. [76,77]

It's good shit!

EXERCISE

Exercise is a super important tactic in nullifying the effects of the dreaded stress and Anxiety. As discussed earlier, the body becomes full of energy and tension when activated by Fear, and this needs to be released.

If, not then it results in tension and also weight gain. Hang on, what?

I know. More fun stuff, hey. I've mentioned tension previously but let me tell you about weight gain.

As the body primes itself for action, it requires plenty of energy to do so.

If that energy is mobilised and not used, then it gets stored as fat and generally heads towards your gut region as the best place to

L.E.T.'S GET PHYSICAL

make itself home. You may see people with excess belly fat around the gut and hips region after prolonged periods of Anxiety and Fear.

Exercise can help use up some of this energy to reduce your fat stores and tension, but the main reason exercise is so powerful is the release of endorphins and enkephalins, both of which make you feel good.

Because endorphins help block pain, they allow for happier body sensations and feelings to enter. This also includes blocking the effects of the Fear and their sensations, making you feel bulletproof.

From a brain's perspective, increased exercise levels promote growth in the Hippocampal region, which helps store new memories and process new information. It also promotes better-thinking processes – helping shift old ideas to new fresher ones. Gee, I wonder if this will help our old Anxiety memories and imperfect ways of thinking? Get ya sneakers on, peeps!

The other enjoyable aspect of exercise is that it can be an opportunity to focus on something else aside from your Anxiety. It can promote happier feelings, and it can also be used as a physical and mental resetter—so many good things.

Once you've had a solid workout and got a bit of sweat going on, the body can release a lot of toxins and mobilise wastes to help detoxify your body. It also allows the worries of the world to melt away because your brain and body have been filled with feel-good chemicals, not the usual negative, Anxious ones that seem to have such a strong influence.

If you haven't exercised for a long time, start slow and work up to higher levels of fitness.

I don't subscribe to anyone not being able to exercise because of physical ailments, as there is always some form of exercise that can be done.

Short slow walks are a good start gradually increasing the distance and intensity. If you are already reasonably fit, then try ramping up the intensity as that's what gives you the high.

You won't necessarily feel great at the time of your actual exercise, as the endorphins kick in once you've stopped and recovered – around 30 minutes post-exercise. Then, kick back and enjoy the free ride of happiness and feeling good.

Go out and go full-on guys!

Ideally, three to four sessions a week for around 45-60 minutes go a long way to achieving this great release of Endorphins. [78,79,80]

INCREASING DOPAMINE LEVELS (THE REWARD CHEMICAL)

This stuff needs to be bottled because it makes you feel bloody good. Some of the ways to help produce it in the body are by taking L-tyrosine (which is a supplement that helps increase levels of dopamine), and it can also be derived from almost all healthy foods. The usual suspects such as meat, dairy, poultry, nuts, bananas, green leafy vegetables, turmeric and avocados are some foods to think about incorporating into your diet.

Gingko Biloba can also help. Exercise, walking, yoga, tai chi, meditation, enjoying music, touch like massage or cuddles and any activities you enjoy participating in are a ripping start. [81,82,83,84]

INCREASING OXYTOCIN LEVELS (THE LOVE CHEMICAL)

This little beauty is one of my favourites, as you will see.

It can be increased by physical touch (both sexual and non-sexual) such as hugging, massage and making eye contact.

Cuddles of pets helps as well. Holding hands, giving gifts, exercising, listening to music, meditation and soaking in a hot bath all get this baby rocking! You can probably work out why I like this one. [87]

INCREASING ENDORPHIN LEVELS (THE PAIN KILLER)

As discussed in the exercise section above. Exercise or runners high (yep, it is a real thing) help get these working for you. I usually get it activated if my workouts are full-on and intense.

Meditation, Tai Chi, Yoga, massage and acupuncture also help release it.

Chilli peppers (capsaicin – the burning bit of chilli) also gets it going. *Have a crack.* [78,79,80]

INCREASING SEROTONIN LEVELS (THE MOOD ENHANCER)

You can increase these levels by doing a few things which help you feel sensational.

1) Get more sunlight, bright light and get outside it is thought to increase levels.
2) Regular exercise certainly improves levels and wellbeing.

Serotonin is made from an amino acid called tryptophan. This stuff can be found in foods such as pork, chicken, turkey, fish, rice, eggs, soya beans, cheese peanuts and vitamin B6. Get into them.

Meditating can help identify negative thought patterns and replace them with healthier, more positive outcomes. *Nice!* [81,82,83,84]

STIMULANTS

Good old stimulants – it's a bit of a loaded word, isn't it!

Don't Panic. Stimulants are a food, substance or drug that primarily stimulates your body and make you feel more alert, awake and active. They can be very beneficial when required to get you through your day either at work, home or study.

They can come in lots of forms such as regulars like coffee, tea (caffeine) and cigarettes. They can also come from natural herbs like guarana.

Alcohol also has a combination of stimulant and then depressive action as it often gets you up and about initially and then creates a slower depressive action if you have enough of it (I think we've all been there).

Alcohol can create a bit of a sneaky trap. It has a significant effect on taking the edge off and settling nerves in different situations. It is probably the most commonly used and available drug that helps people reduce their Anxiety (otherwise known as Dutch courage). However, if I peeled the ears back and had a blinder, my Anxiety in the morning would be ten times worst. The combination of feeling physically shit and potential "unknown" behaviour (things you remember along with things you don't) seem to flare things up more.

Although I still love a great time on the frothies, (beers) I am aware that it can create this backlog of nervous tension and Anxiety from time to time, so I approach with caution and awareness.

There have been studies on the effects of alcohol and Neuropeptide Y (N.P.Y.) – which as discussed earlier has a calming and anti-Anxiety effect on us. Although there is no complete understanding of how alcohol and N.P.Y. work together, it seems that there is a correlation between the two, and the effects they have on each other and our Anxiety, making us feel more relaxed and chilled.

Interestingly, other studies have indicated that people with low levels of N.P.Y. tend to suffer from Alcohol Use disorders and abuse of that alcohol, versus those whose levels are higher with reduced alcohol abuse.

It looks like the grog ticks some unhealthy boxes in treating our Anxiety and also potentially increasing our substance abuse (bummer, I know, but certainly something to think about on your

L.E.T.'S GET PHYSICAL

road to recovery if that applies to you).

At this point, I don't think you need to be Einstein to recognise that drug-related stimulants such as methamphetamine (like ice or speed) that naturally rev your system activate the Fear response tenfold. It's not worth it on so many levels.

These stimulants are like adding fuel to the fire that doesn't need any more fuel. Your body is already wired and geared up enough without any further stimulants.

The aim of activating or increasing these chemicals is to calm your system, not enable it any further. Take this into consideration when choosing to add these to your lifestyle. Do you want their effects increasing your Fear and unwanted stress any more?

I, for one, absolutely love my coffee and would never give it up. However, I do notice the effects it has on me if I drink too many cups. I also recognise the results when I have the occasional energy drink in my system – it often makes me jittery, with increased tension and adds Anxiety. [88,89]

I am always mindful of its potential—something to think about.

SLEEP

Oh my goodness, how good is a good night sleep and the effects it has on you?

When we are suffering Anxiety and Fear, one helpful way of turning the hyper-aroused system off is by becoming relaxed and calm. One of the easiest ways to accomplish this is by getting plenty of rest.

After all, sleep allows our body to rejuvenate and repair, providing us with energy and good health.

That's bloody unhelpful, Chris – how hard is it to sleep when you are stressed and worried?

Even if you do get to sleep straight away, how hard is it to stay asleep without waking in the middle of the night and then not to be able to get back to sleep without a constant barrage of endless mind chatter and racing thoughts?

We are sort of stuffed because we know we need sleep to help us recover and feel better, but also find it hard to sleep properly in the first place.

This only creates more Fear, worry and stress and of course, less sleep! Another fun problem! How can we solve this one?

I know, let's get drunk!

Well, hang on a bit. Alcohol does initially help us fall asleep, and I am sure we have all been in that situation when you 'pass out' from drinking too much and then struggle to wake up.

A healthy sleep cycle is when you move into a period of Rapid Eye Movement (R.E.M.) around 90 minutes later. That is the dream state and the opportunity to recharge and repair. Awesome if this is healthy sleep.

However, alcohol disrupts this R.E.M. cycle and won't allow this deeper type of sleep. That's the reason why we often wake up feeling tired even though we've slept all night. We don't get quality, long-lasting R.E.M. sleep cycles that help the body recharge and restore.

Think twice about using alcohol to get a good night sleep and have a look at these ideas below instead.

To be honest, there is no easy solution, but I have several strategies I use that aid in my sleeping and getting a good night's sleep.

Here are a few to try:

1) Meditation (mindfulness) helps quieten the mind and endless chatter if done before bed.
2) Epsom salts baths or baths help relax you before bed. (Mentioned earlier).
3) Stretching your whole body before bed helps release the tension in your muscles, allowing you to become more relaxed and calmer.
4) Reading a book before bed always makes me sleepy and drift off easy. The reason being is that you focused on the book and distracted from your Fears and Anxieties.
5) Getting physical during the day as much as possible helps me become so physically tired that I am too tired to think.
6) No 'blue screens' or technology an hour before bed. Dim lighting also helps activate the release of melatonin (sleep hormone).
7) Bach flower rescue sleep spray or pastels are very effective (I'll talk more about this below).
8) Difficulty waking in the middle of the night and not being able to get back to sleep. Try the L.E.T.G.O.E., 5 D's or F.E.E.L. G.O.O.D. Strategies for anything related to stress, Anxiety, future events, or general worries as it helps you nip thoughts in the bud and not get too heavily involved in them in the first place.
9) Listening to music can be relaxing.
10) Avoid stimulants like tea, coffee, sugary foods or alcohol before bedtime.
11) Melatonin which is a hormone released by the pineal gland to help us fall asleep. (Safe medication). Your GP can prescribe it as an alternative if all else fails. [90,91,92]

SUPPLEMENTS AND VITAMINS TO HELP OUR ANXIETY

Over time it has become clear that nutritional and herbal supplements can and are effective in helping the treatment of Anxiety and associated symptoms with the reduced risk of side effects of other pharmacological medications on the market.

There is also a possibility that some supplements create a 'placebo effect' allowing the patient to feel better. A placebo effect is a response that creates a positive result in your treatment that is purely psychological. The medication or supplement is either filled with sugar or have a proven non-efficacy. It is demonstrated time and time again in studies that placebo has the same effect of the actual 'medical drug' being assessed. The power of the mind, hey?

Thankfully, there is anecdotal evidence that some of the supplements listed below are very effective for treating Anxiety. In saying that, please seek medical advice before taking any of these supplements or vitamins.

I also advise you to do your research about potential side effects or interactions before taking these supplements or vitamins and as always seek medical advice before taking any medication.

In no particular order of merit, here are a few:

BACH FLOWER

This is a homeopathic remedy that I have first-hand found incredibly useful at helping Anxiety.

It is derived from natural flower essences and developed by Dr Edward Bach in the 1930s. The homeopathic community gets a bad rap for their treatments, particularly in them working more as a placebo then clinically. However, from my experience, I have found these little essences to be more than useful.

Thirty-eight different essences act on various emotional states and work subtly to allow you to move forward and resolve any emotional blocks you have.

The Bach flower website gives you a description of what the essences treat that may relate to you. It can be very specific and helpful.

They are entirely safe and have no side effects and can be taken by both children and adults.

The main two formulas that are readily available in most supermarkets and pharmacies are Rescue Remedy and Rescue Sleep. They are both made up of a combination of different essences and can be taken in either pastel, spray, or dropper form.

There is a lot of positive reviews that you can read, and anecdotally, I can also vouch for their effectiveness. [93,94]

PASSIONFLOWER

Passionflower (Passiflora Incarnata Linn) is a common herbal supplement that is effective in reducing your Anxiety. Recent studies have demonstrated that this herb can be as effective as taking oxazepam a (benzodiazepine).

This herb is excellent at keeping mild to moderate Anxiety at bay.

It can be taken in tablet, liquid or tea form.[95,96]

KAVA

Kava is derived from the plant (Piper methysticum) and has been used for centuries in various countries, especially the Polynesia regions.

The advantage of Kava is that it helps relieve your Anxiety and associated symptoms without a sedative effect.

Studies have demonstrated its effectiveness in treating Anxiety and the positive results it has. Interestingly, it also has some severe side effects that have resulted in it being banned in markets across Europe, the United Kingdom and Canada.

There is potential for severe liver damage and failure to occur. Still, it seems to be a little extreme as the current review supports the view that liver damage is significantly rare. If Kava is taken at appropriate levels, it is well-tolerated across all studies.

Overall this is an excellent product with super positive results in various studies.

As an added note, Kava is legal in Australia and available via supplement or teabag. [96]

ST. JOHNS WORT

St. John's Wort (Hypericm perforatum) comes from the flowers of this plant. It has also been used for long periods and has been linked to treating depression more than Anxiety.

However, due to the overlapping of these two conditions, the effects St. Johns Wort has to assist in your Anxiety can only be of benefit. It can have some side effects if you stop using it abruptly but otherwise seems to be well tolerated. It also has a lot of contraindications with other medications, so always check with your health care professional.

Can be taken in either tablet or liquid form. [96]

L-LYSINE

Lysine is an amino acid that helps build proteins in the body. It also seems to have an impact on serotonin (the feel-good hormone) and decreased cortisol levels (stress hormone) by reducing the levels and gut-brain response to stress.

The net result is that it can help reduce your stress and Anxiety with no reported side effects.

Can be taken in tablet form. [96,97]

MAGNESIUM AND VITAMIN B SUPPLEMENTS

Magnesium and Vitamin B are essential for the proper function of nerves in the body, and I mentioned Magnesium earlier when discussing Epsom salts. The combination of both of these supplements has been proven in several studies to be incredibly useful in reducing one's overall Anxiety and promoting a feeling of calmness and being relaxed.

Vitamin B comes in a variety of different numbers such as B1, B3, B5, B6 and B12. They help reduce the build-up of lactic acid and also assist in regulating mood, especially depression.

Vitamin B is not stored in the body, so it is required to be either increased through diet or supplements.

Vitamin B can be sourced from meat, whole grains, potatoes, bananas, turkey and legumes, to name a few.

Magnesium is a positive charged ion or mineral that assists in many different roles at the cellular level. It helps with muscle relaxation, control of blood pressure, and general tension.

As discussed earlier, Epsom salts baths are a great way of increasing our levels of Magnesium, supplements and food similar to Vitamin B with the addition of fish and seeds. [76,77, 98, 99]

COPPER AND ZINC

It is worth checking out your levels of Zinc and Copper.

They have a unique relationship with each other by sort of "sucking" the other one dry creating an inbalance with each other. These two minerals do a heap of stuff in our bodies helping with growth, mental development and cardiovascular health. They also play a massive role in our Anxiety.

The problem often starts when we have high levels of Copper and low levels of Zinc.

It creates a heap of symptoms that can be fixed or resolved by tweaking a few things.

Excess Copper generally comes from water pipes made from Copper, highly farmed land, pesticides and added Copper to animals in feedlots that we eventually eat.

If we are high in Copper, our Zinc is often low, and symptoms below are often not realised because of these two minerals being out of whack.

They are also very rarely checked.

Check this out:

- Anxiety, Panic attacks and nervousness.
- Depression.
- Fatigue.
- Insomnia and poor sleep.
- Mood swings.
- Constipation.
- Yeast infections (digestive problems).
- Racing heart and palpitations.
- Cramping and body aches.
- Oversensitivity and obsessive thinking.

The high levels of Copper tend to ramp up the Anxiety, Panic and anger acting like a conduit of electricity firing off an already highly-strung system almost making our Anxiety even more "trigger happy". It also has a strong relationship with candida (yeast) infections in your gut as they thrive in high copper environments. Check out the chapter in gut health about yeast overgrowth.

Low Zinc levels stuff up our sleep and often are attributed to depression and other mood disorders.

Interestingly, Zinc is needed for the production of Serotonin (Mood stabiliser) and Melatonin (promotes sleep), if it's low then you can see what can happen.

We all know the feeling of super fatigue and emotions associated with it.

That certainly isn't calmness and happiness (shift worker talk here).

If this is a case for you, then changes to your diet trying to reduce your Candida overgrowth and supplemental changes to your Zinc, Magnesium, and Vitamin B6, C and E. This may be an option to balance these two minerals out and indeed assist in reducing your symptoms. [100,101]

(May need to refer to an Integrated Doctor for assistance)

GABA

GABA is a neurotransmitter that helps you feel calm and settled. It can help with Anxiety, sleep, improved mood and of course, stress. Neurotransmitters are chemicals that allow the neurons to talk to each other by clinging to receptors found on each neuron.

It is referred to as an inhibitory neurotransmitter that essentially calms your farm meaning it slows down the neurons firing off like firecrackers and cools their jets!!!

GABA is used in your brain and is made naturally, and interestingly GABA receptors are found in your gut also. We know the relationship your gut and brain have on each other and the importance of gut health and emotions.

As GABA promotes relaxation, sleep and feelings of calm and happiness when present we want to try and get some of this "bad boy" on board for our little often overworked brains to chill for a bit.

A drug like Xanax and Valium act to fire up GABA neurotransmitters to give us that calm and Anxiety reduced feeling.

So, what can we do to increase or produce the levels of GABA in our brain?

Here are a few things to think about which may help.

Kava activates the receptors with a compound found in it called Kavalactones. (Listed above)

Magnesium is a mineral that aids in GABA activation and essential biochemical processes. (Listed above)

L-theanine is an amino acid that increases the production of GABA found in green tea and supplement form.

Other natural ways to increase your GABA is through meditation, exercise and yoga.

All these little things can help turn down the volume and make you feel a bit more comfortable. [102,103,104]

VALERIAN ROOT

This little ripper is a herb that is great at helping you rest and sleep. It would be something you would take at night to aid in sleeping.

The reason it's good for your Anxiety is that it allows your body and mind to rest overnight, which, in turn, gives you a more positive and settled start to the day. That then reduces the overactive, hyperaroused nervous system that is generally ready to flick off into Anxiety and Panic.

It has little or no side effects and comes in tablet or tea form. [105,106]

ESSENTIAL OILS

Essential oils are another complementary addition to helping with our Anxiety.

Several studies have backed up their great effects and benefits, and part of this comes from the deep breathing involved when inhaling a positive aroma. I have seen the positive results of these oils with myself and my children. Like any complementary treatments, it is a process, and you may find some work better than others.

Here are the oils that worked for me to help calm and relax, thus reducing my Anxiety:

1) Lavender oil
2) Rose oil
3) Vetiver
4) Ylang Ylang
5) Bergamot
6) Chamomile
7) Frankincense. [107,108]

Could you give it a go; it's worth a try?

TEAS

Peppermint, chamomile and green tea are all good to help aid in relaxation and assisting in Anxiety as I have experienced.

They all have properties from their relative plants that aid in relaxing, calming effects on you and your body. [109]

COMPLEMENTARY THERAPIES

Complimentary therapies are precisely that, complimentary. A bit like a sweet gravy on top of your meal, if you get my drift.

There are a wide variety of these therapies out there, and many are effective.

Some complementary therapies have a bad rap or negative stigma attached to them. My advice here is simple and straightforward: if you try something and it works, then who cares! It works! Which is sort of the point?

Often, it's hard to understand specific complementary therapies due to the lack of science or understanding, but that doesn't mean they are not valid.

Practises or treatments such as Meditation, Massage, Naturopathy, Chinese medicine, Yoga, Acupuncture, Aromatherapy and Essential oils all play a vital role, and just some of these may be needed.

There are a plethora of complementary techniques and therapies available. All of us are different and respond differently. So finding your unique way of how your body works and responds is essential.

You are on a journey of discovery, it is yours and so do what is right for you- not anyone else!

Finding your style and practises can help you live in a happier Fear-less world.

CHAPTER 15

SIMPLE, PRACTICAL FIXES

We have discussed at length the effects that high stress has on our already Anxious and worked up body. So, I wanted to put together some different tools you might use that can help reduce your stress levels and naturally bring down your hyperaroused state.

They are not overly complicated steps to follow and, even if followed loosely, can provide a guide to help you tackle some of life's challenges – those you will encounter daily.

Surprisingly, many people don't have a natural process or method to use when faced with specific problems or issues that arise and, because of this, tend to struggle when they happen. I have learnt these skills through personal experience, my professional life and various courses along the way and want to share them with you.

These steps can be a great reference point to use if you find things are getting on top of you and you're trying to work out why. They can be applied at home, school, work or general life.

Below are a few suggestions I have, and I hope they help.

PRIORITISING

This first one is definitely a concept that I see can be applied a lot more and is super powerful in putting things in order – allowing you to be calmer and in control.

First, make a list of all the things you need to do today or shortly.

Then, in one of two ways, either by order of importance (perhaps number them 1 – 10); or label from urgent (done now) to significant (done soon) to unimportant (done eventually).

These orders can, of course, overlap and at times things happen to stop them from getting done so allowance to be flexible is important.

Let's use an example of an everyday scenario.

- Washing clothes
- Posting mail at the post office
- Filling out the form for school
- Shopping for food
- Interview for a new job
- Paying bills
- Yoga.

If you look at the list, there seems to be a lot to do, and that can cause quite a bit of stress as it's a bit overwhelming. I agree, but if you can prioritise what's important and needed, versus not essential, some things can be left until tomorrow or the evening.

Using the numbered Order of Importance, it might look like this:

1) Interview for a new job
2) Shopping for food
3) Washing clothes
4) Filling out the form for school
5) Paying bills
6) Posting mail post office
7) Yoga.

Alternatively, the Urgent to Unimportant method might be this:

1) Interview for a new job (urgent)
2) Shopping for food (important)
3) Washing clothes (important)
4) Filling out the form for school (unimportant)
5) Paying bills (unimportant)
6) Posting mail post office (unimportant)
7) Yoga (unimportant).

As you can see, the job interview takes the main focus for the day. However, it's not until noon so it might be ok to get to the shops, buy food for dinner and put the washing machine on before you go. This is assuming you're prepared for the interview, have your clothes ready and have done your due diligence.

If not, food and washing can wait until after the interview (or get take away dude).

The other tasks can be done after your interview, on the way home, by paying bills at the post office along with posting mail. The school form can be done at night or wait until tomorrow.

And, of course, at the end of a busy day and hopefully successful interview, timeout for Yoga would be perfect.

This is just an example and a relatively simple one, but this strategy is excellent at helping you get things done and keep your head on straight.

Another example I like to use is my sons' homework. They get two weeks to complete eight topics before handing it in. I ask them to prioritise what the most critical issues are, and do them first. Otherwise, if they are all relatively similar, they can break the topics up over eight nights and do one topic each night. This results in minimal stress and ease of completion.

If they wait until the last minute, then eight topics have to be completed in a short time frame and end in stress. We've all been there, hey?

The only reason this strategy doesn't work is that they are not disciplined to do a topic each night. Alternatively, they could do two topics over four nights. Either way, it's all about taking a gradual, stress-free approach.

CONFLICT

This topic sure can create a lot of stress for anyone, let alone someone who isn't confrontational. The ability to work through conflict is a skill that needs plenty of practise and time but has compelling results. Not everyone gets their dukes up for a rumble or likes to charge in like a bull.

Not dealing with conflict often leads to resentment and anger, and that only affects you in the long run. It also drives up your wired brain and fuels your Anxiety.

Here are some tips to follow that can help:

1) Take time to plan your approach and thoughts.
2) Try and speak to the person directly with the issue.
3) Use a non-threatening manner (for example, a calm voice, open body language).
4) Listen to their thoughts without speaking.
5) Try and problem solve the issue.
6) If you can't resolve the issue, aim for a win/win approach.
7) Utilise other colleagues or peers if necessary, to help find a solution.
8) Don't hold a grudge; move on.

The most significant problem individuals face when dealing with conflict is not doing it correctly and often become angry or aggressive to get their message across. Talking calmly and using open body language is more effective in getting the results needed.

There is also an old adage that I like to use 'you get more flies with honey than vinegar'. A little sweetness (and gentle, calm behaviour) goes a long way.

PROBLEM-SOLVING

If only there were a simple way to solve all our problems!

Here are some tips to follow that can help:

1) Identify the problem.
2) Determine the cause.
3) Ask myself, can it be fixed.
4) Look at alternatives and use advice from others if needed.
5) Select a solution to use.

6) Apply the solution.

7) Reassess to see if it works.

Some of the issues people have when solving a problem is working out what the problem is in the first place. This needs to be identified.

It will be impossible to find a solution if you can't find the cause. This is relevant in all areas in your life, including work, relationships or socially. All problems have a reason, some being on an emotional level and others being a little more straightforward and practical.

Once you've identified what the hell is wrong, ask yourself if you can fix it by yourself. If not, seek assistance from others or from different resources to help out.

Decide to choose a solution and apply it. Hopefully, it works.

Otherwise, it's back to the drawing board to tweak maybe or entirely rearrange your original solution.

Here's a simple example:

PROBLEM: The computer won't turn on.

CAUSE: See if it is plugged in and turned on.

CAN YOU FIX IT: The computer is plugged in and turned on, but there's still no power.

ALTERNATIVES: Maybe the power is out, check the fuse box, call electrician.

SOLUTION: Electrician guiding you through fuse box and asking to flick the switch to power the house.

APPLY: Flick fuse box switch and see if computer power is on.

ASSESS: Power to the computer is on.

A SIDE NOTE: If the power to the computer is still not on, maybe call energy company to see if power is out in your area – a different solution.

I think you get the drift of what I am trying to help you with. This list of steps is a guide and may be of benefit when you're stuck trying to find a solution.

TEAMWORK

Working as a team, whether as a family or in the workplace, can have massive advantages in getting things done quickly, effectively and at times in a fun way, without the potential for resentment and conflict (which can happen when someone feels others are not doing their fair share to help out).

If you can get in, get your hands dirty with each other working as a team, there often feels like a sense of closeness or comradeship that only promotes more healthy relationships within the group.

The key is having a go and helping out as much as possible, and you can't go wrong. They are lazy and being slack fuels fire at times, especially when everyone is tired or exhausted:

1) Identify your roles and be flexible with your tasks (we sometimes get shit jobs).
2) Listen to others and complete your tasks.
3) Apply your knowledge if required for specific tasks.
4) Enjoy building relationships and understanding we all have different personalities.
5) Show common courtesy towards your colleagues or family/friends.
6) Build rapport by helping out when you can and asking assistance if needed.
7) Don't stop until the task is completed or everyone agrees to stop.

EFFECTIVE COMMUNICATION

This topic is probably the most significant cause of stress out of everything. Although we are all fluent in speaking, we very rarely communicate effectively. On the contrary, we tend to not relay our messages appropriately in the right context or with the best timing. It is often when we hold everything in and then explode with comments that don't match the crime and end up creating negative relationships and conflict.

It's much better if we address problems early, so they don't manifest into something more significant. Also, the ability to bloody LISTEN is a skill that I have no idea about, but apparently, it's quite effective. Seriously, listen before you speak.

Let's take a look at what we can do to communicate effectively:

1) Listen without responding.
2) Use the right body language.
3) Use effective, slow, calm language and to the point.
4) Be patient and understanding of the other person's comments.
5) Be tolerant of their thoughts.
6) Aim to express and communicate what's on your mind fully.
7) Aim to end in a friendly, peaceful environment.

Let's say you feel like you need to speak to your partner about your feelings regarding lack of affection.

Approach him/her with the topic and state your feelings. Allow him/her to respond without butting in. Be open to their thoughts and comments, and reply in a way which is calm and soft to enable your message to get through and listened. Talk through thoroughly until you find the answer or compromise.

Aim to not 'bottle things up' for too long, as other stronger emotions may interfere with the effectiveness of your communication. If you save up even the smallest frustrations, you make life more stressful for yourself as time goes on.

ACCOUNTABILITY

Being accountable for your actions is the best way to take control of your life and head in the right direction. If you can identify where you are potentially making mistakes or doing the wrong thing, then you can fix the problem and reduce stress in your world.

If you're someone who tends not to be accountable for your actions and have things go wrong often, then perhaps it's time to ask yourself if it's you that is the problem, instead of someone else. It also gives you credibility when you admit you're wrong. We all make mistakes.

It's time to get the old mirror out and have a good look at yourself (Michael Jackson wrote a song about that):

1) Identify the problem that you need to be accountable for.

2) Explain and justify your actions.

3) Take responsibility if at fault.

4) Adopt the policy of Own it, Solve it and Do it.

5) Take the necessary steps to accept responsibility for your actions.

Let's look at another simple example. You tend to enjoy a few beers or drinks now and then. (Oh no, another alcohol example. Yes, shhh, pay attention.) However, you also tend to stay a little later than usual and eventually become drunk.

You get home, and your partner is annoyed and upset with you. This ends in an argument, waking up the kids and making them even angrier. The next morning you are hungover and need to take the kids to tennis practise and find yourself alienated and feeling terrible. Your initial reaction is that it's unjustified – after all, why can't you have a few drinks? You work hard and need a break.

What needs to happen here is firstly realise that having a few drinks is probably fine. It's excessive and intoxicated that needs to be addressed and accounted for.

It would help if you took responsibility for the fact that you drank too much and may have needed to either leave earlier or drink slower, perhaps drank lower strength beer or water for a while. That way, you would be able to make a better, non-intoxicated decision, and you also would have woken up feeling healthier and happier.

Become accountable, accept that you are part of a family; you have commitments and drink alcohol appropriately. This is an example of accountability (and also one that may bite me on the arse in the future now it's on paper!)

MAKING A DECISION

Did you know that making a decision – whether or not it's right or wrong –helps reduce stress in your body and calms down the old noggin.

The reason for this is that once a decision is made, the brain won't have to keep always trying to find the answer or conclusion, and then it can relax.

The brain wants to make the loop go full circle – that is how it's wired.

Think about previous times when you are 'stewing' over a problem and can't make a final decision. How does it make you feel?

Stressed and uneasy, I'd guess. Because essentially you are ruminating your thoughts and not shutting them off. As I've talked about many times now, we are trying to stop constant thoughts spiralling out of control to help reduce your Anxiety.

This is the same thing, but in regards to any decision, you make in life regardless of it being related to Anxiety or not.

CHAPTER 16

DIFFERENT TYPES OF TREATMENTS

GETTING SERIOUS

We're getting to the end of the book, and you may be asking yourself: "OK, I reckon I have a serious Anxiety problem, but where do I go for help? What is the best possible treatment option for me? Do I need to take drugs or medications to help out?"

Let's explore a few alternatives and see if we can come up with an answer, or at least a few ideas.

The first thing we need to do is determine what the problem is in the first place.

The most straightforward and most practical place to start is with your local GP Perhaps have a look at speaking to a therapist to put you in the right direction.

With regards to medication and treatment, I want to make things clear: I think that anti-depressants and benzodiazepines (very addictive sedatives) are not suitable treatment options for Anxiety. My book and workshops are based around effective cognitive techniques, diet, lifestyle changes and gaining a broader perspective on life and where we sit. A holistic approach that you are in control of!

I honestly feel that medications are a Band-Aid solution to the problem and don't resolve our Anxiety.

I am only wanting the best for anyone who suffers from this horrendous, underestimated mental health condition that affects us so dramatically.

Mostly, it's up to the individual: what suits them and their needs, and I advise you to speak with a variety of health care professionals before making your choice.

If medication is required to help you get to a position that is less traumatic and allows you the ability to start thinking clearly, then that's up to you and the health care professionals you feel best with.

People's ability to recover and live life without the burden of Anxiety and Fear varies for each individual.

Many factors alter the time it takes to heal and recover: previous trauma, your mental health status, individual experiences already being exposed to, current physical health status, and longevity of actually suffering from Anxiety.

The critical thing to remember (if you haven't figured it out yet) is that there is no QUICK FIX! I am sorry, but it will take a lot of hard work and dedication regardless of the choice of treatment you choose, but I can assure you the rewards will be liberating and endless.

The alternative is the Status Quo. Nothing will change. Or, worst case, things will continue to get worse.

Having said all of this, let's check out some things we can do:

Health care providers like your GP, Social workers, Psychologist, Nurse practitioner, Counsellors or even Priests are all great resources to help with your quest.

It will be handy to check the provider's training and credentials and level of experience before committing to them.

It is also helpful to feel comfortable with that person, as you are going to expose a lot about yourself to them and that may be confronting (please remember that it is always confidential and it's part of their job description to not judge you, so it's OK to open up to them).

Although I am not keen on anti-depressants and benzodiazepines, I have a list of complementary vitamins and supplements that I feel are less addictive, natural and effective, which were listed in the previous chapter.

COGNITIVE BEHAVIOURAL THERAPY (CBT)

My book and workshops are based on Cognitive Behavioural Therapy (CBT), and this has been demonstrated to be the most effective type of treatment for Anxiety and Anxiety disorders by numerous studies.

CBT is like the specialist for Anxiety in the same way a Cardiologist is a specialist for hearts or Oncologist is for cancer patients.

As you have seen and read, it questions your thoughts and challenges them to be more realistic and helpful.

It also shows you how thoughts affect your behaviour and feelings, and how we can change that if needed.

There is plenty of homework and investigating for both the therapist and patient to do to get results and, as you can see throughout the book, the work is quite useful.

Given that Anxiety is predominantly based on unhelpful/negative thoughts, this is my choice for therapy.

The CBT model involves exposure to the Fear or anxious stimuli, gradually increasing the exposure that eventually desensitises the Fear over time.

It has been well established over a long period and has the results to prove it that are often long-lasting.

Well worth checking this set up out and indeed a fantastic therapist if you chose to try the book first and get stuck.

PSYCHOTHERAPY

Psychotherapy is super useful in helping you deal with things, or previous experiences, that have affected your life in the past or in the present.

Having the ability to deal with other stressors or issues that are affecting your mental health and wellbeing can help reduce your stress, Anxiety and Fear.

It focuses on feelings, thoughts and behaviours that concern you and allows you to flush out what's going on in your head.

The therapist can then offer tools or insight into how you can work towards changing your values or beliefs in a helpful way that gives you the ability to shift previous thought patterns that have been troubling you.

They can often delve into your past and early childhood experiences, sexuality, culture, relationship history, various illnesses and any other concern you have that needs to be explored.

It is a great complementary therapy to have alongside the CBT.

Let's face it, we are emotional creatures, and all have a history of experiences that have created some distress and unsettling in our past.

This often translates to the present and future. Speaking to a therapist can help clear out some old beliefs and emotional distress that's needed to move forward.

It is highly recommended in your path to recovery.

NET (NEURO EMOTIONAL TECHNIQUE)

NET involves understanding the relationship with the body; the environment, nutrition and structure of our bodies.

It is an emotional therapy that helps deal with stress-related physiological responses that create physical illness in the body.

As discussed earlier in the book when I talked neuropeptides, these chemicals are released when we are stressed and help an emotion become connected within the body.

This emotion can be held within the body and, if not dealt with and released appropriately, can end up resulting or creating physical illness.

This emotion can also be activated or triggered at any time even after the event creating a pattern of illness and emotional distress even after the initial situation. It's like it gets stuck and keeps relaying every time similar incidents occur.

The NET technique helps remove or shift emotional blocks that, in turn allows us to heal and move forward with our lives.

Think of it like a technique that helps 'clean out the closet' and start fresh, without the constant patterns of emotional disturbance reoccurring.

I have found this incredibly effective at removing old, stubborn emotion and allowing me to be free of them.

With our new outlook and all of these tools we have learnt throughout the book, we can minimise the need for having emotions stored and not dealt with properly. Our strategies are now effective at resolving the emotion at the start when they occur, stopping the build-up and probability of physical illness developing in the future.

There are plenty of more types of treatment and therapies out there to be researched. The ones listed above are the ones that I have personally used and have found offer excellent results.

INTEGRATIVE GENERAL PRACTITIONER (GP'S)

So you have done it all, seen the CBT therapist and talked to death about your childhood and just about done every type of alternative treatment out there and although there has been an improvement, your still not quite where you want to be.

Let me introduce you to the **Integrative GP.**

These guys are Doctors who have a medical degree and studied everything about the body and tend to look a lot deeper into your problem with "open eyes" and a holistic approach to your condition. In our case, Anxiety.

To give you an example, they would perform a comprehensive history of your birth, childhood, medical and mental health conditions, diet, lifestyle etc.

They then use their "western medicine" with evidence-based practise with natural medicine and other therapies current in mainstream medicine.

It isn't alternative medicine, as it is based on the latest scientific evidence and uses the most current interventions and other allied health practitioners to achieve well being and of course, effective treatment.

Being a holistic approach, it encompasses the social, emotional, environmental, spiritual, psychological and physical health of the patient to determine what can help them.

DIFFERENT TYPES OF TREATMENTS

They are quite expensive, to be honest, but I feel they delve into the biochemistry of your body. i.e. zinc/copper, magnesium levels as well as gut health, mould, fungus and toxins your exposed to. They can determine if your Anxiety is also caused by internal biological problems or dysfunction in your body with science.

They are a real game-changer!!!

HOW A BASE JUMPER SAVED ME

TWO STEPS FORWARD,
ONE STEP BACK.

CHAPTER 17

SNAKES & LADDERS

The old slippery ladder that seems to allow you to climb three rungs up and then slide down four of the bastards!

How often does this happen on our road to recovery, and how unsettling and heartbreaking can it be. It often makes us feel like there's no point in trying to change. Each time I move forward, something always pulls me back to at times a worse position than before.

I used to get quite demoralised when this happened to me and found my motivation would suffer significantly. Setbacks were the enemy to me, and I would try and avoid them at all costs.

However, during the journey, I started to realise that there was some merit in slipping down the ladder and that setbacks were mini-lessons that needed to be learnt along the way to recover.

Admittedly, it did take some time to adjust my way of thinking, but I eventually started to change my view on them, and it made a huge difference. Remember perception, perception, perception! The change came when I had felt Anxiety and Panic free for maybe half a day and was thinking that I was somehow 'cured' all of a sudden and miraculously!

Then out of the blue, I suffered another Panic attack. I was sitting in the park on a beautiful sunny day, for no apparent reason. It was the first time I suffered one without any particular, obvious 'trigger'. At least, that's what I thought at the time.

Although at first, I felt cheated and distraught about the attack, I realised for the first time that my Panic doesn't always have to be affiliated with external stimuli driving this Anxiety and Panic. Of course, I understand how it was all internal and, in that case, very thought driven.

Although I had no answers, strategy or intervention at that particular stage in my world of Anxiety, it gave me a little understanding of my condition.

It was a definite case of three rungs up and then four rungs down in a flash. However, over time and realising that my setbacks are little lessons to assist my recovery, I began to change my perception of them. Now, I even view them in the light of hope and growth, versus Fear and failure.

Even though now I have recovered, there are times that I still experience Anxiety and Panic, and I believe that is inevitable. It is part of the human experience.

Let's look at it from another angle.

What if I was to say you suffer from high blood pressure but have it controlled via your medication. That's great, and it works well. However, there are times, despite taking your medicine and doing the right thing, your blood pressure is high and needs a little attention. This can be seen with almost all types of medical conditions even if you're medicated.

So why should our Anxiety be any different?

Expect the occasional 'set back' or 'flare-up' as with any other condition, but have the confidence that your strategy and newfound understanding will put you back on track. It does not mean you're destined for a life of Anxious hell again.

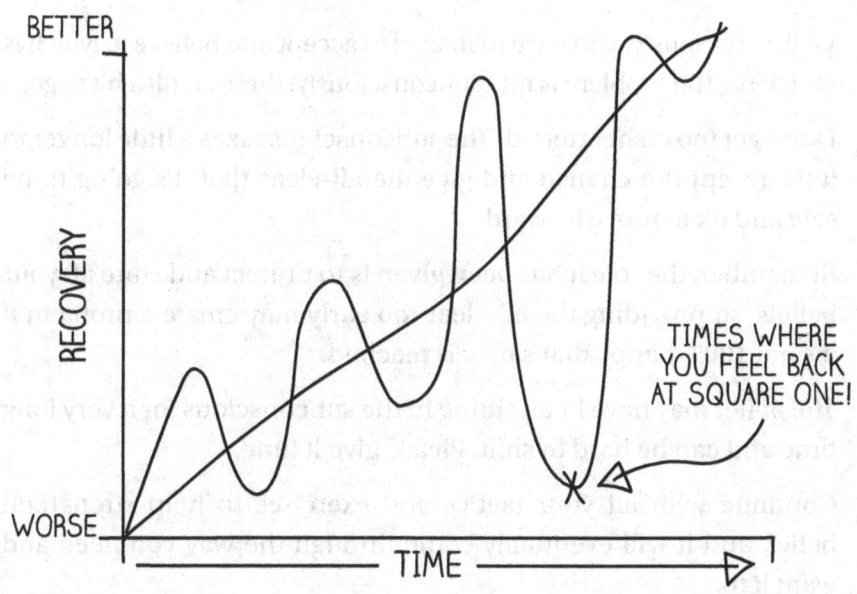

DELAYED PERIOD OF BELIEVING

Let's say you have done all the work smashing out your automatic thoughts, assessing them and fixing them up; you've applied it to your Fear and exposed yourself to that stimulus time and time again…and yet…

It seems that there is a delay in believing that your Fear is bulls#&t! You can't understand why the hell you still have reactions of Fear and all these little setbacks because, in your mind, everything should be back on track and you should be living Fear free.

Well, consciously, you have managed to accept and believe it, which is excellent. The problem is that subconsciously, there is still a bit to go.

Don't get too disheartened. The subconscious takes a little longer to fully accept the change and give the all-clear that it's going to be safe and ok to move forward.

Remember, the role it has been given is to protect and store all your beliefs, so providing the all-clear too early may create a problem if it's not 100% happy that safety is reached.

The belief may have been sitting in the subconscious for a very long time and can be hard to shift. Please give it time.

Continue with all your tactics and exercises to help strengthen belief, and it will eventually come through the way you need and want it to.

Also remember what we discussed in previous chapters about breaking habits and making neurons fire together, wire together and that change takes time.

NEW SYMPTOMS

If you have suffered from Anxiety, the chances are that you have been unfortunate to develop new symptoms and Anxieties along the way (we're just unique like that). It can sometimes feel as though no sooner you have got on top of one symptom or Fear, then another one pops up out of the blue, and you have to start all over again.

If this is the case with you, don't be alarmed. This is simply a sign that you're still highly stressed or hyperaroused from previous Fear and Anxiety, or you're still learning the skills required to kick this problem fair and square in the arse.

The critical thing to remember is that you now have new skills and strategies to use that have never been available to you before. Implementing them takes time to become efficient at and ultimately master.

Secondly, it's also essential to get that new symptom evaluated and assessed medically, to rule out it not being caused by a physical or medical condition.

There are lots of times the physical symptoms create the Anxiety, and then the spiral of Fear and then conversely, the long-term Anxiety creates the physical symptoms and responses.

Either way, it may be hard to identify the reason or cause for the symptom, and it can often be a case of using the process of elimination.

There will be times when, after numerous physical and medical tests and examinations, with no obvious answer that it may become apparent that it's your Anxiety and Fear that is the source of your symptoms.

The time is now: ask yourself what the things you need to change, improve and get cracking towards a better you.

MORNING DREAD

Yep, that feeling when you wake up to and go WTF? I just woke up, and already I feel like an anxious, nervous wreck. I feel butterflies in my guts, I am uneasy and jittery and feel a general sense of doom.

This rooster has been telling me that all my Fear and Anxiety comes from my thoughts and head, and I've been doing great, so why the hell am I feeling this way right now?

Fair call. Let's look at the dreaded morning dread!

Well, although you have been in the feathers, sleeping happily (I hope) and not doing a lot of conscious thinking, your subconscious mind is busy filtering and sorting out all the negative crap you have been pumping into it during your waking hours.

This information and turmoil are all happening behind the scenes without you being conscious of it.

Therefore, if you wake up feeling this crappy Morning Dread, it would be fair to say that there are some underlying, unresolved issues or Fears that have not been fully computed and may need to be addressed.

I used to lay there and try and work it out but generally to no avail. This is probably due to the fact it's coming from the subconscious mind.

I now deal with it differently and get up and start my day without trying to change the situation; otherwise, it ends in a spiral of no result!

It could also be quite obvious what the problem is, and that allows you to put some strategies in place to nail the issue.

IT'S YOUR TURN NOW

So, you have come to the end of the book, and I am guessing that you are spewing that it has finished and you want more of this cracking dialogue and hilarious comedy that I have been providing. (It's like he's in my head, I hear you say!)

I hope you have got to the finish line and have learnt heaps of new strategies and information about your Anxiety, and I also hope you have a new approach to deal with it.

I often see so many people suffering because they have not been able to get the right advice or techniques to combat and defend themselves against such a nasty fun stopper.

The debilitating effects are not easily seen to the naked eye of people who have not experienced this themselves and, to be fair to them, they understandably don't get it and resonate with your situation.

Some of the stuff mentioned throughout the book may help those loved ones empathise with your struggles and help you with the journey you're on.

Anxiety is not fixed overnight, and it probably will be part of your life forever. That being said, although I get occasional 'episodes' of Anxiety and Panic, it certainly has nowhere near the same impact it did when I suffered my Nervous breakdown. My life is full of health and happiness 99% of the time, with more realistic Anxiety presentations rather than exaggerated. I promise you that you won't need to suffer as you have in the past.

The reality is, I find it relatively easy to manage these days as I have become disciplined in my strategies and tactics, and I'm also aware of what exacerbates the Anxiety in the first place.

Over time, you will also get to the same happy place as me and look back at the turmoil and the life you used to have as a distant, fucked up memory.

Hope is here for us to all see, and a lovely guided direction is in front of you.

I appreciate my life far more now, and I live it to the fullest much more these days than I did before my diagnosis. I realise that when life is shit, it is shit and when it's good, it's great.

Therefore, whilst I'm living virtually Anxiety free, I will make the most of my life and follow my dreams as I also realise the fact that Anxiety is purely an illusion, and that is it.

The illusions I now create are ones of happiness and joy without the negativity and Fear.

I want you to get up and look in the mirror and say to yourself:

I am **STRONG, WORTHY AND LOVED.** With the assistance of this book, family, friends and other professionals, I will become the person I have always wanted to be.

This is your first step to recovery, and I wish you well in your endeavours.

God bless and smash this crazy world of Fear away because you have the power and knowledge to do so!

This is your chance to live a Fear-less life!

FREEDOM!!

"LIFE WILL ONLY CHANGE WHEN YOU BECOME MORE COMMITTED TO YOUR DREAMS THAN YOU ARE TO YOUR COMFORT ZONE."

— CHRIS BREEN

CHAPTER 18

CHEAT SHEETS

This chapter is a quick reference guide and resource with cheat sheets all in one handy little spot for your convenience. They are obviously all throughout the book as well in different sections.

I know that there will be times when you just want to qucikly reference these tools without ploughing through the book and this will help make your journey that little bit easier. *Legend!*

Good Luck!

WORKSHEET FOR OUR ANXIETY / FEAR
(THE ONE STOP SHOP)

ANXIETY LEVEL	PHYSICAL SYMPTOMS	BEHAVIOURAL SYMPTOMS	EMOTIONAL SYMPTOMS
RATING (1-10)	(EG: SHORT OF BREATH / INCREASED HEARTRATE)	(EG: RUN / AVOID)	(EG: ANGRY / SCARED)

EVENT: _____

1. WHAT DO YOU THINK WHEN YOUR ANXIOUS IN THIS SITUATION?

_____

_____

2. ASK YOURSELF WHAT IS THE WORST CASE SCENARIO THOUGHT OR IMAGE IN YOUR HEAD?
(remember it is the core root of your Fear and also sets up our spiral of thoughts which are often automatic) - you can't fix what you don't know!!)

_____

_____

3. WHAT HAVE YOU BEEN AVOIDING OR NOT WANTING TO FACE?
(places, people, situations etc – Great working out triggers)

_____

_____

Now we have to question our WORST CASE SCENARIO and argue/rebut the hell out of it!

REBUT BIT:

LIST 3 REASONS WHY IT COULD BE BULLSHIT/ILLUSION:
(SOME THINGS TO ASK YOURSELF):

1. WHERE IS THE PROOF/EVIDENCE OF THIS BECOMING REAL?

_____

_____

2. WHAT IS THE PERCENTAGE / PROBABILITY OF IT HAPPENING?

_____

_____

3. WHAT IS LIKELY TO HAPPEN?

_____

_____

4. WHAT ARE THE ACTUAL FACTS?

_____

_____

5. WHAT IS A MORE REALISTIC/HELPFUL WAY OF LOOKING AT IT?
   (This is great for things like performance in sport, job, social, public events etc., Stuff you begin to realise is more Anxiety than fact)

_____

_____

OK, sometimes you have done all the work above and can't shift or change your way of thinking. I.e. generally stuck in thoughts, serious illness, death, serious accident and it's just pure fact that "WORST CASE SCENARIO" is apparent. Fear is a FACT!

TRY AND LIST HOW YOU WOULD COPE IF WORST CASE SCENARIO HAPPENS.

LIST AS MANY COPING STRATEGIES YOU CAN THINK OF?
Ask others if stuck what they would do? (E.G. visualisation tool, time, space, acceptance etc.)

_____

_____

_____

_____

_____

N.B. you can always utilise a therapist if unable to move forward.

CHEAT SHEETS

ANXIETY & PANIC ATTACKS - 2 FRONTS

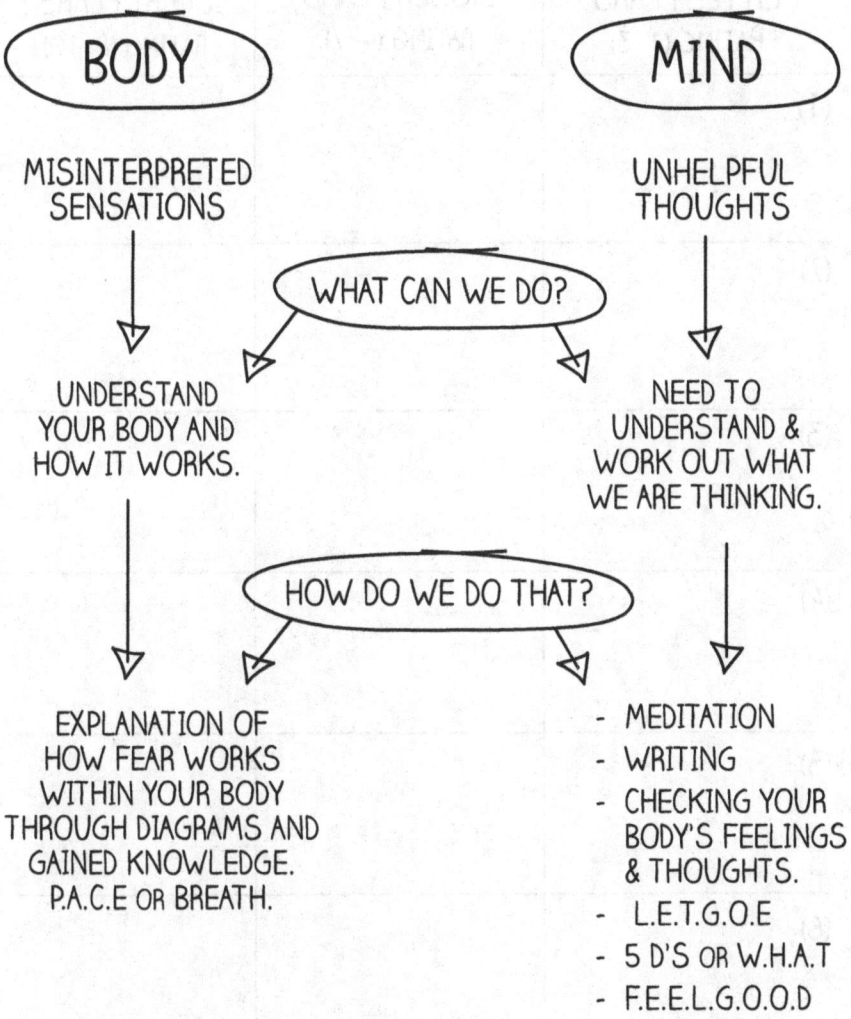

Understand that both thoughts and sensations are allowed to happen without resistance – fighting both will only empower Fear.

FEARS AND WORRIES LIST

LITTLE FEARS RATING (1-3)	BIGGER FEARS RATING (4-7)	SCARY FEARS RATING (8-10)
(1)		
(2)		
(3)		
(4)		
(5)		
(6)		
(7)		

CHEAT SHEETS

BRAVERY REWARD CHART

LIST OF THINGS YOU LIKE - TO REWARD YOURSELF:

_____

_____

_____

_____

_____

_____

_____

FEAR / WORRY (REMEMBER BUILD UP TO IT):

_____

1ST STEP TOWARDS FEAR:

REWARD FOR BRAVERY:

FEELINGS (E.G. HAPPY / PROUD / SENSE OF ACHIEVEMENT):

2ND STEP TOWARDS FEAR:

REWARD FOR BRAVERY:

FEELINGS (E.G. HAPPY / PROUD / SENSE OF ACHIEVEMENT):

3RD STEP TOWARDS FEAR: _____

REWARD FOR BRAVERY: _____

FEELINGS (E.G. HAPPY / PROUD / SENSE OF ACHIEVEMENT): _____

_____

4TH STEP TOWARDS FEAR: _____

REWARD FOR BRAVERY: _____

FEELINGS (E.G. HAPPY / PROUD / SENSE OF ACHIEVEMENT): _____

_____

5TH STEP TOWARDS FEAR: _____

REWARD FOR BRAVERY: _____

FEELINGS (E.G. HAPPY / PROUD / SENSE OF ACHIEVEMENT): _____

_____

6TH STEP TOWARDS FEAR: _____

REWARD FOR BRAVERY: _____

FEELINGS (E.G. HAPPY / PROUD / SENSE OF ACHIEVEMENT): _____

_____

7TH STEP TOWARDS FEAR: _____

REWARD FOR BRAVERY: _____

FEELINGS (E.G. HAPPY / PROUD / SENSE OF ACHIEVEMENT): _____

_____

CHEAT SHEETS

8TH STEP TOWARDS FEAR: _____

REWARD FOR BRAVERY: _____

FEELINGS (E.G. HAPPY / PROUD / SENSE OF ACHIEVEMENT): _____

9TH STEP TOWARDS FEAR: _____

REWARD FOR BRAVERY: _____

FEELINGS (E.G. HAPPY / PROUD / SENSE OF ACHIEVEMENT): _____

10TH STEP TOWARDS FEAR: _____

REWARD FOR BRAVERY: _____

FEELINGS (E.G. HAPPY / PROUD / SENSE OF ACHIEVEMENT): _____

11TH STEP TOWARDS FEAR: _____

REWARD FOR BRAVERY: _____

FEELINGS (E.G. HAPPY / PROUD / SENSE OF ACHIEVEMENT): _____

12TH STEP TOWARDS FEAR: _____

REWARD FOR BRAVERY: _____

FEELINGS (E.G. HAPPY / PROUD / SENSE OF ACHIEVEMENT): _____

P.A.C.E

FEAR FUELS FEAR - CONSENT STOPS IT

That means if you fight Fear with Fear it will grow and grow and grow into the ugly monster you have probably been experiencing.

However, Fear will go missing and lose its power when you **CONSENT** to it, become **PASSIVE** and **OBSERVE** it, get **ANGRY** with it or **EMBRACE** it.

P.A.C.E

P. **PASSIVENESS AND OBSERVATION** of bodily sensations without judgement helps stop the feedback loop and turns off our Fear because there are no thoughts of Fear fuelling it.

A. **ANGER** towards your sensations reduces Fear by sending the message that enough is enough. Once again, this interrupts the feedback loop and helps reduce our Fear.

C. **CONSENT OR PERMITTING** these bodily sensations helps stop the feedback loop of Fear because the message coming through is that it's all OK. We are going to roll with it. There is no fuel to add to the Fear fire.

E. **EMBRACING** the Fear and challenging the symptoms to increase in severity. This might sound terrifying, but it's my favourite tactic and has always been the most effective for me. You might think I'm a giant weirdo, but I also tackle this step with a smile promoting feelings of happiness. Don't judge it 'til you've tried it!

CHEAT SHEETS

P.A.C.E. is the first strategy I use to stop and reduce the effects of my physical symptoms when they are in full swing. Their power and strength are impossible to ignore.

FEAR FUELS FEAR -
CONSENT STOPS IT!

BREATH

RULE OF 4'S is BREATHING IN THROUGH YOUR NOSE FOR *4 SECONDS*, then into your BELLY region and HOLDING YOUR BREATH FOR *4 SECONDS* (activating vagus nerve), and then BREATHING OUT OF YOUR MOUTH FOR *4 SECONDS*. This is a total of 12 seconds per cycle.

OR

If it's tough for you to do 4 seconds, try starting with *2 SECONDS* or *3 SECONDS*, then building up to *4 SECONDS* over time. (If you are hyperventilating, you'll find strong resistance to holding your breath, but it will settle – I promise).

N.B This works excellently for severe Anxiety and Panic!

ANOTHER TECHNIQUE IS:

BREATH HOLDING for *5-10 SECONDS* at a time, then try and breathe slowly, especially whilst breathing out. Do this until symptoms settle, and when you feel you can control your breathing rate again or just to reset your breathing rate in general, which can increase sneakily when you are stressed.

THIS IS A LITTLE RIPPER AS WELL:

PURSED LIP BREATHING is BREATHING IN THROUGH YOU NOSE FOR *4 SECONDS* into your BELLY and then BREATHING OUT FOR *5–10 SECONDS* through pursed lips. This is a little slower in effect but well tolerated until your breathing rate slows down. It's a great tool to help you relax and become calm.

Great little chiller outerer!!

IF YOU ARE HYPERVENTILATING... YOU GUESSED IT, USE: BREATH STRATEGY.

W.H.A.T

A simple tool is by asking yourself W.H.A.T when anxious. This is on the run FIRST AID for our Anxiety.

WRITE IT DOWN Amazing how much things become clear when written down Look at what you have been thinking and ask yourself using:

W.H.A.T

- **W. WHAT** AM I THINKING WHEN ANXIOUS?
  (Worst case scenario image/thought- Root cause Fear)

- **H. HOW** DID I COME UP WITH THIS THOUGHT?

- **A. AM** I USING EVIDENCE TO BACK IT UP?

- **T. TRY** BEING MORE REALISTIC OR HELPFUL IN MY THINKING AND IMPROVE IT.

CHEAT SHEETS

WHAT IS THE % OR LIKELIHOOD OF WORST CASE SCENARIO HAPPENING?

STEP 1) Recognise our WORST CASE SCENARIO thoughts or images when anxious (become aware).

STEP 2) Recognise the 1st and 2nd thoughts as they set up our Anxiety/Fear spiral.

STEP 3) Determine what we are thinking and ask yourself if it's helpful or unhelpful.

STEP 4) Get some backup and evidence to refute or change our thinking to a more helpful/realistic way.
Rebut the fuck out of it.

STEP 5) Put the new you and your thoughts into action from above (you will feel like a brand-new dude).

STEP 6) PRACTISE, PRACTISE, PRACTISE
(steps 1 through 5 on repeat).

L.E.T.G.O.E

THE POWER OF LETTING GO

One of the significant drivers of Anxiety and its persistence is rumination (your constant self-talk and unhelpful problem solving of your Anxiety). Another way to describe it is 'constant worry'. However, we can make massive improvement into our Anxiety if we nip it in the bud at the beginning, before it creates that out of control spiral. Rumination can drain our energy.

The concept is simple: Identify it is an anxious or unhelpful thought... and LET IT GO.

This is as hard as you think it might be at the start because you first need to be aware of your automatic thoughts and then also be able to acknowledge and LET GO.

THIS IS SO POWERFUL AS IT REMINDS THE SUB-CONSCIOUS THAT EVERYTHING IS SAFE AND OK.

CHEAT SHEETS

L.E.T.G.O.E

L. LISTEN
Your first/automatic thought sets up your Anxiety, the second thought starts creating the spiral. Pay attention to what that thought is.

E. EMBRACE
Accept the thought and roll with it. It has happened, you can't change it and your reaction to it the vital part. The action required here is NOTHING (easy, yes?)

T. THINK
Is this an anxious thought? Is this an unhelpful thought? Is this a negative thought? Is this in the future? CAN I CONTROL IT?

G. GET SLOW
Slow, deep breaths that is. This helps activate our Vagus Nerve, which in turn calms the body and allows for rational thinking before jumping to the worst-case scenario. Slow, deep breaths will also reduce overreaction to stimulus.

O. OBSERVE
Imagine you are curiously watching – pay attention to your body's reaction, your feelings and symptoms. Don't judge, observe as they lose strength and power. Refer back to Chapter 4 and 5 and how the body responds to stress (this will help).

E. ENVISION
Imagine that deep in your mind; you are not Anxious. You are confidently coping and working through your Anxiety. As weird as it sounds, try to smile while you are doing this – it helps reprogram the wiring in your brain.

THE 5-DS

THE 5-D'S are similar in many ways to L.E.T.G.O.E, and this straightforward process might be more suited to you:

1. DEEP BREATHING
Your first/automatic thought sets up your Anxiety, the second thought starts creating the spiral. Pay attention to what that thought is.

2. DETERMINE – consider what you are thinking and if it's helpful or not.

3. DISPUTE – replace unhelpful/negative thoughts with new helpful ones.

4. DETECT – observe all symptoms without reaction or embrace them fully and encourage their severity (which, paradoxically, stops them)

5. DREAM – visualise you being non-Anxious in the situation or event and *smile*.

Now you've got the rundown of both physical and mental strategies, here's one more First Aid mnemonic for you to take on board... something the combines all the strategy and reminds you of the space you want to be in (body and mind!)

CHEAT SHEETS

NEGATIVE THOUGHT   POSITIVE THOUGHT

IMAGINE LOOKING AND FEELING EMBARRASED

IMAGINE YOU HAVE NAILED IT! "I FEEL AMAZING"

FEEL GOOD

F.E.E.L.G.O.O.D combines all the strategy and reminds you of the space you want to be in (body and mind!)

F. **FEEL** sensations, understand symptoms and remember they don't harm you (the sensations are produced by a variety of chemicals in your body and are only activated to help, you don't need to Fear them).

E. **EXPECT** Amygdala – understand it's doing its job trying to alert you to Fear (it's the canary in the mine, shooting off messages and chemicals to the body and the cognitive brain most often subconsciously. It's always on alert using our senses ready to pounce being a protector rather than the enemy).

E. **ESTABLISH** proper breathing by learning to breathe into your diaphragm (this gives you time to regroup, adapting your cognitive brain and also calming the chemicals released from the Amygdala shooting off before we have a chance to think about it).

L. **LIVE** in the present – ask yourself if it needs to be dealt with now, today or at a later date. Also, do you need to control it? (remember control of any situation is almost impossible, so why try and increase your stress about it).

CHEAT SHEETS

G. **GET** informed on your thoughts. Ask yourself questions (what are your unhelpful/Anxious thoughts? Are they Worst Case Scenario? Do I need to have control/certainty? Do I require approval? Do I have to be perfect or perform highly? Do I have to get it right? Do I feel Anxious about feeling Anxious? Why?).

O. **ORCHESTRATE** helpful thoughts (it's incredible how negative or incorrect our thoughts when on autopilot!)

Ask more questions:
- Does it matter if it's the Worst Case Scenario?
- Is it that bad?
- Do you have evidence that your thoughts are real?
- What's the probability of it happening?
- What would someone who is not anxious in this situation think?
- What is a more helpful way of thinking?

O. **OPEN** your mind to visualisation and project a positive vision about the outcome. (flip the negative image in your mind to a positive result).

D. **DELAYED** sensations can be expected as the chemistry takes time to resolve from the body (you might have gone through all these steps and are still feeling Anxious. Give it a moment, your body takes time to readjust and the chemistry needs to settle. You are OK).

REMEMBER - all these tricky little acronyms are here to make them easy to remember – especially at a time when your brain is a bit fried. All we are trying to do is cut the power and fuel from those unhelpful thoughts by using a few necessary tools and a strategic process to get your head clear. *You can make up your own if you like.*

TROUBLESHOOTING CHECKLIST

- [ ] Do you feel your understanding of how Fear works with both thoughts and bodily sensations is up to date?

- [ ] Are you able to apply PACE, BREATH, L.E.T.G.O.E., 5 D'S, FEEL GOOD OR WHAT forever?

- [ ] Are you being disciplined with your added background work?

- [ ] Are you continually writing thoughts down as it's the best, quickest route to recovery because of its power to see problem thinking and insert into the subconscious?

- [ ] Are you questioning thoughts every time you're Anxious?

- [ ] Have you identified the Worst case scenario? (the root cause of your Fear).

- [ ] Have you looked at and changed your diet (I will talk about this more shortly)?

- [ ] Are you practising exposure and practising often? It will fail when not done enough. You need to start somewhere and continue with it. Additionally, be aware brief exposure can have a negative effect because it increases your beliefs that your Fear is real.

CHEAT SHEETS

☐ Are you avoiding or escaping thoughts and physical sensations because it only increases your Anxiety? Be aware it won't allow you to understand and accept them. Although escape and avoidance are natural Fear responses, they're not sustainable in the long run. You will have to use strategies not to avoid. Avoidance is a short-term fix that will make things so much worse over time. It prevents Anxiety from declining naturally and decreases the quality of life because you're not living freely, and you feel like crap all the time.

☐ Safety seeking is when you try and prevent a scary outcome through thoughts and behaviours. The big issue is that you're not learning what's unhelpful in your thoughts to address them.

☑ Are you on the piss and telling your Anxiety to fuck off without using your manners? *Lol!*

"FACE EVERYTHING AND RISE."

UNKNOWN AUTHOR

ACKNOWLEDGEMENTS

To my boys, Charlie and Oliver. This is my Legacy to you from a place of pure LOVE. It may serve as a guide to you one day!

To my wife, Tanya. Your constant encouragement and belief in me that has empowered my dream to show the world HOPE is real and achievable. Also for your amazing guidance, illustration and graphic design expertise helping me put this book together — thank you!

To my Mum. You taught me NEVER to give up and allowed our blueprints to cross. You are the most amazing woman someone could ever meet, and you have such fierce determination and refusal of the word NO.

To the rest of my family and close friends (you know who you are). We have crossed many rivers and mountains together—some in excitement and others in distress. However, there has never been a moment I have ever not felt your presence and loyalty in our journeys, and that is the gift no monetary amount could ever replace.

And finally to two of the most amazing and talented women I know who painstakenly spent countless hours editing and providing advice on what is good and not so good! To Kirsten MacDonald and Amy Doak, *I thank you from the bottom of my heart.*

REFERENCES

(1) Stein, M.B. and Stein, D.J., 2008. Social Anxiety disorder. The lancet, 371(9618), pp.1115-1125.

(2) Spitzer, R.L., Kroenke, K., Williams, J.B. and Löwe, B., 2006. A brief measure for assessing generalized Anxiety disorder: the GAD-7. Archives of internal medicine, 166(10), pp.1092-1097.

(3) Etkin, A. and Wager, T.D., 2007. Functional neuroimaging of Anxiety: a meta-analysis of emotional processing in PTSD, social Anxiety disorder, and specific phobia. American journal of Psychiatry, 164(10), pp.1476-1488.

(4) Craske, M.G. and Barlow, D.H., 2014. Panic disorder and agoraphobia.

(5) McNally, R.J., 1994. Panic disorder: a critical analysis. Guilford Press.

(6) Leckman, J.F., Grice, D.E., Boardman, J., Zhang, H., Vitale, A., Bondi, C., Alsobrook, J., Peterson, B.S., Cohen, D.J., Rasmussen, S.A. and Goodman, W.K., 1997. Symptoms of obsessive-compulsive disorder. American Journal of Psychiatry, 154(7), pp.911-917.

(7) Baker, D., Hunter, E., Lawrence, E., Medford, N., Patel, M., Senior, C., Sierra, M., Lambert, M.V., Phillips, M.L. and David, A.S., 2003. Depersonalisation disorder: clinical features of 204 cases. The British Journal of Psychiatry, 182(5), pp.428-433.

(8) Beck, A.T., Emery, G. and Greenberg, R.L., 2005. Anxiety disorders and phobias: A cognitive perspective. Basic Books.

(9) Marks, I.M., 1987. Fears, phobias, and rituals: Panic, Anxiety, and their disorders. Oxford University Press on Demand.

(10) Marks, I.M., 1987. Fears, phobias, and rituals: Panic, Anxiety, and their disorders. Oxford University Press on Demand.

(11) Anglin, J., 2008. Quantum canaries learn to fly. Nature Physics, 4(6), pp.437-438.

(12) Isaacson, R., 2013. The limbic system. Springer Science & Business Media.

REFERENCES

(13) Tortora, G.J. and Derrickson, B.H., 2018. Principles of anatomy and physiology. John Wiley & Sons.

(14) Clark, R.E., 2004. The classical origins of Pavlov's conditioning. Integrative Physiological & Behavioral Science, 39(4), pp.279-294.

(15) Folgering, H., 1999. The pathophysiology of hyperventilation syndrome. Monaldi archives for chest disease= Archivio Monaldi per le malattie del torace, 54(4), p.365.

(16) Sullivan, G.M., Coplan, J.D., Kent, J.M. and Gorman, J.M., 1999. The noradrenergic system in pathological Anxiety: a focus on Panic with relevance to generalized Anxiety and phobias. Biological psychiatry, 46(9), pp.1205-1218.

(17) Turnbull, A.E., 2011. Fear, numbers, and measles. Health communication, 26(8), pp.775-776.

(18) Connolly Baker, K. and Mazza, N., 2004. The healing power of writing: Applying the expressive/creative component of poetry therapy. Journal of Poetry Therapy, 17(3), pp.141-154.

(19) Spielberger, C.D., 2010. Test Anxiety inventory. The Corsini encyclopedia of psychology, pp.1-1.

(20) Horowitz, S., 2010. Health benefits of meditation: What the newest research shows. Alternative and Complementary Therapies, 16(4), pp.223-228.

(21) Gawain, S., 2002. Meditations: Creative visualization and meditation exercises to enrich your life. New World Library

(22) Margolin, I., Pierce, J. and Wiley, A., 2011. Wellness through a creative lens: Mediation and Visualization. Journal of Religion & Spirituality in Social Work: Social Thought, 30(3), pp.234-252.

(23) Gupta, A., Ramdinmawii, E. and Mittal, V.K., 2016, December. Significance of Alpha Brainwaves in Meditation examined from the study of Binaural Beats. In 2016 International Conference on Signal Processing and Communication (ICSC) (pp. 484-489). IEEE.

(24) Barker, W. and Burgwin, S., 1949. Brain wave patterns during hypnosis, hypnotic sleep and normal sleep. Archives of Neurology & Psychiatry, 62(4), pp.412-420.

(25) Behrend, G., 2009. Attaining Your Desires: By Letting Your Subconscious Mind Work for You. The Floating Press.

(26) Burton, L. and Lent, J., 2016. The use of vision boards as a therapeutic intervention. Journal of Creativity in Mental Health, 11(1), pp.52-65.

(27) D'Argembeau, A., Renaud, O. and Van der Linden, M., 2011. Frequency, characteristics and functions of future-oriented thoughts in daily life. Applied Cognitive Psychology, 25(1), pp.96-103.

(28) Mommaerts, J.L., 2020. Your Mind As Cure: Autosuggestion for everyone. AURELIS.

(30) Draganski, B., Gaser, C., Busch, V., Schuierer, G., Bogdahn, U. and May, A., 2004. Changes in grey matter induced by training. Nature, 427(6972), pp.311-312.

(31) Chambers, R.A., Potenza, M.N., Hoffman, R.E. and Miranker, W., 2004. Simulated apoptosis/neurogenesis regulates learning and memory capabilities of adaptive neural networks. Neuropsychopharmacology, 29(4), pp.747-758.

(32) Kempermann, G., Kuhn, H.G. and Gage, F.H., 1997. More hippocampal neurons in adult mice living in an enriched environment. Nature, 386(6624), pp.493-495.

(33) Heilig, M., McLeod, S., Brot, M., Heinrichs, S.C., Menzaghi, F., Koob, G.F. and Britton, K.T., 1993. Anxiolytic-like action of neuropeptide Y: mediation by Y1 receptors in amygdala, and dissociation from food intake effects. Neuropsychopharmacology, 8(4), pp.357-363.

(34) Morgan III, C.A., Wang, S., Southwick, S.M., Rasmusson, A., Hazlett, G., Hauger, R.L. and Charney, D.S., 2000. Plasma neuropeptide-Y concentrations in humans exposed to military survival training. Biological psychiatry, 47(10), pp.902-909.

(35) Sabban, E.L. and Serova, L.I., 2018. Potential of intranasal neuropeptide Y (NPY) and/or melanocortin 4 receptor (MC4R) antagonists for preventing or treating PTSD. Military medicine, 183(suppl_1), pp.408-412.

(36) Morales-Medina, J.C., Dumont, Y. and Quirion, R., 2010. A possible role of neuropeptide Y in depression and stress. Brain research, 1314, pp.194-205.

REFERENCES

(37) Charney, D.S. and Deutch, A., 1996. A functional neuroanatomy of Anxiety and Fear: implications for the pathophysiology and treatment of Anxiety disorders. Critical Reviews™ in Neurobiology, 10(3-4).

(38) Lopresto, D., Schipper, P. and Homberg, J.R., 2016. Neural circuits and mechanisms involved in Fear generalization: implications for the pathophysiology and treatment of posttraumatic stress disorder. Neuroscience & Biobehavioral Reviews, 60, pp.31-42.

(39) Jager, W., 2003. Breaking bad habits: a dynamical perspective on habit formation and change. Human Decision-Making and Environmental Perception–Understanding and Assisting Human Decision-Making in Real Life Settings. Libor Amicorum for Charles Vlek, Groningen: University of Groningen.

(40) Allom, V., Mullan, B., Smith, E., Hay, P. and Raman, J., 2018. Breaking bad habits by improving executive function in individuals with obesity. BMC public health, 18(1), pp.1-8.

(41) Lynch, B., 2017. System and method for training the subconscious mind. U.S. Patent Application 15/004,893.

(42) Lach, G., Schellekens, H., Dinan, T.G. and Cryan, J.F., 2018. Anxiety, depression, and the microbiome: a role for gut peptides. Neurotherapeutics, 15(1), pp.36-59.

(43) Foster, J.A. and Neufeld, K.A.M., 2013. Gut-brain axis: how the microbiome influences Anxiety and depression. Trends in neurosciences, 36(5), pp.305-312.

(44) Gershon, M.D., 1999. The enteric nervous system: a second brain. Hospital Practise, 34(7), pp.31-52.

(45) Scott, T., 2011. The AntiAnxiety Food Solution: How the Foods You Eat Can Help You Calm Your Anxious Mind, Improve Your Mood, and End Cravings. New Harbinger Publications.

(46) Chaitow, L., 2003. Candida Albicans: The non-drug approach to the treatment of Candida infection. HarperCollins UK.

(47) Maker, B., How Anxiety & Depression Can Come From Our Gut.

(48) Lee, Y.K. and Salminen, S., 2009. Handbook of probiotics and prebiotics. John Wiley & Sons.

(49) Tuohy, K.M., Probert, H.M., Smejkal, C.W. and Gibson, G.R., 2003. Using probiotics and prebiotics to improve gut health. Drug discovery today, 8(15), pp.692-700.

(50) Bakken, J.S., Borody, T., Brandt, L.J., Brill, J.V., Demarco, D.C., Franzos, M.A., Kelly, C., Khoruts, A., Louie, T., Martinelli, L.P. and Moore, T.A., 2011. Treating Clostridium difficile infection with fecal microbiota transplantation. Clinical Gastroenterology and Hepatology, 9(12), pp.1044-1049.

(51) Ott, S.J., Waetzig, G.H., Rehman, A., Moltzau-Anderson, J., Bharti, R., Grasis, J.A., Cassidy, L., Tholey, A., Fickenscher, H., Seegert, D. and Rosenstiel, P., 2017. Efficacy of sterile fecal filtrate transfer for treating patients with Clostridium difficile infection. Gastroenterology, 152(4), pp.799-811

(52) Schmidt, E.K., Torres-Espin, A., Raposo, P.J., Madsen, K.L., Kigerl, K.A., Popovich, P.G., Fenrich, K.K. and Fouad, K., 2020. Fecal transplant prevents gut dysbiosis and Anxiety-like behaviour after spinal cord injury in rats. Plos one, 15(1), p.e0226128.

(53) Brandt, L.J., 2013. American Journal of GastroenterologyLecture: Intestinal Microbiota and the Role of Fecal Microbiota Transplant (FMT) in Treatment ofC. difficileInfection. American Journal of Gastroenterology, 108(2), pp.177-185.

(54) Luo, J., Wang, T., Liang, S., Hu, X., Li, W. and Jin, F., 2014. Ingestion of Lactobacillus strain reduces Anxiety and improves cognitive function in the hyperammonemia rat. Science China Life Sciences, 57(3), pp.327-335.

(55) Hadizadeh, M., Hamidi, G.A. and Salami, M., 2019. Probiotic supplementation improves the cognitive function and the Anxiety-like behaviors in the stressed rats. Iranian Journal of Basic Medical Sciences, 22(5), p.506.

(56) Cowan, C.S., Callaghan, B.L. and Richardson, R., 2016. The effects of a probiotic formulation (Lactobacillus rhamnosus and L. helveticus) on developmental trajectories of emotional learning in stressed infant rats. Translational psychiatry, 6(5), pp.e823-e823.

(57) Knott, G.J. and Doudna, J.A., 2018. CRISPR-Cas guides the future of genetic engineering. Science, 361(6405), pp.866-869.

REFERENCES

(58) Tu, Z., Yang, W., Yan, S., Guo, X. and Li, X.J., 2015. CRISPR/Cas9: a powerful genetic engineering tool for establishing large animal models of neurodegenerative diseases. Molecular neurodegeneration, 10(1), pp.1-8.

(59) Ledford, H., 2016. CRISPR: gene editing is just the beginning. Nature News, 531(7593), p.156.

(60) Almeida, O.P., Flicker, L., Lautenschlager, N.T., Leedman, P., Vasikaran, S. and van Bockxmeer, F.M., 2005. Contribution of the MTHFR gene to the causal pathway for depression, Anxiety and cognitive impairment in later life. Neurobiology of aging, 26(2), pp.251-257.

(61) Bjelland, I., Tell, G.S., Vollset, S.E., Refsum, H. and Ueland, P.M., 2003. Folate, vitamin B12, homocysteine, and the MTHFR 677C→ T polymorphism in Anxiety and depression: the Hordaland Homocysteine Study. Archives of general psychiatry, 60(6), pp.618-626.

(62) Anderson, S., Panka, J., Rakobitsch, R., Tyre, K. and Pulliam, K., 2016. Anxiety and Methylenetetrahydrofolate Reductase Mutation Treated With S-Adenosyl Methionine and Methylated B Vitamins. Integrative Medicine: A Clinician's Journal, 15(2), p.48.

(63) Gillespie, N.A., Kirk, K.M., Evans, D.M., Heath, A.C., Hickie, I.B. and Martin, N.G., 2004. Do the genetic or environmental determinants of Anxiety and depression change with age? A longitudinal study of Australian twins. Twin Research and Human Genetics, 7(1), pp.39-5

(64) DiMauro, J., Domingues, J., Fernandez, G. and Tolin, D.F., 2013. Long-term effectiveness of CBT for Anxiety disorders in an adult outpatient clinic sample: A follow-up study. Behaviour research and therapy, 51(2), pp.82-86.

(65) Albano, A.M. and Kendall, P.C., 2002. Cognitive behavioural therapy for children and adolescents with Anxiety disorders: Clinical research advances. International review of psychiatry, 14(2), pp.129-134.

(66) Walker, S. and Walker, D., 2010. Chiropractic technique summary: Neuro emotional technique (NET).

(67) Karpouzis, F., Pollard, H. and Bonello, R., 2008. Separation Anxiety disorder in a 13-year-old boy managed by the Neuro Emotional Technique as a biopsychosocial intervention. Journal of Chiropractic Medicine, 7(3), pp.101-106.

(68) Cuijpers, P., Donker, T., van Straten, A., Li, J., Andersson, G. and Cuijpers, P., 2010. Is guided self-help as effective as face-to-face psychotherapy for depression and Anxiety disorders? A systematic review and meta-analysis of comparative outcome studies.

(69) Borkovec, T.D. and Ruscio, A.M., 2001. Psychotherapy for generalized Anxiety disorder. The Journal of Clinical Psychiatry.

(70) Cook, N.D., 2002. Tone of voice and mind: The connections between intonation, emotion, cognition and consciousness (Vol. 47). John Benjamins Publishing.

(71) Tulen, J.H.M., Boomsma, F. and MAN IN TVELD, A.J., 1999. Cardiovascular control and plasma catecholamines during rest and mental stress: effects of posture. Clinical Science, 96(6), pp.567-576.

(72) Hackford, J., Mackey, A. and Broadbent, E., 2019. The effects of walking posture on affective and physiological states during stress. Journal of behavior therapy and experimental psychiatry, 62, pp.80-87.

(73) Deshmukh, V.Y., Health Benefits Of Stretching.

(74) Nelson, A.G. and Kokkonen, J., 2020. Stretching anatomy. Human Kinetics Publishers.

(75) Koch, L., 2005. Iliopsoas-The Fight and Flight Muscle for Survival.

(76) Edward, F., 10 Health Benefits of Epsom Salt.

(77) Chalker-Scott L. "Miracle, myth, or marketing: epsom salts." Washington State University. wsu.edu. 2007. Accessed 18 Jan. 2018.

(78) Harber, V.J. and Sutton, J.R., 1984. Endorphins and exercise. Sports Medicine, 1(2), pp.154-171.

(79) Leuenberger, A., 2006. Endorphins, exercise, and addictions: a review of exercise dependence. The Premier Journal for Undergraduate Publications in the Neurosciences, 3, pp.1-9.

REFERENCES

(80) Veale, D.D.C., 1987. Exercise and mental health. Acta Psychiatrica Scandinavica, 76(2), pp.113-120.

(81) Field, T., Hernandez-Reif, M., Diego, M., Schanberg, S. and Kuhn, C., 2005. Cortisol decreases and serotonin and dopamine increase following massage therapy. International Journal of Neuroscience, 115(10), pp.1397-1413.

(82) Kulkarni, S.K., Bhutani, M.K. and Bishnoi, M., 2008. Antidepressant activity of curcumin: involvement of serotonin and dopamine system. Psychopharmacology, 201(3), p.435.

(83) Hoebel, B.G., Hernandez, L., Schwartz, D.H., Mark, GP and Hunter, G.A., 1989. Microdialysis Studies of Brain Norepinephrine, Serotonin, and Dopamine Release During Ingestive Behavior Theoretical and Clinical Implications a. Annals of the New York Academy of Sciences, 575(1), pp.171-193.

(84) Wood, P.B., 2008. Role of central dopamine in pain and analgesia. Expert review of neurotherapeutics, 8(5), pp.781-797.

(85) Yuen, A.W. and Sander, J.W., 2017. Can natural ways to stimulate the vagus nerve improve seizure control?. Epilepsy & Behavior, 67, pp.105-110.

(86) Simon, B.J., Errico, J.P. and Raffle, J.T., ElectroCore LLC, 2014. Non-invasive vagal nerve stimulation to treat disorders. U.S. Patent 8,918,178.

(87) Neumann, I.D., 2007. Stimuli and consequences of dendritic release of oxytocin within the brain.

(88) Thorsell, A., 2007. Neuropeptide Y (NPY) in alcohol intake and dependence. Peptides, 28(2), pp.480-483.

(89) Robinson, S.L. and Thiele, T.E., 2017. The role of neuropeptide Y (NPY) in alcohol and drug abuse disorders. In International review of neurobiology (Vol. 136, pp. 177-197). Academic Press.

(90) Le Bon, O., Staner, L., Hoffmann, G., Kentos, M., Pelc, I. and Linkowski, P., 2001. Shorter REM latency associated with more sleep cycles of a shorter duration in healthy humans. Psychiatry research, 104(1), pp.75-83.

(91) Steiger, A., 2010. Sleep cycle. The Corsini Encyclopedia of Psychology, pp.1-2.

(92) IGUCHI, H., Kato, K.I. and IBAYASHI, H., 1982. Age-dependent reduction in serum melatonin concentrations in healthy human subjects. The Journal of Clinical Endocrinology & Metabolism, 55(1), pp.27-29.

(93) Walach, H., Rilling, C. and Engelke, U., 2001. Efficacy of Bach-flower remedies in test Anxiety: a double-blind, placebo-controlled, randomized trial with partial crossover. Journal of Anxiety disorders, 15(4), pp.359-366.

(94) Chancellor, P.M., 2013. Illustrated handbook of the Bach flower remedies. Random House.

(95) Akhondzadeh, S., Naghavi, H.R., Vazirian, M., Shayeganpour, A., Rashidi, H. and Khani, M., 2001. Passionflower in the treatment of generalized Anxiety: A pilot double-blind randomized controlled trial with oxazepam. Journal of clinical pharmacy and therapeutics, 26(5), pp.363-367.

(96) Saeed, S.A., Bloch, R.M. and Antonacci, D.J., 2007. Herbal and dietary supplements for treatment of Anxiety disorders. American family physician, 76(4), pp.549-556.

(97) Smriga, M., Ando, T., Akutsu, M., Furukawa, Y., Miwa, K. and Morinaga, Y., 2007. Oral treatment with L-lysine and L-arginine reduces Anxiety and basal cortisol levels in healthy humans. Biomedical Research, 28(2), pp.85-90.

(98) Sartori, S.B., Whittle, N., Hetzenauer, A. and Singewald, N., 2012. Magnesium deficiency induces Anxiety and HPA axis dysregulation: modulation by therapeutic drug treatment. Neuropharmacology, 62(1), pp.304-312.

(99) Lakhan, S.E. and Vieira, K.F., 2010. Nutritional and herbal supplements for Anxiety and Anxiety-related disorders: systematic review. Nutrition journal, 9(1), p.42.

REFERENCES

(100) Russo, A.J., 2011. Decreased zinc and increased copper in individuals with Anxiety. Nutrition and metabolic insights, 4, pp.NMI-S6349.

(101) Bouayed, J., Rammal, H. and Soulimani, R., 2009. Oxidative stress and Anxiety: relationship and cellular pathways. Oxidative medicine and cellular longevity, 2.

(102) Lydiard, R.B., 2003. The role of GABA in Anxiety disorders. The Journal of clinical psychiatry, 64, pp.21-27.

(103) Nemeroff, C.B., 2003. The role of GABA in the pathophysiology and treatment of Anxiety disorders. Psychopharmacology bulletin, 37(4), pp.133-146.

(104) Aroniadou-Anderjaska, V., Qashu, F. and Braga, M.M., 2007. Mechanisms regulating GABAergic inhibitory transmission in the basolateral amygdala: implications for epilepsy and Anxiety disorders. Amino acids, 32(3), pp.305-315.

(105) Hadley, S.K. and Petry, J.J., 2003. Valerian. American family physician, 67(8), pp.1755-1758.

(106) Jacobs, B.P., Bent, S., Tice, J.A., Blackwell, T. and Cummings, S.R., 2005. An internet-based randomized, placebo-controlled trial of kava and valerian for Anxiety and insomnia. Medicine, 84(4), pp.197-207.

(107) Setzer, W.N., 2009. Essential oils and anxiolytic aromatherapy. Natural product communications, 4(9), p.1934578X0900400928.

(108) Ali, B., Al-Wabel, N.A., Shams, S., Ahamad, A., Khan, S.A. and Anwar, F., 2015. Essential oils used in aromatherapy: A systemic review. Asian Pacific Journal of Tropical Biomedicine, 5(8), pp.601-611.

(109) Moss, M., Jones, R., Moss, L., Cutter, R. and Wesnes, K., 2016. Acute consumption of Peppermint and Chamomile teas produce contrasting effects on cognition and mood in healthy young adults. Plant Science Today, 3(3), pp.327-336.

(f) Facebook.com/ Chris Breen - Fear Less
(📷) instagram.com/ chrisbreen_fear_less
(@) email: chrisbreenauthor@gmail.com

Chris Breen's career in nursing and paramedicine, spanning over 25 years, is a testament to his dedication to mental health and support for others in the community, particularly in the context of men's mental health in Australia. His journey, beginning with a personal struggle against severe Panic attacks, agoraphobia, and Anxiety in 2001, has shaped him into a compassionate mentor and educator. His experiences, both professional and personal, offer him a unique perspective on the complexities of mental well-being, including stress, Panic disorder, and social Anxiety.

As a paramedic in Australia, he has witnessed the suffering of his patients, gaining a deeper understanding of mental health challenges, encompassing conditions like obsessive-compulsive disorder, post-traumatic stress disorder and Panic attacks. This experience, coupled with his own journey, makes him an empathetic guide in the area of mental health, advocating a ***drug-free*** approach with a strong emphasis on cognitive behaviour therapy techniques. His debut book, "How a Base Jumper Saved Me," reflects this blend of personal narrative and professional insight. The book is not just his story but a hopeful guide for those battling Anxiety, offering practical advice and research-based strategies for self-help.

His message is clear: with the right approach, anyone can overcome Anxiety and it's mental health challenges with education, time and effort. His book is a tool for empowerment, providing insights and methods to manage Anxiety and reclaim control of your life.

www.ingramcontent.com/pod-product-compliance
Lightning Source LLC
Chambersburg PA
CBHW011152290426
44109CB00025B/2578